About this book

With Cyprus joining the European Union in 2004, the pressure is on political leaders to resolve forty years of conflict between Greek Cypriots and Turkish Cypriots, and to erase the brutal Partition Line that scars the island, fostering nationalist hatred and impeding communication. The 'EU moment' has already triggered a startling decision to open checkpoints on the Green Line for day crossings, an opportunity eagerly seized by ordinary citizens. But a permanent peace agreement is elusive.

This scholarly but lively study is a gendered analysis of conflict and peace processes in Cyprus, based on extensive interviews and group discussions with women living both north and south of the Line. Their memories evoke nationalist attacks on Turkish Cypriots in the 1960s, the violent expulsion of Greek Cypriots in 1974, and the gender-specific experience of being a refugee. We see in today's Republic of Cyprus and the unrecognized Turkish Republic of Northern Cyprus, rivals in continual stand-off, a gender order in which patriarchy, nationalism and militarism combine to keep women on the margins.

The Line traces the fortunes of a remarkable Cypriot women's project working for peace, using the Internet to defy the barriers to communication placed between them. In the future Cyprus of their imagining we will no longer draw arbitrary and damaging lines to separate so-called ethnic groups, or to differentiate men and women, creating hierarchy, exclusion and inequality. The study will be relevant to all who teach about, think about and strive to put an end to racist, sexist and militarist oppression and violence in this and other regions of the world.

Cynthia Cockburn

The Line: Women, Partition and the Gender Order in Cyprus

Zed Books
LONDON · NEW YORK

The Line: Women, Partition and the Gender Order in Cyprus
was first published by Zed Books Ltd, 7 Cynthia Street,
London N1 9JF, UK and Room 400, 175 Fifth Avenue,
New York, NY 10010, USA in 2004.

www.zedbooks.co.uk

Cover designed by Lee Robinson, Ad Lib Design, London N19
Set in Bembo and Futura Bold by Ewan Smith, London
Printed and bound in Malta by Gutenberg Press Ltd

Distributed in the USA exclusively by Palgrave Macmillan, a division of
St Martin's Press, LLC, 175 Fifth Avenue, New York, NY 10010.

A catalogue record for this book is available from the British Library

Library of Congress cataloging-in-publication data available

ISBN 1 84277 420 4 cased
ISBN 1 84277 421 2 limp

Contents

Acknowledgements

The help I have received in the course of the research project on which this book is based has been more generous than I can say, and has come from many sources. First, the project could not have occurred at all without funding granted by the following organizations, to whom I wish to express my sincere appreciation. My four principal funders were the Barrow Cadbury Trust, the Ajahma Charitable Trust, the Allan and Nesta Ferguson Charitable Trust and the Network for Social Change. I also received important contributions to the project from the Lipman-Miliband Trust, the Lansbury House Trust Fund, the Maypole Fund, the Scurrah Wainwright Charity, the William A. Cadbury Charitable Trust, the Eleanor Rathbone Charitable Trust and the Amos Trust. To all of them my warmest thanks.

Second, how can I thank enough the women of the organization Hands Across the Divide? You welcomed me as a member (which I hope I shall long remain). You were flexible and open-minded enough to allow me to turn you into a subject of research, and loving enough to make sure it did not spoil our friendships, the candour of our many conversations or the fun we have together. The names of Hands Across the Divide members appear in note 6 of the Introduction – though some members, whose company and co-operation I have also enjoyed, have joined since that list was drawn up. Among HAD members I would specially like to mention Sevgül Uludağ and Katie Econo-midou who first invited me to Cyprus and encouraged me to think of continuing the connection in a research project. All of us are very grateful to the British Council and the United Kingdom High Com-mission in Nicosia for supporting the seminar that made the birth of Hands Across the Divide possible.

Something from which I have gained greatly during the periods I have spent in Cyprus is an informal connection with three academic institutions, mediated by very special colleagues and friends who work in them – Maria Hadjipavlou at the University of Cyprus, Myria Vassiliadou, director of the Mediterranean Institute for Gender Studies at Intercollege, both in Nicosia, and Fatma Güven-Lisaniler and Sevin Uğural at the Eastern Mediterranean University in Fama-gusta. Please know, each of you, how grateful I am for your unstinting generosity. It made me feel secure and grounded to have access from time to time to your advice and to your well-respected institutions.

The outcome of any qualitative research depends finally on the willingness of those on whom the researcher leans for information. I was fortunate in obtaining the generous co-operation of 142 women in my data gathering. They were invariably thoughtful and patently honest in their replies to my persistent and sometimes, I am sure, painful questions. I cannot name them all here. Many appear by name in the text. But my thanks to every one of them are very sincere. I would also like to thank those eleven meticulous typists who transcribed my tapes; several women who helped me with interpretation; those who hosted group discussions for me; and others, including Oya Talat and Ayla Gürel, who were kind enough to have me to stay in their homes. In this respect I would like to thank Gülay Kaşer in particular for opening her house to me for a long period in a way that made me feel I really belonged. In south Nicosia I stayed on several occasions at the ultra-supportive Cyprus American Archaeological Research Institute, than which there can be no more hospitable lodging for a visiting researcher.

This text went through a strenuous pummelling before it saw the light of day. Though no doubt errors of fact and dubious authorial opinions still remain in it, they are due to my recidivism. The book would have been a sorry object indeed without the improvements suggested by many perceptive and clear-minded women who read and commented on it. Forty copies of the manuscript were out and about, under scrutiny, at one point. How can I mention everyone who helped get this text into shape? Yet I feel I want to mark up my special gratitude to some who did a page-by-page job on sections of the manuscript and gave me substantial comment, while hoping this will not make others feel their help has not been appreciated. They are Ann-Sofi Jacobsson-Hatay, Anthoula Papadopoulou, Fatma Güven-Lisaniler, Floya Anthias, Kate Young, Maia Woodward Dyason, Maria Hadjipavlou, Myria Georgiou, Myria Vassiliadou, Nana Achilleos, Netha Kreouzos, Nina Nissen, Nira Yuval-Davis, Nora Räthzel, Olga Demetriou, Rita Pantazi, Selma Bolayır, Sevgül Uludağ, Sue Lartides, Susie Constantinides, Tabitha Morgan and Zehra Nalbantoğlu.

Finally, I would like to thank Robert Molteno and others at Zed Books, who for the second time have taken a manuscript of mine and seen it most professionally through the processes of editing, printing and distribution – taking special care of the reproduction of my photographs, which I know add to their burdens. Thank you, Zed.

The photograph on page 165 is reproduced by courtesy of the *Cyprus Mail*; the lower photograph on page 164 and the upper one on page 200 are reproduced by courtesy of *Yeniçağ*; the lower photograph on page 200 is reproduced by courtesy of Oya Talat. All other photographs, with the exception of historical photos on pages 81, 120 and 121, are by the author.

Introduction

When the poem utters the big word
all the weapons will hush at once...
War will die of shame (Neşe Yaşın)

The rope snakes across the floor, then lies inert. The dancer steps beside it, stumbles across it, her feet exploring its meaning, what it says about her freedom and her confinement. Arianna Economou, in her performance, *Walking the Line*, is conversing with the Partition of Cyprus. What strikes me about this scene is that the dividing line seems to be alive. The rope slithers and slides, now one thing, now another. This helps me to see how a geo-political partition is not just armoured fencing, it is also a line inside our heads, and in our hearts too. In fact, the physical fence is a manifestation of these more cognitive and emotional lines that shape our thoughts and feelings. The inner lines express who we think we are, and who is not us, whom we trust and of whom we are afraid. When we are very afraid or very angry, at some identifiable moment, a line springs out and plants itself in the earth as a barrier. It becomes The Line, and passage across it is controlled, by uniformed men, at a Checkpoint.

This book is about the marking of difference and categorizing of people, and about partition as a strategy for dealing with conflict. Cyprus is an extraordinarily rich source of experience on these subjects, from which those of us who live elsewhere can learn a great deal. We shall see how the distance between people of 'Turkish' and 'Greek'[1] cultures on the island was widened in a number of political projects (colonial, nationalist, international), so that they became increasingly separate from each other physically and socially. In the 1960s the majority of the population of Cyprus (approximately four-fifths) was 'Greek Cypriot'. The most important minority (a little less than one-fifth of the population) was 'Turkish Cypriot'. There were, besides, much smaller minorities of Armenians, Maronites and Latins. The many scattered communities in which the Turkish Cypriot minority lived till the mid-twentieth century, adjacent to or even integrated within Greek Cypriot neighbourhoods, were gradually consolidated under pressure of physical threat and political manipulation into mono-communal areas. We shall see how ephemeral cultural

'lines' were redrawn, becoming harder, clearer and more physical
in the process, circling round Turkish Cypriot enclaves. Finally, in
1974, following an abortive *coup d'état* by Greek Cypriot extremists
associated with the Greek military *junta*, Turkey launched a military
intervention.[2] Greek Cypriots were ousted from their homes in great
numbers. People were moved this way and that to create two 'ethnically' homogeneous regions, and separated by a high fence running
from the western shoreline of Cyprus to its eastern coast.

The book is about contemporary realities too, the way those living
either side of the fence have gone on to experience their separate
worlds. It looks at similarities and divergencies between north and
south Cyprus. It considers the significance of relatively new populations on the island, Turks from Turkey in the north, Asian and other
migrants in the south. Above all I have been interested in the inner
processes of line making, line negotiation and line melting, so far as
people are able to express their thoughts and feelings. And I speculate
about the future of lines.

The book is woman-centred and gender-analytical. It is based
on participant observation, interviews and group discussions with
women. One good reason for this female focus is that gender differentiation, like ethnic differentiation, is a political project that involves
drawing a line. Political, I mean, in the sense that it involves power,
purpose and collective action. The gender order,[3] like the ethno-
political order, involves the exploitation of certain material facts together with stories from the past, to dichotomize men and women,
and create privilege and dependency. Evading gender demarcation,
being a free thinker in a free body, is not easy, in Cyprus or anywhere
else. One more thing that is striking about Arianna's dance is that the
body of the dancer is androgynous. She says, 'perhaps the dancer's
dream is to be not a woman. To be neutral. To find *presence* – a body
in space and time.' She made me feel that we might, at a stretch, say
neither/nor to the limiting models of feminity and masculinity on
offer. And in liberating our capacities, we might reshape power.

So *The Line* is a book about Cyprus seen through women's eyes.
The speakers differ in their social positioning, so they perceive and
relate to ethnic and class lines in a variety of ways. But whatever else
situates them, all the speakers are, being women, *relatively* peripheral
to power. (I remember Arianna saying of herself, 'I am an artist on the
margins.') Nobody I spoke with failed to observe that Cyprus is male-

dominated – is there a country that is not? – but they put men's pre-eminence down to a variety of causes. Depending on which cause they stress, they are more or less likely to consider gender hierarchy something they can contest. The protagonists of the book are a particular cluster of women who have formed a small organization to work for co-operation between women in Cyprus in the pursuit of peace, equality and human rights. These women do, as we shall see, refute the legitimacy both of gender subordination and the Partition Line.

Partition: stasis and change

The line that divides Cyprus, like that which separates the state of Israel from Palestinian territories, is called the Green Line. The internationally recognized independent state that has sovereignty, in principle, over the whole island is the Republic of Cyprus, with its seat in the centrally placed city of Nicosia. But the Green Line partitions the island in such a way that the government of the Republic in fact has control over only half the capital city and the southern 63 per cent of the land area. The authority controlling the northern 37 per cent is an entity, recognized only by Turkey, known as the Turkish Republic of Northern Cyprus (TRNC).[4]

The Green Line is in fact a double line, with an area of no man's land between two parallel fences. Greek Cypriots call this the 'dead zone', but it is not altogether barren. The United Nations has its offices and barracks in there, and its blue-beret soldiers patrol the barbed wire. In spring and early summer, the Green Line lives up to its name. The grass and shrubs run riot between the fences. Much of it is an unnatural nature reserve, a refuge for warblers and buntings, flycatchers and hoopoes. There are also choice game birds, francolin and *chukar* partridges. Consequently, the buffer zone, despite or because of its minefields, has been an adventure playground for some men who, in the hunting season, like to dress in camouflage fatigues, slip through the wire and shoot the creatures they have hunted almost to extinction in the rest of the island. A UN colleague tells me these men also enjoy provoking little incidents with 'the other side', with the pleasurable by-product of winding up the UN squaddies.

In Nicosia, the Line cuts right across the Venetian ramparts of honey-coloured stone. The buffer strip is narrow here and you can catch a glimpse of individuals 'over there' going about their business. Tourists in south Nicosia would walk down a pedestrian shopping

The Partition Line that divides Cyprus from shore to shore is two fences separated by a buffer zone. It is patrolled by a United Nations peace-keeping force, **UNFICYP.**

In some places the Line is fierce with razor wire, at others it lapses into rusty iron sheet and oil drums. Here it becomes Fatma's garden fence.

street and find, at the end of it, a timber structure specially constructed for them to climb up and view 'the occupied territories' through a peep-hole. One day on my first visit to Cyprus in 2001, I joined a tour group on the platform. It was unpleasant, somehow, as though we were in a hide, peering at wild animals in their habitat.

For almost twenty-nine years the Green Line was a closed border with only two checkpoints. One was in Nicosia. Here a Greek Cypriot and a Turkish Cypriot guard post are separated by a hundred yards of neutral territory in which the former Ledra Palace hotel stands, an imposing old building with mock-Crusader detailing, well past its prime, now in the hands of the UN administration. The other checkpoint controls passage through the unique buffer-zone village of Pyla, an hour's drive from Nicosia, towards the eastern seaboard. The frequency of crossings has varied from time to time, but permission has always been required. Exceptions are made for the staff of foreign embassies, who pass under diplomatic arrangements, and tourists who have been allowed to cross from south to north at the Ledra Palace checkpoint, on foot, on day passes (in at 8 a.m., back before the clock strikes five). Some Turkish Cypriot workers are allowed to cross at Pyla on a daily basis to jobs in the south. Ordinary Turkish and Greek Cypriots, however, have not been allowed to move freely through the checkpoint. It has at times been very difficult to get a permit from the administration of the Turkish Republic of Northern Cyprus to cross in either direction, and, besides, few Greek Cypriots have been willing to appear to recognize the 'pseudo-state', as they term the TRNC, by filling in the official form involved.

Suddenly, without any warning, on 21 April 2003, the authorities of the TRNC announced that the Line, this formidable obstacle to movement and communication, would simply be opened. Any citizen of north or south might cross to the other side between 8 a.m. and midnight, no permit required, on presentation of an identity document. The news was greeted on both sides with amazement, jubilation and suspicion in equal measure. The government in the south was slow to react, but did not contradict the move. Extraordinary days followed. On Wednesday 23 April, the first day of the opening, people flocked to the Green Line from both sides. At first the waiting time in the queue to get through the checkpoint was as much as eight or ten hours, but even this did not deter people who had longed for such a moment and were afraid it might not last. The weather was unseasonably hot. People fainted in the queue. The United Nations, jumping to attention after so many years of relative inaction, erected a long canopy to provide some shade along the way, together with toilets, drinking water dispensers and pink plastic sacks for litter. As it became apparent that the authorities were not about to change their minds, and indeed the permissiveness was gradually extended, the UN also opened additional checkpoints and repaired roads to carry motor traffic.

In the first three weeks a staggering 350,000 crossings were recorded (*Cyprus Weekly* 2003a). Some Greek Cypriots would not consider taking advantage of the relaxation, holding fast to their decades-long refusal to recognize the TRNC by submitting their documents to the border officials. But many thousands made emotional pilgrimages to homes they had had to abandon twenty-nine years before. Northerners crossed southwards, also searching for their pasts. In many cases, on both sides, they were greeted generously by the people they found there. But euphoria was mixed with pain, and many people reported feeling disturbed and depressed after the visit. Seeing your former home, knowing that the opening of the Line does not mean an agreement permitting 'return' and realizing too the even harder truth that return does not mean restitution of the past – for the place where you used to live has become in many ways a foreign land – these were painful experiences. Nevertheless, there was a widespread feeling that the opening of the Line was irreversible, and that it was a step towards a better future. It initiated a new kind of debate in Cyprus. In place of the endless circling around the issue of partition – how to deal with it, how to maintain it or how to end it – the new preoccupation was the meaning of the opening: why it had happened, how to interpret it, the risks involved, and what to anticipate.

An important factor associated with the opening of the Line was the process of the Republic of Cyprus's accession to the European Union. Shortly before the announcement of the opening, at an important ceremony in Athens, the Republic of Cyprus along with nine other new entrants had been welcomed to membership of the European Union. The many years of accession negotiations were complete and it was now a certainty that Cyprus would take its place in 'Europe' with effect from May 2004. For many months, in the run-up to this date, those in both south and north who most want to normalize relations on the island had been engaged in strenuous lobbying to use this auspicious period to achieve a peace agreement and a new constitution. The leaders had reopened talks, under the auspices of the United Nations, in January 2002. Regular meetings had continued for fourteen tense months. The UN, to force the pace, had eventually drafted a peace agreement, the Annan Plan, and presented it to both sides in December 2002. But on 16 April at a meeting in The Hague, Rauf Denktaş, political leader of the TRNC, rejected the plan. Tassos Papadopoulos, President of the Republic, was able to lay the blame for failure of the negotiations on Denktaş, but popular opinion in the south was by no means united on the Plan. It appeared all but inevitable now that Cyprus would enter the EU still divided. The north, like Turkey, would remain on Europe's margin – some of its population wanting in, others seeking a different kind of national identity. Those Cypriots[5] who dearly wanted a solution to the 'Cyprus problem' (as it is termed) had been left empty-handed yet again, afraid of what the future might hold.

In the fourteen months during which the leaders had been meeting face to face, there had been increasing popular agitation in northern Cyprus. The opposition parties and trade unions organized demonstrations that drew crowds of unprecedented size. The figures reported seemed to suggest that as many as a quarter of the whole population of north Cyprus were on the streets calling for an agreement to enable Cyprus to join the EU federally unified. There were also very large counter-demonstrations in support of Denktaş, for the Turkish Cypriot population was divided on the issue. It was speculated that the move to open the Partition Line was designed by Rauf Denktaş to defuse protest and keep hold of the initiative. It seemed as though he were saying, 'We can do without the UN and its Annan Plan.' Those who were suspicious of his motives believed he intended, far from doing away with the Line, to normalize it and give it legitimacy as an international border. It was clear to all that the opening of the Line did not solve the 'Cyprus problem'; it may well have compounded it. There were many, north and south, pointing out that the sticking points on which negotiations had foundered so many times over three decades – such as the fair division of land and resources, the return or compensation of refugees, rights concerning investment in property, land and enterprise, the structure and distribution of powers in a federal or confederal state – had yet to be negotiated. A slender opportunity still remained for an agreement to be signed before May

2004, the final-final moment of the Republic's accession to the European Union, but a great deal of hard bargaining would be needed in the interval for this to come about.

My research in Cyprus began at a time when the Line was a rigid barrier, resistant to any significant breach, seemingly eternal. It ended a few weeks after this entirely unanticipated opening. The book deals with Partition as it affected the lives of some women during the period of my study, March 2001 to April 2003. I will return to the subsequent 'opening' in the final chapter where I explore possible futures, but it remains important to understand experience of people separated on the basis of ethnic name, living for long years in adjacent areas, and particularly the difficulties faced by those who struggle for reconnection.

A women's initiative: addressing division

There is a history in Cyprus, going back to the late 1970s, of what is termed 'bi-communal activity'. At first, moves towards contact between the two sides were spontaneous. From the late 1980s, however, third parties, mainly institutions from the USA specializing in conflict resolution, brought together small groups of Cypriots from north and south. Sometimes they were able to organize their encounters in the buffer zone, sometimes it was necessary to meet overseas. Over two decades these externally mediated contacts resulted in perhaps three thousand individuals acquiring 'reconciliation' experience, gaining contact, even friendship, with individuals in the other zone. Women have been particularly active in this process and may even be a majority of bi-communalists. But those, women or men, actively seeking contact with their counterparts the other side of the Line have been a small minority of the population of either community. Meanwhile, a whole generation of young people has grown up without first-hand knowledge of those who live the other side, and their schooling has continued to convey a sense of 'them' as a source of enmity and danger.

The women's organization Hands Across the Divide (HAD), that is the focus of my research and of this book, was a late development in the bi-communal tradition. HAD, however, is an unusual project in three ways. First, unlike most bi-communal groups it is not mediated by a foreign institution; in this sense it is autonomous. Second, its members prefer not to term their project 'bi-communal' - that is, being linked groups, one in south Cyprus, one in north Cyprus. Rather, flying in the face of Partition, they have attempted from the start to work and structure themselves as a unitary organization. They were thus the first to find a way round the regulations that had hitherto made a formal organization with members in both parts of Cyprus a legal impossibility. Third, they have focused less on 'reconciliation' than on synchronized political action. As women, they have called on their politicians to 'solve the Cyprus problem now' and have been prepared to demonstrate publicly to drive home their point. They were in fact on the street in advance of the mass demonstrations in the north. One of the demands in their first press statement had been for freedom of communication across the Line. Though they are few in number, they have thus been symptomatic of the movement for change.

Hands Across the Divide originated in a particular event held in Nicosia in March 2001. Two women had come across my writing on gender and national identities in situations of armed conflict (Cockburn 1998). They invited me to facilitate a bi-communal seminar in Nicosia. My initial contact was with Sevgül Uludağ, a Turkish Cypriot journalist from the north of Cyprus, and Katie Economidou, a Greek Cypriot activist and conflict resolution trainer from the Republic of Cyprus. They had formed a friendship across the Line when meeting outside the island at bi-communal events. After several stalled initiatives, they now wanted to make a new start, organizing among women either side of the Line. Meanwhile, other women, also known for their bi-communal work and keen to frame up a new initiative addressing issues of conflict and gender, had been in touch with the British Council office in Nicosia.

The resulting seminar, organized by the British Council and funded by the United Kingdom High Commission, was titled *Communication in Divided Societies: What Women Can Do*. Our aim was to give it an activist more than an academic character and I suggested inviting as speakers women working across frontiers in Ireland, Bosnia-Herzegovina and Israel/Palestine. A planning group of women, north and south, was convened who in turn drew to the seminar a varied list of activists and academics, individual women and women involved with organizations, women both with and without experience in bi-communal work and younger women, including students. The idea was to locate the first day of the two-day meeting in the south, at Intercollege, and the second at Cyprus International University in the north. Thirty women participants would be crossing the Line in each direction. This was highly unusual, since contact between south and north had recently been limited to meetings under UN auspices in the buffer zone.

Arrangements, however, did not go according to plan. The Turkish Cypriot authorities, two days before the seminar was due to take place, arbitrarily reduced from thirty to ten the number who would be granted permission to cross the Green Line. In the south, threatening articles in the Greek Cypriot press criticized the seminar as interference by a foreign power. They censured the organizers for choosing Cyprus International University as a venue, which, they said, constituted recognition of the illegal northern regime. The women participants now had to make a difficult decision. They had to decide whether to accept the northern authorities' terms and make the invidious selection of ten of their number to cross the Line, or withdraw from the seminar. Those in the south had to decide whether they were prepared to run the gauntlet of angry nationalists in their community. Instead of being chaperoned across the line in British official vehicles, as a group, they would now have to go individually through the checkpoint and be faced with completing the hated official form that is felt to imply recognition of the 'pseudo-state'. Should we call the seminar off? For me at this moment the Line was clearly delineated for the first time. I felt for myself its stark power to maim relationships. I experienced it then as inhumane, barbaric, in a way I will never do again – because you quickly get used to it, and bend your mind around it. We thought seriously of cancelling the seminar, but eventually women on both sides persisted in the arrangements with great good-will and sense of purpose.

It was only after the seminar was over that I realized how innovatory, ambitious and unlikely it had been. Against all the odds, it was a success. A decision was made in the closing session that did indeed seem to promise a fresh start in women's bi-communal activity in Cyprus. The women present committed themselves to a movement of women with an attempt at some kind of unitary organizational structure to link them. The first step was to create an e-mail network. It would turn out to be a vital cross-Line organizing medium. A core of around twenty-five of the more committed women took forward the group that eventually named itself 'Hands Across the Divide'.[6]

Action and research: the approach

After the seminar I went back to the UK and wrote a proposal for a two-year full-time project of participatory action research (Reason 1998).[7] I agreed it with colleagues in Cyprus and approached possible funders. As the group in Cyprus began to coalesce, in the summer of 2001, there was energetic activity on the e-list, of which I was a part. We discussed the nature of my relationship to the group with some care. We clarified that if any conflict of interest were to arise between my research and Hands Across the Divide, the group's interests would take priority. We were agreed that my role in relation to the group was not one of 'mediation' or 'conflict resolution'. Not only did the group not want mediation, it is something for which I have neither qualifications nor skill. Rather, I would be working with them as a researcher and writer in the field where gender studies and peace/ conflict studies intersect, and as a feminist activist in the international women's movement against militarism and war. I would be a member, as fully involved in the group's activity as my movements in and out of Cyprus permitted, and contribute whatever competence I had that was found useful.

The ways I could be of service included, for instance, using my e-links to the worldwide network of women's anti-war movements to inform a wider world of the continuing 'cold war' in Cyprus, and of women's aspirations for change. I was able to use my experience in drafting project proposals as a basis for raising grants and by this means managed to obtain support, in cash and in kind, from various friendly sources (see Acknowledgements) to fund some of the activities described in Chapters 6 and 7. When in Cyprus I was now and then used as a carrier pigeon, using my freedom as a 'tourist' to cross the Line from south to north, carrying messages to and fro. The fact that I lived for periods of time in both parts of the island also I think contributed to communication within the group. On occasion, when asked, I would take a turn facilitating meetings. In general, in my relationship with HAD, my policy was to hold back from decision-making, since my commitment to Cyprus inevitably lacks the longevity of that of other members. But I felt free to make an input to developing a workable structure and good group process. With the help of civil society support organizations in the UK I eventually helped frame a constitution for the group.

It was agreed that while being actively engaged with HAD I would be gathering research material. In participant observer mode, I would monitor the progress of Hands Across the Divide itself, assess the impediments it would certainly encounter, observe its achievements and analyse its shortcomings. In this sense it was a continuation of work I had done previously among women's organizations in other situations of ethnicized conflict (Cockburn 1998). Secondly, through interview and group discussions, I would try to gain an understanding of the context in which Hands Across the Divide was working. I do not claim that the interview sample was representative. My aim was to make HAD members the focus, while including also other women of a range of ages and ethnic names. Members of HAD in the north are either affiliated to or sympathetic to the opposition political parties that campaign for *rapprochement* and an early agreement between south and north Cyprus. In the south the membership is in the main less oriented towards political parties, which are in any case less polarized in their politics than in the north. The southern women vote more eclectically for those who seem to promise progress towards a solution. The non-HAD interviewees were selected to include a range of political affiliations, identified from the nature of parties and non-governmental organizations with which the women in question were known to be connected. My aim in this information-gathering was to hear some of the remembered and recounted histories that are inevitably brought to cross-Line working, and to grasp what I could of women's perceptions of gender and 'ethnic' relations in Cyprus today – the better to understand where HAD is coming from, the world in which HAD wants to be effective today, and what might logically, therefore, be a HAD perspective on the future.

With the organization's help I eventually interviewed sixty-one women. Eight of the interviews (five in the south and three in the north) were contextual, with women to whom I went for information due to some institution they represented. The remaining fifty-three (twenty-two in the south, twenty-nine in the north and two in London) were personal, in-depth interviews which characteristically ran for a couple of hours, and covered the more important features of the subject's life, her memories of conflict, her feelings about many aspects of Cyprus today, most importantly the Partition, and her hopes for Cyprus tomorrow.[8] In age, the interviewees ranged from early twenties to over eighty.[9] Twenty-two of the personal interviews were with HAD members.

In terms of 'ethnicity' it is difficult (and inappropriate) to pin my research subjects down. It will become clear in Chapter 1 that I interpret cultures as changing and indistinct phenomena, and the naming of ethnicities as a mobilizing of cultural difference for political purposes. The logic of Partition in Cyprus means that the overwhelming majority of those inhabiting the south call themselves and are called by others 'Greek Cypriots', while those in the north are identified as 'Turkish Cypriots' and 'Turks'. But what exactly do these categories mean? Facts of birthplace, parentage and partner usefully complicate and enrich the picture. What I can say for sure about the fifty-three women with whom I conducted personal interviews is the following. Forty were born in Cyprus, nine in countries of the Cypriot diaspora and four in Turkey. Parentage is relevant too: eighteen were born to a mother and father both of whom were described as 'Greek Cypriot' and four to 'Greek Cypriots' married to partners of other identifications. Twenty-six were born to a mother and father both of whom were described as 'Turkish Cypriot'; in three cases both parents were 'Turkish'; and in one case they were 'Kurdish'. One was born to a 'Turkish Cypriot' married to a 'Turk'. In terms of their own relationships, of those thirty-three women who spoke of a current husband or partner, in six cases his ethnicity was something other than 'Greek Cypriot' or 'Turkish Cypriot'. Most significantly, there was no one among my interviewees who was either living within, or was an offspring of, a 'Turkish Cypriot'/'Greek Cypriot' union. Such mixed liaisons have never been common in Cyprus. Finally, I regret, now, that I did not achieve any interviews with women of the ancient minority groups in Cyprus, the Armenians, Maronites and Latins; with distinctive groups such as the 'Pontic Greeks'; or Eastern European migrant women; or Roma women.

In addition to individual interviews, I conducted twelve group interviews, seven in the south and five in the north. Each group comprised women who were, in one way or another, similarly situated. Those in the south were women of Relatives of the Missing; Greek Cypriot women displaced from the north in 1974, living in a refugee housing complex; Asian workers at the Immigrant Support Action Group; secretarial students at Intercollege; social science students at the University of Cyprus. I met with (two) young women of the Greek Cypriot nationalistic students' group, Independent Student Bastion; and women of 'Women Walk Home', a movement

that actively confronted the Green Line in the 1980s. In the north
the groups were women of the trade union ÇAĞ-SEN; users of the
Kayad Community Centre; women of the Republican Turkish Party
(CTP); widows of men massacred by Greek Cypriots in the southern
village of Tokhni in 1974; and (two) Kurdish students. Taken together,
these groups represented a wide range of age, class positioning and
political opinion.

As well as these group interviews, I set up and recorded round
table discussions, in which characteristically a group of between four
and eight women would meet for an evening in someone's home.
Of the participants, two-fifths were members of HAD, the remainder
other women selected by them and me to bring a range of political
affiliation. I chose the topics of discussion - exactly the same in the
north and south. In parallel discussions of 'power' we thought about
how women are situated in relation to all the dimensions of power in
the Republic of Cyprus and the TRNC. In twin round tables on 'violence' we explored the many manifestations of violence in Cypriot
society (including militarism) and how violence bears on women's
lives. The third theme was 'identity', and here women were invited
to share their feelings on different aspects of their sense of self and
belonging. We talked a lot about being or feeling 'Turkish Cypriot',
'Greek Cypriot', 'Cypriot', a mixture of these, or something else altogether. We also talked about our identities as women. 'Bodies' was the
fourth topic. We shared ideas on how as women we 'live our bodies' in
Cyprus. These discussions covered image and fashion, love, sex, sexuality, marriage and reproduction. Finally, I invited women to discuss
'futures'. We focused on what women really mean by a satisfactory
'solution' to the Cyprus problem – going beyond mere constitutional
arrangements to think about language and schooling, work life and
home life, racism and multiculturalism, security and demilitarization.

In total sixty-three women participated in the group interviews
and forty-seven in the round tables – 110 in all. Of these twenty-nine
were also the subject of in-depth interview, while eighty-one were
new faces. Thus the number of women included in my data-gathering
as a whole totalled 142.[10] I assured everyone I interviewed or involved
in discussions that I would not quote their words in print, or write
anything about them that would identify them, without returning to
them first to make sure they agreed.[11] And I kept my promise in this
respect, returning to Cyprus in the spring of 2003 to reconnect with

my many research contacts, all of whom agreed their 'sound bites'. Six women decided to appear in the text under pseudonyms, while the remainder are identified by their own names.

About the book

In evolving an analytic strategy for handling the resulting material, I thought about the logic of participatory action research. I believe that the most useful thing a researcher can do is to identify and tease out what Chairman Mao liked to call the 'main contradiction'. What was the main contradiction in the activity of Hands Across the Divide? To me it took the form of this question: if our main concern is pressing our politicians to obtain a fair solution to the Cyprus problem, why are we a *women*'s group – why not include men? It can be expressed in reverse form: if we are a women's group, why are we focused on the *Cyprus problem*, which is not, on the face of it, a 'women's issue'? To address this contradiction we need to be clear in our political thinking and actions about the concepts of gender and ethnicity, and how in theory and practice they interlink. For they are intimately related, in such a way that one will always find a gender phenomenon within an 'ethnic' one, and vice versa; and for that reason change in one of those relations will involve change, or tension, in the other. In short, I believe the Cyprus problem is gendered and women's problems in Cyprus are not separate from other dimensions of relationship, including relations between Greek and Turkish Cypriots and 'others' on the island.

In Chapter 1, therefore, I introduce some of the terms that will be needed when discussing the experiences women recount in later chapters. In doing so I have tried to write in a way that achieves two (perhaps incompatible) aims. First, I hope academic readers will feel able to trust the soundness of the theory despite the necessarily skimpy handling of weighty matters. Second, I hope the non-academic reader will not be dismayed by abstraction, and will emerge from Chapter 1 grasping a few 'thinking tools' that seem usable in her or his own situation. Concepts and theories are implicit in political practice, but in the moment of action they are not always conscious or clear. The aim of a moment of research could be to articulate, and feed back into the action, concepts and theories in a form clear enough to help the choosing of strategies.

In this first chapter, then, I discuss the pleasures and dangers inherent in difference and differentiation, and the ways in which individuals acquire a sense of self in relation to ethnic and gender identities. I sketch possible meanings for ethnicity and gender, and the dangerous tendency in both sets of relations to dichotomize, drawing sexist and racist lines between 'self' and 'other'. My aim throughout the book has been to test the idea (already widely debated) that gender and ethnic differentiations involve comparable processes, that the similarities and differences between them are significant – we can learn something from them. The chapter ends with a brief consideration of partition as a political strategy for dealing with conflict and of transversal politics in the renewal of dialogue.

The following two chapters are historical, and show something of the sources of the ethnic enmity and separation that a group such as Hands Across the Divide attempts to overcome. We get glimpses of the traditional patriarchal family in which women of today's older generation lived as little girls, and begin to see just how gendered and familial were ethno-national processes. In Chapter 2, dealing with the period 1960 to 1973, women describe a period in which nationalist movements and international pressures turned tension into enmity between Greek-speaking and Turkish-speaking Cypriots. In Chapter 3 the focus is on 1974, the year of the Greek Cypriot *coup* and the Turkish military action that brought about Partition. The many lines that already circled Turkish Cypriot enclaves were transformed into a single Line, extended from one side of the island to the other. It took physical form, became fixed and impermeable. We see, in women's words, how large movements of population took place, resulting eventually in an ethnically homogeneous Turkish Cypriot north and Greek Cypriot south. Two masculinities, one that had been dominant, the other subordinate, each now acquired undisputed hegemony over its separate space.

The next pair of chapters describe contemporary realities in Cyprus, as women (members of HAD and others) perceive them, and develop a more detailed understanding of the prevailing gender order and gender cultures. Chapter 4 gives women's analysis of the political, economic and military realities of contemporary Cyprus. I draw out their gendered evaluation of the authority systems they live under, and how these differ in the two parts of the island. Chapter 5 addresses the family and marriage, the politics of sex and the body. I explore with women the changes they detect in the gender order in Cyprus – a relaxing of the familial codes of traditional patriarchy, yet an adaptive reproduction of male dominance in forms viable for the twenty-first century. Women explore the reasons for the weakness of feminist movements on either side of the Line.

Underrepresented in the formal structures, some women have found scope for self-expression in civil society. Chapter 6 recounts grassroots *rapprochement* activity in Cyprus, those bi-communal projects I mentioned earlier, bringing Turkish Cypriots and Greek Cypriots into contact for purposes of peace-building. This and the following chapter then tell the main events over two years in the life of Hands Across the Divide. I review the difficulties this project met and members' efforts to deal with their differences. From their experiences I believe something can be learned for other struggles in other places to overcome the effects of a partition and mobilize women's energies for gender transformation and for peace.

In the final chapter I come back to the opening of the Line in April 2003 and the prospects for a solution. I look at current expressions of ethnic identity and cast forward to the implications for identities if and when an agreement is signed to bring the two communities into closer contact. Women relate very variously to ethno-national belonging, some cherishing it, some indifferent, others passionate about evading it. I suggest that changes in ethno-national and gender identifications are likely to affect each other. In and after peace negotiations women are likely to press for the implementation of United Nations Security Council Resolution 1325 of 2000, which calls for women to be included in peace-making and peace-building, so that post-war society may embody new values. I try to foresee the nature of the feminist movement that HAD seems logically to foreshadow – transformative, prefigurative and ethnically inclusive – that could be an actor in the reconstruction of society in a future Cyprus.

Those Greek and Turkish Cypriots who want to see Partition ended speak of themselves today as 'Cypriot', aspiring to an identity no longer semi-detached from Greece and Turkey but fully grounded in the island. I explore who and what a 'Cypriot' may turn out to be. First, when the name is spoken, will it suggest a woman? Second, whom will it include? It is the urgent desire of Turkish Cypriots and Greek Cypriots to find and relate to each other in a complementary mode that history has never till now permitted. But will that mean a narrow and exclusive (if hybrid) sense of self? The presence on the island of large new communities of migrants interestingly challenges the binary opposition of Greek Cypriot and Turkish Cypriot. How will the Turkish minority in the north and the growing number of Asian and other migrants in the south be defined in relation to the new Cypriot self? What potential is there for a politics of alliances based on values – feminist, anti-racist - rather than on identity? I close with some thoughts about Cyprus in 'Europe' and what women in Cyprus and other European countries could each bring to the other's movements.

§

It has been in my favour that, as a foreigner, I have been able to live and work with women equally in south and north Cyprus, something that has been all but impossible for a Cypriot. English is the common language in which a group of Greek Cypriot and Turkish Cypriot women are obliged to work. This factor, negative in excluding from dialogue the majority of the population, has been positive for me, making my involvement feasible. All the same, I was very aware in writing the book that my exposure to Cyprus has been relatively short and that because I do not speak or read Turkish or Greek there may be a great deal I have missed or misunderstood in the story I am trying to tell. My account is, besides, a necessarily 'situated' and partial one, from the standpoint of an English feminist working within the framework of political sociology. If it has any plausibility it is due to the generous guidance of Cypriot women themselves, especially members of Hands Across the Divide, and of a number of academic colleagues in Cyprus and elsewhere, whom I name and thank in the Acknowledgements.

The principal audience I have had in mind for the book is an informed but not necessarily academic reader, active for (or simply concerned about) social change, particularly in gender power relations and in the way we deal with identities and conflict. I would like it to be seen as a sketch, inspired by the pioneering work of Cypriot feminist writers, on which they will soon construct more substantial accounts of Cypriot women's perspectives. I would like to think it might encourage the growth of an inclusive and outward-reaching women's movement in Cyprus, help make feminism a more say-able word, and feminist change a more thinkable thought. I hope it may help to make Cypriot women's work for peace better known internationally. And more generally I would like it to be one more reminder to a neglectful world of the situation of this island that has for so long been caught midway between war and peace. There is a great deal we can learn from the struggle of progressive Cypriots to deal creatively with their web of inimical identities, tangled over and over again by the game play of bigger masculinist powers on the stage of the Ottoman Empire, the British Empire, the Cold War and now this new world order, in which the violent global strategies of the USA govern all our chances.

Notes

1 Although I do not consistently place quotation marks around ethnic names, because it would make tedious reading, I do so where I want to remind the reader that these, wherever they are used, are no more than labels, identity tags, and do not have an essential or fixed meaning. See page 29 for a discussion of ethnicity.

2 There are informal codes of practice, differentiating north and south Cyprus, concerning the words used to describe many contested phenomena. The events of July and August 1974, for instance, which Greek Cypriots call the 'Turkish invasion', many Turks and Turkish Cypriots call the 'peace operation'. Throughout the book I have chosen neutral terms – in this case 'intervention' – while recognizing that some readers may consider this practice itself evidence of political bias.

3 Concepts such as 'gender order' and 'ethnic order', useful in understanding gender and ethnicity, are introduced in Chapter 1.

4 Opinion on the politically correct way to represent the Turkish Republic of Northern Cyprus (TRNC) is sharply divided. The majority of Greek Cypriot authors understandably place quotation marks around the term to indicate the internationally unrecognized nature of this political entity, founded through the forceful expulsion of Greek Cypriots from part of the island. (Conversely, many Turkish Cypriots take care to refer not to the 'Republic of Cyprus' but to the 'Greek Cypriot administration'.)

Among non-Cypriot authors some place quotation marks round TRNC, and some do not. I have chosen to omit them, and regret that this will distress some readers. I am persuaded, however, by the arguments of Greek Cypriot authors Costas Constantinou and Yiannis Papadakis. They suggest that the official discourse of recognition 'has been employed by both regimes as a means of prohibiting or strictly regulating cross-ethnic contact that in effect normalises ethnic division both on the ground and as mentality. In doing so, the two sides misappropriate the international law of implied recognition and continue their historical reification of each other. By denying or giving specific "recognitions" of the other, Cypriot regimes of power thus naturalise what they do or say about each other' (Constantinou and Papadakis 2001: 129).

5 I use the term 'Cypriot' in most contexts as a general and inclusive category comprising both Greek Cypriot and Turkish Cypriot, together with the 'old' minorities on the island, Armenian, Maronite, Latin and Roma. However, in the final chapter I introduce a more politically conscious use of the word that is currently gaining salience, where Cypriot is a conscious ethno-national identity intended to transcend the divisions generated in Cyprus's history of conflict and partition.

6 Membership of Hands Across the Divide has changed from time to time. The following were those who eventually signed the constitution at a founda-

tional meeting in London or were subsequently named as founding members at the inaugural meeting in Pyla. Many of them will be mentioned and cited in subsequent chapters. Members resident south of the Line were Alexia Zinonos, Anna Agathangelou, Anthoula Papadopoulou, Georgette Loizou, Katie Economidou, Magda Zenon, Maria Hadjipavlou, Maria Salousti, Myria Vassiliadou, Nana Achilleos, Netha Kreouzos, Neşe Yaşın, Rita Pantazi, Sofia Georgiou, Sue Lartides and Tina Adamidou. Members resident north of the Line were Bahire Korel, Cemaliye Volkan, Derya Beyatlı, Fatma Azgın, Gülay Kaşer, Mine Yücel, Selma Bolayır, Sevgül Uludağ and Zehra Nalbantoğlu. The overseas members were Ayşe Simşek, Cynthia Cockburn, Destine Korak, Emine Ibrahim, Floya Anthias, Myria Georgiou, Olga Demetriou, Susie Constantinides and Tabitha Morgan.

7 Participant observation involves the active and self-conscious engagement of the researcher in the world that is the subject of her study. It is a particularly useful approach where the research focus is human meanings and interactions viewed from the perspective of insiders to particular situations and settings (Jorgensen 1989). Participatory *action* research, in particular, can be said to have two aims, first to 'produce knowledge and action directly useful to a group of people', and second to 'empower people … through the process of constructing and using their own knowledge' (Reason 1998: 269). Approaches to action research are highly diverse (for a typology see Hart and Bond 1995). My own interpretation of the methodology, involving membership of and engagement within a small non-governmental organization, will I hope become apparent as the text unfolds.

8 In two cases, a daughter was present at the interview with her mother, helping to interpret for her. The daughters also contributed material about their own lives and opinions, but are not included in the total of interviews.

9 Seven of those I interviewed in this personal vein were in their twenties, seven in their thirties, twenty-two in their forties, twelve in their fifties, three in their sixties and two in their eighties.

10 In a third of the individual interviews and in most of the group interviews, I had the help of an interpreter. The round tables were conducted mainly in English, but women helped each other by occasional interpretation. Seventy-five of my eighty-three data-gathering encounters were tape recorded. I worked from handwritten notes only when the interview subject asked me not to run a tape, or when the physical circumstances prevented it. On return I had these many hours of tape transcribed in full, resulting in around 4,000 pages of single-spaced typescript – a mass of qualitative data that I then coded thematically myself. With the help of the NUDIST NVivo computer program I sorted and cross-related the content of these transcripts, along with similarly theme-coded fieldwork narratives and notes from readings of books, academic papers, articles, leaflets and news cuttings.

11 The quotations from interviews and discussions that I use in the book are in many cases not exactly as they were originally spoken. This is because some women were speaking through an interpreter, others were speaking hesitant and imperfect English and, besides, some accuracy must be expected to have been lost in transcription. But, crucially, the reliability of the quoted remarks depends upon my having returned to each speaker to clarify her meanings. I have used three dots where some of the spoken text has been omitted, and square brackets to indicate a comment or question I inserted.

1 | Self and other: kinds of line

On 'UN Day' each year, the United Nations peace-keeping force in Cyprus opens the grounds of the Ledra Palace for a festival. Thousands of women, men and children from both sides have crossed the checkpoint on this unique occasion in the Cypriot calendar, to spend a few hours in the buffer zone with former friends and neighbours, and perhaps to prove to themselves they could reach at least the midpoint on the coast-to-coast journey they promised themselves would be possible again some time in the future.

As the crowd dispersed after dark on UN Day 2001, two elderly couples came out together and took leave of each other before crossing back to their respective parts of Nicosia. I walked southwards with the Greek Cypriot husband and wife. 'We come and meet up with these Turkish Cypriot friends of ours once each year,' they said. 'How crazy it is that we can't invite them home to our house for a cup of coffee. How good that would be!' I thought to myself, the two families live within a few hundred yards of each other. They breathe the same air. The same moon shines on both. Why can these friends not live together in daily contact, in civility?

This question can be approached from two directions. It can be explained as an effect of history, in which certain events in the past have led to certain realities in the present. And that is the approach I take in the chapters that follow. But it can also be approached conceptually, by exploring notions like 'difference', 'otherness' and 'identity'. These are abstract concepts whose meanings refer to a wider world than Cyprus, but they have a material, and very painful, specificity on the island. The historical approach will be more meaningful if these concepts are brought into play at the start, giving us a language in which to consider the events that took place in the past and the damage they have done to the present.

Difference and differentiation

Difference: this is a word loaded with trouble and with desire. Difference is inevitable and necessary. It is the source of much pleasure and cultural richness in human life. It is when we experience differences that we learn something new and may be able to overcome the narrowness of our horizons. Human encounter is a constant play and negotiation of difference and sameness. We can fall in love with difference. Yet, difference is often constructed as insurmountable otherness. We can hate for difference. Such divisive differentiation is usually an exploitative project of politics and power.

The making and marking of difference between human beings is not only unavoidable – it is an achievement. It is both a psychic and social process. It arises first in infancy as the child learns to differentiate herself or himself from the primary care-giver (most often the mother) and gain a sense of separateness, of being an individuated self in relation to that overwhelmingly significant other that gives or withholds nourishment and attention. The differentiating process continues into childhood, adolescence and adult life, as a person acquires and modifies a sense of self in more and more complex sets of relations among siblings and peers, parents, teachers and other adults. Social being involves acquiring and continually modifying one's personhood, through learning certain affinities and belongings (we are 'girls', we are 'Muslims') and understanding who one is not, who is deemed 'other' (they are 'boys', they are 'black', we are 'not adults').

The focus of this book on the concept of 'line' takes us beyond apparently innocent questions of difference and draws us on to the clearly political ground of active differentiation, where *identity* is at stake, the constitution and uses of identities in relations of power. The key political question is not whether we make and mark difference between us – of course we do. But how do we do it? What is the *mode of differentiation*? What is implied in the way we draw our lines, for inclusion and exclusion, closeness and distance, love and hate? A good deal of new thinking has been done on 'identity' in the last ten or fifteen years, extending its relevance from the domain of psychology into that of sociology and political science. Some of the new perceptions about identity are of profound political importance, particularly for those who struggle with exclusion, inequity and violence in relations of gender and ethnicity. Below, I draw mainly on the work of Stuart Hall (for instance Hall 1996) but also on that of Jonathan Rutherford (1990), Avtar Brah (1996; Brah et al. 1999) and others.

First, an individual's identity is not given by biology, by the family into which one was born or by cultural inheritance. The individual does not have an essential self that is there waiting to be uncovered, discovered. Rather, the sense of self is something we achieve as we grow and alter, responding to different encounters over time. It is dynamically constituted. Second, there is an element of chance in who we come to see ourselves as being, and also an element of necessity, where we are up against constraints and imperatives. Most importantly, there is an element of agency, of choice and investment, in the building of an identity. The individual may unquestioningly take up and live the name she hears herself called. Or, in certain circumstances, she may rebel and reject 'identification with' this or that belonging, or strive to rewrite its meaning.

Further, collective identities are constructed in and through discourse. We are surrounded by stories that bid for our attention. We hear words of warning, words of praise, about what it is to be 'a good woman', 'a worthy man', a 'true Turk' or a 'new Cypriot'. And we narrativize our selves as well, giving an account of ourselves in a story that is not finished till we die. But a sense of self is not the same thing as an identity: the obituary we would write if we had the chance would most likely reveal a self at odds with ascribed labels. For one thing, a sense of self is complex, built up of several interlocking (sometimes even contradictory) belongings and attachments. Ethnicity is only one of them. Pick a person from the street: 'she' may feel herself to be not only 'a Greek Cypriot', let us say, but also 'a Londoner', 'a teacher', 'a mother', 'secular' and so on, each of these identifications shaping the way she lives the others.

Finally, a discomfiting fact: important aspects of our selfhood are constituted not merely through differentiation but through exclusion, defining a 'we' and 'they'. It is particularly true of gender identity and ethnic identity (of which more below) and in certain circumstances also class. Once we have acknowledged that the forming of a significant component of identity involves the drawing of a line of separation, two questions unavoidably arise. If this is a self, who is the not-self it defines? What kind of line is drawn between this self and that constitutive 'other' or 'others'?

A line of differentiation may be relatively rigid or flexible, relatively permeable or impermeable. It may be sharply dichotomous, a matter of 'us and them', or involve pluralities so that one sees oneself as belonging to just one among many comparable communities. The other it separates from the self can be a little different or profoundly different, interestingly different or threateningly different, merely alien or utterly inimical. William Connolly has done useful groundwork here in distinguishing *antagonism* from *agonism* in the question of identities. Antagonism occurs when one identity group, let us say one defining itself by ethnic, political or religious belonging, aims for nothing less than conquest or conversion of the other, and mobilizes its power to define the other down. By contrast, agonism means caring struggle and strife, in which a collectivity sees dialogue and engagement with its 'different other' as necessary to its own fulfilment. Connelly suggests we are capable of choosing democratic identity processes in place of violent ones (Connolly 1991). This may seem idealistic, but it is an idealism without which the world may not have much of a future.

In the construction of gender identities, likewise, different modes of differentiation are possible. Different forms of masculinity and femininity exist within a given culture. One may be hegemonic, others subordinated or marginal. Some masculinity/femininity dyads may be more dichotomous than others. A man may have a great deal invested in a masculinity that is sharply differentiated from femininity. It could be he is proud of embodying, or trying to attain, qualities he and others in his culture admire as specifically masculine. Alternatively he might startle traditional opinion by distancing himself from the cultural norm of masculinity and valuing quite other qualities he finds in himself. He may look upon a woman not as someone complementary to himself but as, like him, a member of a category called 'people' whose senses of self mostly diverge a little or a lot from the binary gender norm.

One might think, then, that difference should always be minimized, since to stress it will only, ever, strengthen the line of exclusion. But this would be to lose all the creative energy of difference, the play of sexual self-expression, the enriching interactions of cultures. And in any case, once lines are drawn, those who are positioned 'the wrong side of the line' by a stronger identity group that benefits from excluding and distancing them, may reasonably want to reinforce their own sense of their collective difference and speak up in protest from their marginal position. Many women today feel they need to identify and organize as women in order to understand their position better, disclose the inequities of gender, and work for change. A subordinated ethnic minority may feel a similar impulse at a given moment.

A concept of difference, then, can never be put out of political play (Bacchi 1990; Cockburn 1991). The base-line for justice is that social arrangements should as far as possible respect and satisfy our individual specific needs as we ourselves perceive them – in the way architectural design should take account of people of varying heights, for example. Some specific needs are shared by a collectivity of people (women of a certain age menstruate, adherents of certain religions may not eat particular foods). Social arrangements should accommodate these group needs too. A subordinated or marginal collectivity or identity group must retain the right to point out where a line is being drawn to its disadvantage. It is when a dominant collectivity or identity group uses difference to draw a line *in its own interests* that we should begin to be suspicious. It is humane to differentiate in order to satisfy a need, inhumane to pile on to a tangible specificity (menstruation, say) a load of secondary negative characteristics (irrationality, unemployability) that disadvantage the group in question. It is acceptable to draw attention to *differentiation*, a process in which difference is being constructed and used to separate, subordinate and exclude. It is unhelpful to make assumptions about someone's *difference*, label her with an identity tag ('She's a Charlie', i.e. a British Cypriot); more constructive to leave space for her to show who she feels herself to be ('I was born in London but I feel more Cypriot than English').

The new thinking on identity has given us a refreshing sense of shifting possibilities. It has also presented us with a tough challenge, suggesting an irreducible need for responsible awareness of the perils of 'identity' as we do political work. If the making and marking of lines of differentiation is continually in process, and if it may be done in different modes, then outcomes (though subject to fierce pressures) can never be certain, and there is always scope for changing, through discourse and through practice, who we and others sense ourselves to be, and to whom and how we feel connected.

Gender lines, ethnic lines

In this book I am concerned with two particular dimensions of identity: gender and ethnicity. Although they are not the only components from which people construct a sense of self, they are specially important. First, they are universal – everyone everywhere is obliged to negotiate a relationship to the man/woman dyad, and no one can avoid being caught up in accepting or refusing ethnic 'names'. Second, both involve the drawing of lines to mark and separate people as 'different'. A third factor in the significance of these two dimensions of identity is the power and pervasiveness of the social forces that define and seek to enforce them.

It is by now widely accepted that environment and culture are profoundly constitutive of the differences we see between women and men – differences of appearance, behaviour and life course. Genes, chromosomes and hormones play a part in shaping men and women into different social beings, but there is too much variation in gender difference between periods and between places for biology to be its principal source (Brannon 1999). The relationship between the body and culture turns out to be a two-way affair, and the interactions are complex. R.W. Connell best captures the relationship when he describes the body as an arena or a site 'where something social happens' (Connell 2002: 48) And the something social is formidable in its persistence and power, and the range and complexity of the effects it generates. Cultural practices shape our bodies – life experience influences the fleshy structures and neural pathways of the brain, sport enhances men's musculature, beauty products soften women's skin. 'Ideal type' differentiations of men and women in some cultures produce creatures that can seem to be not merely different genders but inhabitants of different planets. On the other hand there are plenty of variations among the differentiations of gender and, besides, many individuals escape the formulae and do their own thing. As Bob Connell puts it: 'There is certainly enough gender blending to provoke heated reminders from fundamentalist preachers, conservative politicians and football coaches … that we ought to be what we naturally are, dichotomous. There are whole social movements dedicated to re-establishing "the traditional family", "true femininity" or "real masculinity". These movements are themselves clear evidence that the boundaries they defend are none too stable' (Connell 2002: 5).

Gender expectations and prescriptions vary and change from one time and place to another. So people do not 'get' a gender once and for all. To be acceptable and effective in the world in which they live they must 'do' gender as they go along, learning and practising gender competence (Butler 1990). In this they have a degree of agency, to achieve new expressions of old differences, sometimes to bend the rules. But their freedom is limited by structures – enduring and widespread patterns among social relations, such as a traditional family form, religious dogma or state policy. Cyprus is no exception, and we shall see a great deal of such structures in coming chapters. They tend to be hard to shift, being expressions of the interests of those who benefit from the system of power as it is. What is more, the inertia resides within us too, in so far as each of us has taken on board and internalized social expectations.

In parallel with this shift in the way gender is perceived, away from an essentialist view of given and fixed difference, there has occurred an equally important turn in the way culture and ethnicity may be understood. An earlier (though by no means superseded) understanding took cultural and ethnic distinctiveness, like gender difference, at face value. A 'people' of a historically given culture, seen as definable and distinguishing, were taken unproblematically to be of a given, even primordial, ethnic belonging. In reality there are no hard and fast lines between cultures, but instead much overlap and continual change. The alternative 'take' on ethnicity has a different starting point, asking how is an ethnic name *produced* through systems of meaning and structures of power? From this perspective, 'culture is no longer understood as what expresses the identity of a community. Rather, it refers to the processes, categories and knowledges *through which communities are defined as such*: that is, how they are rendered specific and differentiated' (Donald and Rattansi 1992: 4; my italics). Ethnicity, in other words, is best seen as an investment in cultural differentiation by particular social actors, often elites, with a political intention. For this reason, ethnic names – 'Serb', 'Chechnyan', 'Welsh' – can never be taken at face value. Ideally, they should be written with quote marks around them.

In Cyprus, the most significant (though not the only) ethnicizing process has been the dichotomizing of 'Greek' and 'Turk' and the simultaneous marginalizing of cultural variations that diverge from these two stereotypes. It is paralleled by a gendering process that (as elsewhere) differentiates masculine from feminine in such a way as to box varied people into two reductive and inescapable categories of human 'being'. Both processes have been socially damaging and impoverishing, resulting in power structures that have generated inequities and injustices, resentment, incomplete development and violence. They are, besides, more than merely contiguous, going along side by side. They are interconnected and mutually reinforcing. Gender is always constituted in a culturally specific form, and an ethnicity always pronounces its norms for manhood and womanhood (Anthias and Yuval-Davis 1992; Yuval-Davis 1997). Our oppression as women is enacted in ethnically specific ways. We shall see Cypriot women, for instance, struggling with the expectations of women in their families of origin.

That gender and ethnic relations, being intertwined, are sensitive to mutual change, is a central proposition of this book. Both, too, are potentially affected by economic change. For one thing, this has brought more women into the labour market. And as traditional patriarchal family codes have been undermined by modern consumer cultures, the marking of difference and inequality between women and men has continued, but in an adaptive form. What makes the line of the gender dichotomy so hard to challenge in such cultures today is less a surviving belief in its 'god-given' nature than that it is pervasively represented as the primary source of delight and pleasure: '*vive la différence!*' Heterosexual love and desire constitutes the most massively celebrated, propagated and commercially exploited theme in 'Western' cultures. From within the institution of heterosexuality, which gives primacy to the couple, and generates rivalry between women for the attention of men, it remains difficult and costly for women to identify politically with each other. In societies that are most opposed to Western capitalist cultural and consumer imperialism, one aspect of resistance is often the reinforcement of traditional gender dichotomy and hierarchy.

Gender and ethnicity: similarities and differences

There are both similarities and differences between gender and ethnicity in the processes they involve and the effects they produce. They are alike in tending towards an 'othering' process in which a non-self is defined and excluded in the very process of defining the self. Simone de Beauvoir was one of the earliest and most articulate to reflect on alterity, 'otherness'. She wrote: 'No group ever sets itself up as the One without at once setting up the Other over against itself … Jews are "different" for the anti-Semite, Negroes are "inferior" for American racists … the subject can be posed only in being opposed – he sets himself up as the essential, as opposed to the other, the inessential, the object' (de Beauvoir 1972: 16). But de Beauvoir's main concern was gender. For her, woman was the absolute case of alterity. In an assertion that galvanized a generation of women she wrote: 'She is defined and differentiated with reference to man and not he with reference to her; she is the incidental, the inessential as opposed to the essential. He is the Subject, he is the Absolute – she is the Other' (de Beauvoir 1972: 16).

A second likeness between ethnicity and gender is that the mode of differentiation they involve varies similarly along a continuum. Jan Nederveen Pieterse has shown how ethnic identities may be more and less politicized, belongings felt with more and less passion. A certain ethnicity may be a low-intensity affair involving little more than the celebration of certain cultural features such as cuisine. Or a culturally identified group may be highly self-aware, yet inward-looking, with few political aspirations. But given certain stimuli, people may awake to feel they are being in some way 'named' and inferiorized. They may begin mobilizing in that name, generating a discourse of difference, entering into rivalry with 'others' over resources and opportunities. Imaginations may turn to nationhood, such that ethnicity becomes *ethno-nationalism* and visionary politicians embark on a project of nation-statehood. They may take up arms to achieve it. And finally there may emerge a collectivity with the power to impose monocultural control, denying validity to others' identity claims, or casting other named groups in specific and inferior societal roles (Pieterse 1997).

There is clearly a resonance here with gender relations. Gender difference in some cultures is laid back, so casual that gender-benders may play, with relative impunity, with divergent ways of living 'man' and 'woman'. In others it is ferociously enforced and policed. When such gender extremism occurs it often coincides with and forms an intrinsic part of political projects of ethnic cultural differentiation – as in fundamentalist religious movements.

There are, however, certain important differences between ethnic differentiation and gender differentiation. One is in their relation to a physical referent. In matters of gender, taking a cue from our two-part reproductive biology has led us to represent human beings in a strictly dichotomous way (there is male/masculine and there is female/feminine, end of story). This blinds us to the more messy reality: our physical and neurological dimorphism is slight compared with our human similarities – and compared with the range of variation among women and among men (Brannon 1999). Besides, biological sex itself is not always unambiguous: an estimated 1.7 per cent of new-born babies are intersexed (Fausto-Sterling 2000: 51). It has also made us reluctant to diverge from the dichotomous schema to acknowledge variants of sexual orientation – lesbian, gay, bisexual, transgender, transsexual. Ethnicity is different from gender in this respect. First of all there are numberless cultures that can potentially be identified and mobilized under distinctive ethnic names. And secondly, although some may claim physical difference for themselves and their 'other', belief in a link between a cultural collectivity and a phenotypical feature such as hair or skin colour is even more difficult to sustain than the link between gender and biological sex. Many individuals belie their ethnic stereotype.

However, perhaps the most significant difference in the two differentiating processes is that while communities who consider themselves ethnically distinct may move apart, to a greater or lesser extent, to dwell in mono-communal groups, men and women have been held by heterosexual reproductive relationships into cohabitation. Gender separatism, as in single-sex religious establishments, is relatively rare. While an ethnic line, such as the line that encircles a ghetto or the partition line that splits a country, may almost totally separate two cultural groups, the gender line that differentiates men from women operates in another way. It achieves its effects within a myriad day-to-day interpersonal interactions. The gender line runs through every institution, every street, every building, every bedroom – even the bed itself.

The *ethnic line* separating those two couples who attended UN Day at the Ledra Palace was totally tangible: to walk home they had to pass through a barrier flanked by barbed wire. The *gender line* that separated each woman from her husband was hidden, a suppressed and ill-articulated matter appearing to concern only her and him. Who knows how gender difference is negotiated between them, what they feel and say (or never do say) to each other about their relative responsibility, choice, privilege and authority, about different expectations for their daughter and their son? This dissimilarity in the form taken by differentiation means that the logic and practice of struggle *against* othering and inferiorization, too, are bound to be dissimilar in the two cases of ethnicity and gender.

The ideal effect of an ethno-national partition line such as that of Cyprus is the separation, legitimated by a perception of 'danger' and a history of violence, of populations on the basis of supposed cultural distinctiveness. To imagine, in the case of gender, a line as total as this, one would have to imagine women withdrawing from, or expelled by, men to live in a separate region, marked by barbed wire, with state control of border crossings. It is unthinkable. The very unthinkability, though, provokes two further observations. First, ethnic *apartheid* is equally ridiculous, since as we have seen it is impossible to say definitively who is in one 'ethnic' group, who in another. One culture is lived in a multitude of ways. It is one thing in the heartlands, another on the fringes. It may be unique or hybrid. As individuals, many of us are of 'mixed blood', live in 'mixed marriages', are less or more religious, live in a culture different from the one in which we were raised, and so on. Second, we should not assume from the unthinkability of gender partition that the line as it is drawn between women and men in contemporary societies is relatively unproblematic. Its effects are often *less* tolerable precisely because women and men are chained together in intimacy, in a domain labelled 'private'. When gender tensions result in clinical depression or violence, as they often do, the damage is hidden from view and often goes unremedied.

Gender and ethnicity: useful terminology

The study of gender has produced some terminology that will be useful in thinking about Cyprus. For instance, the Australian sociologist Jill Julius Matthews, in a path-breaking book *Good and Mad Women*, wrote of the *gender order*, using this term to mean the power relations in any given society that establish a basic sexual division of labour, an initial social differentiation by gender that permeates and underpins all other distinctions (Matthews 1984). Of course she points out that it is not logically necessary that a society's gender order should be hierarchical or oppressive to one sex or the other. In fact, however, all the ones which we know advantage men to a greater or lesser degree. R. W. Connell has taken up Jill Matthews's concept of gender order and refined it by the further term *gender regime*, to designate the gender arrangements in any given institution (Connell 1987). The particular gender relations between individuals in the armed forces, for instance, may well differ from those in a hospital or a school.

It is important to examine our societies meticulously with a gender lens if we want to change them. The gender order in contemporary Cyprus, as in most if not all other societies, is characterized by male dominance. Such a system is often called, for short, *patriarchy*, rule by the fathers (from the ancient Greek *pateras*, father). The term was more appropriate in the past, in monarchies and theocracies where power passed through the hands of the father in a family-based system. Carole Pateman, in a usefully gendered reconsideration of the transition from feudalism to capitalist modernity and electoral democracy, shows how men's dominance over women did not diminish. Rather, power passed from the patriarchs to men as a whole – in the state, business corporations, the institutions of civil society, and heterosexual relations inside and outside marriage. She represents this key moment in the long and changing history and prehistory of gender orders as marking a shift from patriarchy to fratriarchy – the rule of the brothers (Pateman 1998). But 'patriarchy' continues to be used in everyday speech and since it has the merit of familiarity I use it in this book.

A further gender concept that will be useful in the chapters that follow is the notion of the *patriarchal dividend* – the advantage that accrues to men, as individuals and as a collectivity, from a gender order in which men and masculinity are dominant (Connell 2002). The dichotomous and unequal relations between men and women are not the only divisive effect of a patriarchal system. It also involves massive hierarchies that place men themselves in rank order, greatly to the disadvantage of those at the bottom. In other words, some men bank more of the patriarchal dividend than others. *Patriarchal bargain*, too, is a useful concept. Within systems of male power women are obliged to strategize and negotiate, taking as much as they can, sacrificing as little as they must, within the constraints of their situation (Kandiyoti 1988). The result is that most women accommodate to male authority and actively promote patriarchy. The effect of any partition is not only to separate the two sides, but to sow seeds of division within each side. Bitter divisions are likely between those who sign up to the patriarchal bargain and those who do not.

We can see how these various gender concepts might usefully be applied to the ethnic arrangements prevailing in a society and its institutions. Thinking in terms of the *ethnic order* would enable us to identify a hegemonic ethnic group holding sway over subordinate ones, and be aware of historic moments of ethnic tyranny. It would enable us to distinguish strictly hierarchical and reductive differentiations, similar to those of caste, from liberal and fluid regimes where ethnic distinctions do not matter very much and do not entail great inequalities or injustices. The notion of *ethnic regime* would enable us to compare the ethnic practices of one institution such as the police with those of another such as the social welfare system. We might also think in terms of an *ethnic dividend* (how much, for instance, has cultural 'Englishness' benefited an individual or group in Cyprus at given moments?) and an *ethnic bargain* (when one ethnic group provides services to another in exchange for patronage or protection, something we shall see occurring in the relation between the British and the Turkish Cypriots in the 1950s).

Two further terms I shall use in the chapters that follow may need some explanation: *sexism* and *racism*. I use 'sexism' to mean on the one hand an ideology, a mind-set that marks an inflexible binarism between men and women, stresses inequality between them, and makes it the basis for certain norms of behaviour. On the other hand it is a practice – that of deploying the notion of sex difference in a way that results, whether it is intended or not, in exclusions, inequalities and power-play. As sexism marks gender difference and sustains the gender hierarchy, so 'racism' is the ideology and practice that marks ethnic difference and sustains an ethnic ordering. The words sexism and racism both have an old-fashioned ring, due to an apparent reference to physique: biological sex on the one hand and phenotypical variance (particularly darkness versus fairness) on the other. As the understanding of sex difference has shifted in recent years to a focus on culture, something similar has happened in the matter of 'race' (Solomos 1989; Anthias and Yuval-Davis 1992). Today it is generally accepted that race is not a valid mode of categorizing people: features such as height, hair colour and skin tone vary on a continuum. Yet we cannot dispense with the term racism, because racist thinking and practices continue to damage people who may look alike but are distinguishable by their *culture* – 'cultural racism' (Balibar 1991; Rattansi 1994). Nationalism, even ethno-nationalism with its ambitious agenda of statehood, cannot be reduced to racism. But ethnocentrism and racism are intrinsic to it. Ethnocentrism gives primacy to the worldview of the imagined 'people', marginalizing others and silencing their discourse, while racism actively marks the boundaries and sustains the sense of who is 'one of the people' and who is not.

Partition as a political strategy

Worldwide, territorial lines have been drawn between populations for a number of different reasons. Imperial powers have sometimes found it convenient to divide people the better to rule them, or in order to mark out their spheres of influence against those of other colonists. They have also at times (as in the case of India and Pakistan) separated potentially conflictual ethnic groups as a prelude to shedding responsibility for rule. Partition of Cyprus was certainly considered by the British as a 'divide and quit' strategy as they prepared to relinquish control of the island in the 1950s. But international interests instead, as we shall see in the following chapter, brought Cyprus independence as a single state. Partition only came later, as power-sharing failed.

Enforced separation is not always 'ethnic' but may occur, motivated by political and ideological rivalries, within a population that considers itself ethnically homogeneous. The forty-year Cold War between the capitalist 'West' and communist 'East' following 1945 resulted in the partitions of Korea, Vietnam and Germany. The eventual healing of such political divisions presents its own kind of problem, as studies of German reunification have shown (Berdahl 1999). But during the late 1980s, as the political unity and economic viability of the communist bloc crumbled, lines laid down in the Cold War began to seem a crime that should not be repeated. The dismantling of the Berlin Wall was the dramatic high point of a popular revolt against partition. There was a space of a few years in the early 1990s in which the United Nations and other institutions responded to this new spirit, rejecting partition as an answer to armed conflict and promoting a methodology termed 'renewable peace' (Kumar 1997a). The Oslo Accords of 1993 in relation to Israel and Palestine and the Good Friday Agreement of 1998 in Ireland, reflected a new commitment to seeking practical opportunities for renegotiating old partitions, starting programmes to widen the common terrain and engaging regional actors in taking responsibility for solutions.

However, not too far into the 1990s some international relations theorists and politicians were already beginning to reassert the legitimacy of partition. This partitionist view from above and outside responded to certain shocking facts occurring on the ground – genocidal violence by groups in the name of particular ethno-national identities, such as 'Serb' or 'Hutu', in pursuit of domination, autonomy or separateness. Those who argue for partition represent it as 'the lesser of two evils': in certain circumstances, they say, if peoples do not separate there will be mass murder. Chaim Kaufmann, for instance, supports not only the principle of partition but also a policy of judicious transfer of ethno-national groups, arguing that when partitions fail it is often because (as in Ireland) the separation of peoples into defensible enclaves was insufficiently complete. In such circumstances, he says, people feel insecure and do not relinquish their vigilance, so that fear of renewed violence hangs over the peace (Kaufmann 1996; 1999). Daniel Byman castigates the United Nations and the United States for ignoring the option of partition. 'Sadly,' he writes, 'there is a tremendous bias for the continuation of current borders even in the face of repeated mass killings' (Byman 1997: 29).

The case against partition, however, is made by other analysts with equal energy. Radha Kumar argues that the partitions in India, Palestine and Ireland 'rather than separating irreconcilable ethnic groups, fomented further violence and forced mass migration' (Kumar 1997a:24; see also Butalia 2000). Partition, besides, tends to produce undemocratic entities, hampers the redevelopment of economies after war, and embroils international institutions in peace-keeping exercises that are difficult to end (see also Lewis 1995; Woodward 1999).

Cyprus is cited as evidence in support of both positions. Kaufmann, for instance, claims that 'only' twelve killings since 1974, even without a peace agreement, is proof that partition and population transfer save lives. The Turkish Republic of Northern Cyprus, he believes, ranks 'about average' among its eastern Mediterranean neighbours on measures of democracy (Kaufmann 1999: 248). By contrast, Kumar argues: 'While the number of deaths can be said to have been restricted since [the *de facto* partition], the division of Cyprus consists of little more than a prolonged stand-off which is not only dependent on the continuing presence of UN troops but remains in a state of constant readiness to erupt' (Kumar 1997b: 28).

In this book I do not take a position in the debate as to whether, as many Turkish Cypriots felt in 1974, partition of the island was necessary for their security as an imperilled minority or whether, as many others felt then and since, the drawing of the Green Line and removal of people from their homes was not only a violation of human rights but also unnecessary in terms of Turkish Cypriot security and development. I do not offer a conclusion that would support either side in the debate on partition among international relations theorists. What I have chosen to do is simply to contribute information about some of the effects of a long partition, to add to the evidence available to those who make decisions. What happens to ethnic relations during the long years of apartheid? When their development has diverged so long and so markedly, how can two populations make connections across the obstacle of partition? We see, through women's eyes, how, once made, a partition is very difficult to reverse. It generates divisions not only between but within each side, not least between those who adopt the new separate identities and those who refuse them. Cyprus can teach the world a lot about what happens when people live segregated lives for decades and, since the recent precipitate opening, when contact is permitted once again.

A physical partition, in a way, is frozen time. Events in Cypriot history first suggested the Line as a possibility, then planted it in the ground. Of course, it could not impede all development. Some aspects of life blew on past it. But others got tangled in the wire and have been left behind, waiting for some future wind to release them. Significant among the retarded elements are ethnicized identities – selves and their others – for in a way they *are* the line in its non-physical form. It is significant that the organization on which this book focuses chose to call itself Hands Across the Divide. They knew they had to reach across the hostility-gap between people of two 'names'. But to do this, as in all such projects, they had to reach across a reality-gap too, the gap between ascribed identity and the individual actor's actual sense of self. I have shown elsewhere how this was done by women in three other countries, and how difficult it was to find a path between, on the one hand, sensitivity to the significance of 'names', and, on the other, the danger of taking them at face value, being trapped and trapping others in them (Cockburn 1998).

The term *transversal politics* has recently come into use among groups seeking to forge alliances of differently-identified groups resisting racism, fundamentalism, nationalism and war. With Lynette Hunter, I have described it elsewhere as follows:

> It answers to a need to conceptualize a democratic practice of a particular kind, a process that can on the one hand look for commonalities without being arrogantly universalist, and on the other affirm difference without being transfixed by it. Transversal politics is the practice of creatively crossing (and re-drawing) the borders that mark significant politicized differences. It means empathy without sameness, shifting without tearing up your roots. (Cockburn and Hunter 1999: 88; see also Yuval-Davis 1997)

Part of the empathetic process will be a retreading of the history behind the warring identities, and an acknowledgement of injustices. A practice of transversal politics, however, has to take account of more than identities. Difference of *position* in relation to power is also a factor. A given ethnic order, for instance, may be one in which differences of ethnicity and socio-economic class are superimposed, so that one 'side' in the dialogue speaks from a position of relative wealth or authority. Other factors of positioning, within and between identity groups, can be sources of power as well, including age and, if the group is of both women and men, gender. If such differences of position are not acknowledged they will derail the process, however careful the handling of identity (Yuval Davis 1999). Power-positioning and identity sometimes overlap in complicated ways, as when one 'ethnic side' is exploiting the other economically.

Furthermore, an alliance across difficult differences has to be forged on the basis of shared values. Within any name group or power group there will be members of contrasted political ethos. Some may be authoritarian, for instance, some may be egalitarian. Some may be of the left, some of the right. Some may seek more unity, some may desire more separateness. It is thus not everyone of a given ethnic name that will be willing or able to forge an alliance with those of its 'other'. How inclusive membership of a project of alliance can be, or how selective it must be, becomes a crucial issue. We shall see the question of values arising for Hands Across the Divide in Chapter 7, and it will become a major issue in the last chapter.

Finally, when a successful dialogue takes place across difficult differences it is because the participants have come to understand the plurality of truth. Donna Haraway has usefully coined the term 'situated knowledges' to remind us how all knowledge springs from a particular situation, and each voice speaks its own truth. Even a discourse that pretends to a universal truth – and those of the world's white male ruling classes are particularly prone to this – is partial, however much the fact is disguised. It is no truer than the truths of those it marginalizes or silences. Indeed it is likely to be less so, because, as Donna Haraway puts it, 'the god trick' is a recipe for imperfect vision. It is only when brought together and negotiated that our many truths begin to approximate something more trustworthy (Haraway 1991: 193). What is more, co-operation in an alliance for change calls for more than combined knowledges, it demands a shared vision of the nature and goal of the dialogue, including a sense of a shared future. This can only be the product of *imagination*. Imagination too is 'situated' (Stoetzler and Yuval-Davis 2002). An important question in Cyprus today (as we shall see in Chapter 8) is from what position (feminist? bi-communal? multicultural?) is societal change being imagined, within Hands Across the Divide and elsewhere? From a given standpoint, what future can we foresee – and perhaps bring about?

The seriousness for Cypriots of the Cyprus Partition Line can scarcely be exaggerated. The recent opening to individual movement has not diminished this, but rather dramatized it. At the most personal level, what side of the Line you live is an inescapable component of your sense of self. You may try to transcend the dichotomy by taking a plane to the diaspora, but the escape is never complete, because the Line lives, though in varying forms, wherever Cypriot communities have taken root. At the geographical level it constitutes two opposed ethno-national patriarchal polities, differentially shaping the lives and chances of hundreds of thousands of people. And at the global level, it has symbolic meaning as the fence between the West and the Rest.

2 | The production of enmity

I met two young women, Andri Andreou and Efthymia Thrasyvoulou, activists in the Independent Student Bastion. This is a student group in the University of Cyprus, unattached to any of the political parties, that stresses the Greekness of Cyprus. They told me how they recruit new members. They believe 'education' is the place to begin, especially an education in history, 'the identity of the island', as they put it. And they are certainly right, for history is where nationalist politics stakes its first claim. Andri said:

> A student might think that Cyprus belonged to Turkey geographically because it's near to Turkey. It's Greek, we belong to Greece. By culture, by language and by history. The Greeks came here in the twelfth century BC, they came peacefully and they settled the land. You can see evidence of that continuity, the language is the proof. The successive conquerors who came didn't change our language or our religion.

'Ancient history' is never dead and buried. Narratives of what happened or did not happen in very early times often carry even more political freight than accounts of what happened yesterday, because they are about 'who we really are'.

That the Hellenistic connection in Cyprus is strong, and was particularly flourishing in the Classical Age (475–325 BCE), contributes importantly to the cultural wealth of the island. But the Achaean or Mycenaean civilization was not the first. There was human habitation on Cyprus from at least 6000 BCE, flourishing Neolithic and Bronze Age cultures that cannot be termed 'Greek'. And during the first millennium BCE many other incoming peoples followed the Achaeans, as the island was ruled in turn by Assyrians, Egyptians and Persians. In the two millennia that followed, there would be Arabs, French and English Crusaders, Lusignans, Genoese and Venetians. But Efthymia and Andri, like other 'Hellenistic' Greek Cypriots, choose to stress the arrival of Greek culture in the twelfth century BCE, and say 'Cyprus is part of Greece just the way Crete is'. They add, 'We feel Greek', and that is important. Because as we see above, this has a very contemporary significance. It means one thing in particular: feeling 'not Turkish'.

For it is often to counter claims of a Turkish and thus Islamic identity for the island that the claim of Greekness is so fiercely made. And Greek Cypriots may say without fear of contradiction that Cyprus was Christian long before it was Muslim – indeed, before Muhammad was even born. St Barnabas and St Paul brought the Gospel to Cyprus in the first century of the Christian era. The church of Cyprus eventually became a (self-governing) part of the Orthodox Church based in Byzantium (Stamatakis 1991). So it was not only through pre-Christian settlement from the Peloponnese but also, in a rather different way, through adopting Orthodox Christianity that Cypriots of those times came to see themselves as 'Greek'. The island remained Orthodox until the late twelfth century CE, when the island was seized by Franks and for 400 years a succession of Roman Catholic rulers from the western Mediterranean drove Orthodoxy into retreat.

The next invaders in Cyprus's restless history were the Ottomans. Warrior Turkmens migrated westwards from the Asian steppes during the fourteenth century, gradually extending their control over the Balkans and Anatolia. In 1571, a date that all Cypriot schoolchildren know, the Ottomans, by now a well established and culturally diverse empire, seized Cyprus from Venetian control (Goodwin 1999). It is ironic, given contemporary tensions between Christians and Muslims, that the Orthodox Christians at first welcomed their arrival as an improvement on Catholic domination. The Ottomans drafted to the island a substantial population from Anatolia, but did not, it seems, ever seek to establish a demographic majority (Oberling 1982). The Graecophile Independent Student Bastion, intent on the unique claim of Greeks to Cyprus, will tell you that Turkish Cypriots are the descendants of these colonizing Turks, and thus genetically as well as culturally distinct from 'Cypriots'. Efthymia said, despite more than 300 years of Ottoman control, 'neither the Greeks nor the Turks affected each other. We didn't become Turks, and they didn't become Greeks.' And it is true that in all regions of the Ottoman Empire the practice of the sultans was to allow Christianity, Judaism and other religions to operate each within its own distinct cultural space – the millet system.

The story as told by Bastion would be affirmed by right-wing, Turcophile northern Cypriots, who prefer to consider themselves a subset of 'Turks'. But others, who like to think of Turkish-speaking Cypriots as 'Cypriot' before 'Turk', would say that, as in Bosnia and other parts of the Ottoman Empire, some of the pre-existing inhabitants of the island converted to Islam as a way of climbing the ladder to economic prosperity and social influence in the Ottoman regime. If this is so, the forebears of many of today's Turkish Cypriots were 'Cypriot' (or even 'Greek' if that is what you suppose early Cypriots to have been) before they were 'Turkish'.

Bahire Korel, of Hands Across the Divide, whose son suffers from thalassaemia, tells me many who study this inherited disease believe that its prevalence in both Turkish Cypriot and Greek Cypriot populations indicates that they are of the same physical stock. However, if genes are thus to be recruited for politics we should add that Cypriots are widely differentiated in appearance, a reminder that Phoenicians, Egyptians, Persians, Romans, Franks, Venetians and British each contributed to the gene pool and changed the cultural mix. All of which suggests it is a good thing to keep separate and analyse with care, in the calculation and naming of ethnic belonging, the cross-cutting factors of population flow, phenotype, material culture, language and religion.

So far, this account of history and prehistory has been told, as Andri and Efthymia tell it, in terms of what we would today call 'ethnicity' or cultural differentiations, movements and conquests, with religion and language pre-eminent among the determinants of culture. But we could also delve for a gender history and prehistory. And in this respect, women as women can scarcely celebrate 'being' either 'Greek' or 'Turk'. For the Greekness cherished by Andri and Efthymia – the Hellenism of the first millennium BCE revered by the West as 'classical Greece' – is the epitome of patriarchy. No less misogynist were the Byzantine and Frankish Christian regimes that followed. And the Ottoman heritage that some Turkish Cypriots might wish to give more legitimacy as an element within 'Cypriot' identity was an extreme case of a militarized imperialist, and polygamous, male power system.

What is more, there is evidence that for several millennia until around the middle of the second millennium BCE a more gender-equal civilization had existed in Minoan Crete, in Anatolia (as evidenced by excavations of neolithic Çatal Hüyük and Halicar) and other areas of the eastern Mediterranean (Platon 1966; Mellaart 1975). Diane Bolger concludes from her research on burial excavations that Cyprus in the fourth millennium BCE had a village-dwelling farming society, egalitarian and based on kinship. Already by the third millennium it was giving way to one based on lineage, with a degree of hierarchy and bureaucracy. Changes observable in mortuary practices suggest to her that this was accompanied by increasing birthrates and a growing gender division of labour, adversely affecting the status of women (Bolger 2002). When in the second millennium the Achaeans arrived in Crete, and the Hittites in Anatolia, they brought military cultures, substituting throughout the region a cult of masculine gods of thunder and war for the fertility goddess of the agrarian civilization that went before (Hawkes 1968; Eisler 1987; Vassiliadou 1997). Archaeologists studying those Achaean landings in Cyprus mentioned by Andri and Efthymia, which occurred around the twelfth century BCE, note a 'heroic spirit' evident in the pottery of the period which shows 'scenes commemorating various "macho" activities ... connected with Greek male society' (Bunimovitz and Yasur-Landau 2002).

In the late nineteenth century, the Ottoman Empire was in decline. In 1878 the Sultan ceded administrative rights over Cyprus to Britain and in 1925 it became a British colony. This little patch of earth in the eastern Mediterranean embarked on a new career as a valuable asset in the power-play of Britain, and eventually of the North Atlantic Treaty Organization (NATO) and the United States of America. Cyprus has also been a heated issue between the modern nation-states of Greece and Turkey. And it is worth remembering at this point that the drawing of lines between 'Turks' and 'Greeks', with consequent forced migrations, did not begin with the partition of Cyprus. In the nineteenth century, Greece and Turkey had considerably intermixed populations. But Turkey's geographical sway diminished and Greece launched a struggle for independence from the Ottomans in 1821. It was in the grip of an irredentist vision, its Megali Idea, the 'great concept' of a nation whose borders would enclose all lands where 'Greeks' were living – not excluding Istanbul. In the first two decades of the twentieth century by warfare and by treaty Greece did in fact gain considerable territory, and doubled its population (Close 2002).

Popular memory is selective. Many of those who recall these times tell one half of the story, that of their own people's suffering, and forget the other. Greeks also suffered at the hands of Turks. The Great War of 1914–18 marked the end of the Ottoman Empire, but the Treaty of Sèvres in 1920 restored Izmir, Eastern Thrace and certain islands to Turkish rule, and Kemal Atatürk followed through with a military campaign against Greece in the process of founding the secular republic of Turkey. As a result, an extraordinary exodus from Turkey of an estimated 1.3 million Orthodox Christians took place. In the contrary direction, possibly half a million Muslims living in Greece were forced to resettle in Turkey (Close 2002).

The memory of such events in Greece and Turkey, told and retold, permeates Greek Cypriot and Turkish Cypriot cultures, colours their fears and shapes their reactions today. Women in particular remember the tales of their mothers and grandmothers, because this ethnic cleansing, as would be the case a few decades later in Palestine and Bosnia, was an assault on everyday life, the household, the domain of women. Men were the wielders of force in these episodes, and widely used the weapon of rape to destroy the morale of enemy men through defilement of 'their' women. Here is the vicious crux of the intersection of gender and ethnicity.

Enosis, the Greek and Greek Cypriot project for the union of Cyprus with Greece, was born of the Megali Idea. Militant agitation against British rule by the Greek Cypriot majority on the island first erupted in the 1930s but intensified in 1955, when a spate of bombing in Nicosia launched a fierce revolt by the National Organization of Cypriot Fighters, EOKA, led by the rightist Colonel Georgios Grivas. It was energetically suppressed by the British who at one point had 30,000 troops tied up in this operation (Ehrlich 1974: 20). Cyprus's anti-colonial campaign, however, differed in two ways from some other liberation struggles. First, EOKA had no element of leftism. Indeed, the leadership of the Orthodox Church was deeply involved in the movement, and Greek Cypriot communists and Marxists were its targets not its allies. Second, independence was never the goal. This was purely Greek ethno-nationalism, and it was not only the British but also the Turkish Cypriots that EOKA wished to see gone from the island. These differences may be the reason why the concept of women's liberation, an important component of some anti-colonial revolutions (Jayawardena 1986), had no part in the ideology of EOKA.

For their part the Turkish Cypriots harboured a hope that when the British eventually gave up colonial rule of Cyprus the island would be ceded to Turkey, as successor to the Ottoman Empire. As *enosis* had its EOKA, the nationalists on the Turkish Cypriot side had the movement for *taksim*, its aim the division of Cyprus between Turkey and Greece. In 1957 an armed group, Volkan, was set up to

The day the Greeks rose up against the Ottomans in 1821 is celebrated as a national holiday in Cyprus.

pursue this ideal by violence. It would later form an element of the Turkish Defence Force, the TMT (Hitchens 1997).

By the 1950s, many colonies were winning freedom from their colonizers; but Cyprus was in Europe and, with the Cold War at its height, its case was seen in a different light. The Soviet Union dearly wanted access to the Mediterranean. Britain and the USA, allied in NATO, therefore feared Soviet designs on Greece, where the communist movement was strong, and on Turkey, which bordered on the USSR. Arab nationalism was a growing threat to Western access to oil. Cyprus was a crucial link in the chain of British bases in the Mediterranean, the Middle East and beyond. Britain had to hold on to it (O'Malley and Craig 1999).

British strategy: divide and rule

Britain has something to answer for as regards the state of ethnic relations in Cyprus today. Traditionally, the two communities identified not as Cypriots but as 'Greeks' and 'Turks' living in Cyprus. As Zenon Stavrinides put it, they had not regarded themselves as 'compatriots' but rather as 'neighbours' (Stavrinides 1976: 15). Britain did not seek to develop a singular Cypriot identity; rather, its colonial strategy was to maintain the Ottoman practice of delegating authority over community affairs to traditional community leaders, which had the effect not only of underscoring the division between Turkish and Greek Cypriots but also of reinforcing the subordination of women. The education system, municipal councils and electoral rolls were segregated on religious lines. It is not surprising that the communal identities thus strengthened became, in the course of the anti-colonial struggle, ethno-national identities, pitched as much against each other as against the British (Pollis 1979).

It did not help inter-communal relations that the British employed Turkish Cypriots in the police force used to repress the Greek nationalist revolt. In British uniforms Turkish Cypriots were fair game for EOKA. The British were increasingly disinclined to trust Greek Cypriots as public employees and Greek Cypriots were disinclined to employ Turkish Cypriots. This was brought home to me by Canan Öztoprak, a Turkish Cypriot psychologist, who told me how her father had made his living driving a bus that transported Greek Cypriot workers to the copper mines each day. As tensions increased in the late 1950s, these workers deserted him for a Greek Cypriot who started a competing bus route. Canan's father then joined the British police. 'Where else could he earn a living now?' It is a typical story. At the same time, 'divide and rule' being a well-tried strategy for holding on to power, Britain clearly had an interest in favouring Turkish Cypriots. Many Turkish Cypriots signed up to the ethnic bargain, sharing the British priority of defeating Greek nationalism in the belief that, once the *enosis* project was defeated with their help, the world would hand Cyprus to Turkey (Hitchens 1997).

In the last years of British rule the population of Cyprus was largely rural. Traditional family values placed many constraints on women. Anthropologist Peter Loizos first observed village life in Cyprus in the 1960s, but his description implied little change from a decade, or even a century, before. The gender line was deeply scored. The public open spaces and streets of the village were the men's world, he writes. Women moved through them unobtrusively, with eyes downcast. Men's place was in the coffee shop, women's in the home: 'The proper company for a woman was other women, for a man other men.' In the house, women did not sit at table with the men, but served them. Loizos's uncle told him: 'We hope we are Europeans in most things, but in matters of honour, that is where our women are concerned – we are happy to be Middle-Easterners' (Loizos 1981: 28, 35). Turkish and Greek Cypriots shared some distinctively Cypriot customs, including some similarities in cuisine, music and dance, and a certain vocabulary common to the two languages. These things distinguished them from the Greeks of Greece and the Turks of Turkey. But there was a clear differentiation of one community from the other, and women, as in other patriarchal societies, were actively involved in the cultural processes of everyday life that marked the ethnic boundaries (Yuval-Davis 1997).

Except for a small elite, Cypriots at this time were poor. Women now in their late forties or older remember how it was when they were children. They tell me now, 'To have a car was something special, then. There were no fridges, no televisions. It was another world.' But this does not mean there was equality in the poverty. Few women had a wage or a salary at their own disposal. Their labour mainly produced goods and services for use within the home, and they depended on husbands and fathers for cash.

British rule did little to shift patriarchal oppression in rural, traditional Cypriot families. The Greek Orthodox Church maintained its authority and influence. The Church allowed a husband to divorce his wife if she proved to be not a virgin – a law which remained in place until 1979 (Pyrgos 1993). Since not even elementary education was compulsory for either sex, families continued to prioritize schooling for sons over the education of daughters. In 1911 twice the number of boys than girls were enrolled in elementary school. Men were three times more likely than women to be literate. In 1946 no more than 7 per cent of women were in full-time employment with a further 13 per cent part-timing (Cyprus Social Research Centre 1975). However, Britain was having a modernizing effect on the wealthier class and in urban areas. The colonial institutions provided some employment opportunities for educated women. At eighty years of age, Feyziye Hulusi was the oldest woman I interviewed in Cyprus. The well-educated daughter of a cultured Turkish Cypriot family, as a young woman she was employed to type and translate for the British Information Office. In accordance with the rules prevailing at the time, when she married in 1942 she was required to resign from government employment. The exclusion of married women was relaxed after the war, however, not only in the colonies but also in the UK, and Feyziye had a long career in the public service. Her last post was in the Cyprus Broadcasting Service, where, during the EOKA campaign, she narrowly missed death in a bomb attack directed, she believes, at her as a Turkish Cypriot 'lackey of the British'.

Despite the cultural separateness of the two communities, it was shocking to many ordinary Cypriots when in 1955 armed conflict broke out on the island and they found themselves on different sides of it. Many of the northern women I interviewed had lived in the south of Cyprus in those days. Wherever in the island they were, Greek Cypriots had been living not far away. They think back to when they were little girls, how their mothers and fathers would barricade the door at night for fear of raids by EOKA terrorists. In many cases 'my earliest memory' was an event so traumatic for a four- or five-year-old that it would never be erased. Canan Öztoprak used to walk home from infant school alone. She remembers the terror she experienced one day when she was still out on the street as the sirens sounded the curfew, and a military vehicle approached, loudspeaker blaring. She was crying, hammering at the door, calling for her mother to let her in. 'It was only two minutes, perhaps, but to me it was a lifetime.'

Greek Cypriots, despite being the majority, did not live free from fear. The British suspected every Greek Cypriot of complicity in rebellion. Those like Arianna Economou, whose parents were leftists, were caught between hammer and anvil. She remembers being out with her grandmother, caught up in tear-gas as the British forces quelled EOKA-inspired riots. She remembers the British raiding their home, searching for weapons, ransacking cupboards and drawers. But, as well, there had been EOKA extremists, rooting out the 'traitor' leftists, breaking down the door, smashing the television set and confiscating any other commodity (including hoolah-hoops, Arianna remembers) reviled as British. In addition there was the threat from the TMT. Many Greek Cypriot women told me of the shock of finding that individuals and families of the Turkish Cypriot community they had trusted till now as neighbours and friends, had joined the underground and were armed.

The British colonists lacked respect for Cypriots, without much regard to ethnicity. Lawrence Durrell illustrates their lofty attitude with a passage from a nineteenth-century author. The people of Cyprus, wrote W. Hepworth Dixon in *British Cyprus* (1887), are

> an indolent, careless and mimetic people, but without a spark of Turkish fire, without a touch of Grecian taste. With neither beauty of body nor sense of beauty in mind – with neither personal restlessness nor pride of origin – with neither large aspirations nor practical dexterity of hand, they live on in a limpid state, like creatures of the lower types clinging to life for life's own sake; voluptuaries of the sun and sea; holding on by simple animal tenacity through tempests which have wrecked the nobler races of mankind. (Durrell 1957: 176)

While perhaps (let us hope) this is an extreme case, something of this scorching British superiority lived on into the 1950s and damaged the self-respect of both Greek and Turkish Cypriots (particularly men, whose masculinity it diminished). But it did not unify them. There are many Turkish Cypriots who think now they were mistaken to side with the oppressor against their neighbours, that they should have joined the Greek Cypriots in a liberation struggle. But would that have saved them from EOKA's second project, their pogrom against the people they saw as the ruler-before-the-last, the Ottomans? This was, after all, a nationalist and racist war as well as an anti-colonial struggle.

Independence: the unsolicited gift

Within five short years of the onset of this late-colonial mayhem, a Republic of Cyprus was brought into being. Following the national-ization of the Suez Canal by Egypt, and Britain's ill-conceived military response, relations between Britain and the USA soured. Britain's in-fluence in Middle Eastern politics declined, and the USA became the major influence in Cyprus's affairs. World opinion was by now favour-ing decolonization. But military facilities in this crucial corner of the eastern Mediterranean must at all costs be retained to scotch Soviet encirclement of NATO, and oil supplies from the Middle Eastern oil fields remained vital to Western interests. On these things the USA and Britain had no disagreement (O'Malley and Craig 1999).

There followed a complex series of diplomatic moves in which various policy options were considered, including partition of the island, to protect the interests of NATO. Greek and Turkish rivalry on this and other issues was 'a festering sore affecting the organization's defensive strength' (Ehrlich 1974: 35). What strategy could relieve Britain of this costly colony, maintain future stability and secure the bases for the West? The Greek Cypriot leader Archbishop Makarios, through US mediation, was returned from a British-imposed exile. The premiers of Greece and Turkey, at conferences in London and Zurich in 1959, under the eye of the British and US governments, agreed a series of treaties that brought into being a Republic of Cyprus the following year.

Under these agreements, the British would own, in perpetuity, 99 square miles of the island for a military base, while provision was made for a garrison of 950 Greek and 650 Turkish soldiers. The inde-pendence deal was designed to steer Cyprus between the hazards of *enosis* and *taksim*. It named Britain, Turkey and Greece as guarantors of the new republic with an obligation to take action if necessary to pre-vent breaches of the agreements. This solution was one the USA had worked hard behind the scenes to achieve. Though Archbishop Mak-arios, reluctantly, signed up to the agreement, the people of Cyprus were not party to the new arrangements for their governance. There was no referendum (Joseph 1997). Had there been, women would not have been eligible to vote in it.

So Cyprus joined other ex-British colonies among the nation-states of the Commonwealth. The 'line' that marked its borders was now in principle the sea coast. But the system Cypriots were handed was going to prove very difficult to operate. The cost of unity was institutionalized dualism. The distinctive interests of Greek and Turkish Cypriots were accommodated by means of an 'ethnic' principle running through the new structures at every level. There would be a Greek Cypriot president and a Turkish Cypriot vice-president, elected by separate ethnically-defined constituencies. The Council of Ministers was to have seven Greek Cypriot members and three Turkish Cypriot, appointed respectively by the president and vice-president, either of whom could veto the other on significant issues of policy. The two legislative chambers were also to be separately elected by, and given power over, the two communities as regards religion, education, cultural affairs, and personal and civil codes. The cities would have split municipal authorities (Joseph 1997).

In recognizing the equality of the two communities, the constitution established quotas for representation and, 'having a bi-communal character it naturally gave greater representation to the Turkish-Cypriot community in the institutions of government than their absolute numbers could be said to have warranted' (Dodd 1993a: 5). For instance, the Greek Cypriot proportion of posts in the public service and police was to be 70 per cent and in the army 60 per cent, both well below the known proportion of Greek Cypriots in the population – 77 per cent. These percentages would later prove a source of aggravation to Greek Cypriots. If there was a good deal of scope in the constitution for disagreement between Turkish and Greek Cypriot, however, its dichotomous structure was also an affront to the several thousand 'others' – Maronites, Armenians, Latins, Roma – who were not provided for at all. To have citizenship rights, and to vote, an individual was obliged to choose one or other of the only two identities on offer (Sirmen 1979). Thirty-five years later the division of post-war Bosnia would apply a similar constitutional model, reducing diversity to an exclusive and reductive ethnic version of citizenship.

Women gained little in these momentous changes. As we have seen, the movements for *enosis* and *taksim* in Cyprus were not so much liberatory as reactionary movements for union with a motherland, and the gender dimension of their ideologies was patriarchal, as is characteristic of ethnic nationalisms (Yuval-Davis 1997). As Myria Vassiliadou put it, 'the struggle … in Cyprus in the 1950s was created by men, ordered by men and carried out by men. It was a patriarchal struggle on a patriarchal island' (Vassiliadou 2002: 459). Many women supported and assisted the fighters, but they did not characteristically bear arms.

When independence came about, the Cypriot constitution gave women the right to vote and to stand for election, but it gave them little more (Pyrgos 1993). The political leaders who negotiated it, and those whose interests it embodied, were men and the process had been blind to gender. The fair representation of the two principal ethnic groups had consumed their attention, but there had been no parallel attempt to assure the representation of women in the executive or legislature. Civil, familial and personal affairs, including marriage and divorce, remained as in the colonial period, in the hands of traditional community structures, in such a way that patriarchal control over women was perpetuated. Women might have gained some relief from a regime of unremitting masculine violence, active or latent, had the end of the anti-colonial struggle brought a demilitarization of Cyprus. But we have seen that the huge investment in the island of the British armed forces was to continue under the new regime. And, while the constitution-writers hoped they were diminishing the significance of the paramilitary forces on the island, they were simultaneously introducing and legitimating the presence of two new armies – those of Greece and Turkey.

The power-sharing constitution proved unable to hold Greek and Turkish Cypriots together for long. In 1963, frustrated by the Turkish Cypriot veto over policy-making, President Makarios proposed a series of amendments that would have the effect of turning Cyprus into a unitary state, with arrangements for the representation of Turkish Cypriots less as a full partner than as an ethnic minority (Ehrlich 1974). Turkey reacted fiercely, Fazıl Kücük, the Turkish Cypriot vice-president, rejected the proposals, and violence broke out in Nicosia and elsewhere between the TMT and Greek Cypriot official and unofficial forces. The TMT now numbered 5,000 men, with Turkish officers, and was led by the feared Kemal Coşkun, known as Grey Wolf. It was, however, greatly outnumbered by Greek Cypriot forces. Turkey massed troops, ships and aircraft along its southern shore. The Greek Cypriots attacked Turkish Cypriot communities in the northern coastal area to curtail their access to the sea. In retaliation the Turkish air force bombed Greek Cypriot positions in the region (Patrick 1976).

There followed several months of inter-communal fighting in

which 364 Turkish Cypriots were killed, a death rate ten times higher than that of Greek Cypriots, who lost 174 (Oberling 1982). Some 20,000 Turkish Cypriots abandoned their homes and livelihoods in this period and joined others in enclaves, each pulling its defensible ethnic 'line' close around it. Nicosia was partitioned. In response to Makarios's appeal to the United Nations, the Security Council resolved to send in a mediator and a force of 6,500 UN peacekeepers. Most of the combatants, the dead and wounded in these episodes had been men. Women's experience had been predominantly of flight, loss and sexual vulnerability.

The mid-1960s were troubled years. Turkish Cypriots, refusing Makarios's proposed amendments to the constitution, were excluded from parliament; they in turn withheld co-operation, administering their own municipalities separately; each side blamed the other (Dodd 1998). Social separation increased too. In 1890, 515 out of 629 Cypriot villages had had both Greek- and Turkish-speaking neighbourhoods. By 1960 this had fallen to 114. By 1974 many of these had been abandoned and 60 per cent of Turkish Cypriots were clustered in thirty-nine self-ruling enclaves (Brewin 2000). They had become increasingly impoverished, due to the economic sanctions imposed on the enclaves by the Greek Cypriot government, and also to loss of employment – for many Turkish Cypriots were dismissed from their jobs by Greek Cypriot employers and others found it too dangerous to travel to them (Patrick 1976). The police and the civil service had become *de facto* Greek Cypriot organizations. Despite its cavalier treatment of the constitution, the Greek Cypriot administration continued to be treated by the international community as legitimate – a fact greatly resented by Turkish Cypriots (Dodd 1993a).

Between 1963 and 1967 there was intense intra-communal strife within the Greek Cypriot community between those who still sought *enosis*, by violent means if necessary, and those who by now preferred an independent Cyprus (Patrick 1976). On 21 April 1967 a group of colonels seized power in Athens and placed Greece under military dictatorship. Georgios Grivas, now in command not only of the Greek army contingent in Cyprus but also the Cypriot National Guard, attacked two Turkish Cypriot enclaves in the south, causing many casualties. An international war between Turkey and Greece was narrowly averted by US intervention. Some Greek troops were withdrawn from the island to placate Turkey (Hitchens 1997). But the

Turkish Cypriot leadership now formalized their own Provisional
Turkish Cypriot Administration, funded by Turkey.

In the early 1970s, in reaction to a move by Makarios to improve
relations with Turkish Cypriots, and with the support of the Greek
junta, EOKA was revived as 'EOKA-B'. The extremists pursued violent tactics against President Makarios and his administration, against
the Greek Cypriot left and against Turkish Cypriots. On 15 July 1974
they staged a *coup d'état*. Makarios narrowly escaped assassination and
fled the island. Although within a matter of days this fascist attempt on
power would fail and lead also to the fall of 'the colonels' in Greece, it
would not stop Turkey, this time, sending troops into Cyprus – a traumatic and formative moment to which I return in Chapter 3.

Divergences: allocating blame

A retrospective allocation of blame for these events of the 1960s
and early '70s is a factor in present-day tensions between Greek and
Turkish Cypriots. Most, but not all, Turkish Cypriots primarily blame
the Greek Cypriot leadership for having behaved as an arrogant, oppressive majority, undermining the power-sharing provisions of the
1960 constitution, reducing them to stateless persons with diminished
civil rights and encouraging their emigration. The Greek Cypriot
side is blamed for permitting violent attacks on the Turkish Cypriot
community, forcing them to gather in enclaves for protection, so that
eventually they were living on a negligible percentage of the land for
eleven years, virtual prisoners within their villages and districts, separated from each other by armed soldiers manning checkpoints. Above
all, Turkish Cypriots blame Makarios and his supporters for having
failed, until it was too late, to halt the penetration of the Greek *junta*'s
fascism deep into the fabric of life in the island (Hitchens 1997: 73).

By contrast, most but not all Greek Cypriots blame the Turkish
Cypriot leadership both for Turkish Cypriots' misfortune, and for the
disaster that later befell even greater numbers of Greek Cypriots. They
say Turkish Cypriot politicians after 1960 unreasonably used their
power of veto, rendering the constitution unworkable and obliging
Greek Cypriots to govern alone, while they ran a virtual secessionist
state. A contemporary Greek Cypriot political figure, Antigoni Papadopoulou, said to me in interview: 'If the minority has more rights
than the majority, where does democracy go? Democracy means
one person one vote: the majority rules.' They also blame the Turkish

Cypriot leadership (who denied the charge) for having subsequently driven their own people into enclaves as a prelude to *taksim* (Patrick 1976).

There are many Cypriots both north and south, however, who prefer not to join this mutual ethnic blame game. They place the burden of guilt on the 'motherlands'. Greece and Turkey were both using Cyprus as a pawn in their own long-running conflict. Both countries had their sights on control of half, if not all, of the island. In 1964 Greece had infiltrated 10,000 troops into Cyprus, more than ten times the number permitted under the constitution, to be followed in 1967 by a further 8,000, who would work closely with EOKA-B. In the *coup d'état* in 1974 the tanks were Greek army tanks under the command of Greek officers (Hitchens 1997: 84). On the other hand, Cypriots of this point of view also remember the perennial thrust of Turkey to control affairs on the island, the proximity of its ports and airfields, only 40 miles from the coastline of north Cyprus, and the overwhelming military capacity with which it was able to outface Greece and fly threatening sorties over Cyprus.

Above all, however, Cypriots I spoke with emphatically pin the blame for Cyprus's plight on bigger actors on a wider stage. Britain is one, seen as being at fault for failing to carry out its responsibility to Cyprus as guarantor of the constitution it had itself drafted. The colonial power, besides, had failed to lay the foundations for future unity, so that, long after British rule was ended, Turkish Cypriot and Greek Cypriot children continued to be educated separately, in different languages, with textbooks imported from Greece and Turkey. There was not even provision for an individual to marry a partner from the 'wrong' group. Little in communal life was shared. If there was anything at all that held Cypriots together across the widening ethno-political divide (and many told me of individual friendships that survived all this), it was the good nature and good humour of many individual Cypriots.

The United States is bitterly blamed by Cypriots on both sides of the island as a malign influence in the region. It unconscionably supported the dictatorship in Greece, while the *junta* in return leased the US port facilities and contributed funds to Richard Nixon's election campaign. Afraid that Makarios would become another Fidel Castro and afford the Soviet Union a foothold in the Mediterranean, they gave the plotters a free hand in Cyprus. But when the *coup* failed, the

USA switched strategy and played the Turkish card. It had long toyed with the notion of partition. The Line that would eventually become concrete and barbed wire was already alive in the imaginations of US policy-makers (Hitchens 1997: 57). Having held Turkey on a short leash when it suited them, by 1974 they had begun to believe that Turkish military intervention in Cyprus would be to their own, and NATO's, best advantage (Hitchens 1997; O'Malley and Craig 1999). It was a defining moment in a long history in which, as Adamantia Pollis puts it, 'foreign intervention can be traced as the ultimate cause of even the innermost Cypriot phenomena' (Pollis 1979: 119).

The child who heard the gunshots

How did women experience the troubled times of the 1960s? You seldom read their point of view on these formative years. The political histories I referenced above were, all but one, written by men, and the one by a female author did not differentiate experiences by sex. Among the women I interviewed it was those now in their middle years – say, between forty and sixty years of age – who had the most graphic memories of this post-Independence decade, in which the partition between the two ethnic groups began to be first sketched, then inscribed and over-inscribed on the island, turning cultures into interests, interests into enemies. Their memories have a special potency because in the main they are childhood memories. What is remembered now is a sequence of particular moments of anguish or fear that have the power to survive the filtering of many years of adult life. Many of these women say their parents had told them little about what was going on, out of a wish to shield youngsters from adult worries. But this meant, of course, that the children heard the shots and explosions in 1963 and experienced the new rules of caution and curfew, but usually had insufficient information to understand the new reality. For both Turkish Cypriot and Greek Cypriot children of this generation, a bogey had come to inhabit their nightmares: 'The Greeks will get you'; 'The Turks will get you'. As Ayşe Hasan, a Turkish Cypriot, remembers it: 'We were feeling unsafe, scared of the Greeks. Because they might jump any minute through the door and kill your father and mother.' The enemy had a face. Like most other children, she knew that some neighbours or passers-by were 'them'. 'We couldn't trust them,' Ayşe said.

Degrees of trust and mistrust, however, depended a good deal on the politics or temperament of significant adults in a girl's life. Parents and grandparents are mentioned as an influence, so too are school-teachers. Women of both ethnic groups vary in their accounts of the past partly in accordance with the positioning of their parents in relation to political divisions. Several mention the influence of a father whose occupation had furnished him with good relationships among colleagues of the 'other' group. The effect was the same at both ends of the social spectrum. Intellectuals and professionals might understand themselves to share a sophistication and modernity that overrode ethnicity; while rural women from poor farming communities might simply remember, 'We shared the irrigation water. We picked lemons together.' Those who had normal daily relationships with the others were slower to accept the growing separation, were more ready to see that there were 'good' as well as 'bad' individuals on both sides.

Among Greek Cypriots there were children of Greek nationalist parents who would have seen the symbol of the blue and white flag of Greece flying over Greek soldiers' barracks and depots, and seen EOKA's gunmen, too, as a source of protection. Others, who had been the children of left-wing parents, refused to name Turkish Cypriots as the enemy, seeing them rather as manipulated by a populous and powerful 'motherland'. They saw the Greek fascists and their local supporters as enemies more immediately menacing than either Turkish Cypriots or Turks. This was particularly the case after the *junta* took power in Greece in 1967. Arianna Economou, for instance, says of this period:

> I was very fortunate. I had a good teacher, who fled from Greece during the *coup*, a leftist. And she was always telling us the truth about human rights. [But in the school] we had these little spoilt girls, quite fascistic I would say. They were mixing with soldiers, flirting you know, with these Greeks. You knew who they were, they were from the *junta*. And they were influencing these young girls … They would come to the school and say 'Can I go out with you'.

Arianna, even then, deplored this girlish nationalism of her fellow pupils, this seduction by the men in uniform. Her left-wing parents would have believed, with others I spoke to, that politicians and indeed ordinary people who co-operated with the forces of reaction in Greece, far from being protectors, had betrayed the interests of Cyprus by 'letting the *junta* in'.

Among Turkish Cypriots, too, there were differences of opinion and, since opinions were actively rewarded or ruthlessly punished, crucial differences of experience. There are those women who remember, as children, their parents believing the Greek Cypriots were the problem, the Turkish Cypriot leadership, local defence forces and the TMT the solution to it. And there are those, on the other hand, whose parents deplored the terror tactics Turkish Cypriot men were being recruited to, and believed, even then, that the enclaving of Turkish Cypriots was a strategy of their own leadership who had nothing but *taksim* and union with Turkey in their minds. Oya Talat believes now that small incidents, a scatter of assassinations that may even have been the work of *agents provocateurs*, were used by the Turkish Cypriot leadership to legitimate their own recourse to violence. She remembers being shocked one day to see her teacher arrive in the village with a group of armed men. He said, 'Don't be afraid, we are going to protect the village. Please return to your houses.' Later she learned he had joined the TMT. Oya says, 'All the young men were organized. They were beginning to exercise and march, to form an army. Officers came from Turkey, and they were organizing together. Every village began to have its own *mücahitler* "the fighters", as they called them.'

Who could know, now, which of the local men, even which members of your family, might be in the clandestine militia? The impotence women felt when it came to preventing their sons and brothers being drawn into the fighting paralleled that of many Northern Irish women I have talked to, as their sons grew out of adolescence and entered the recruitment zone of the Loyalist and Republican paramilitaries.

Sevgül Uludağ and her family fall into this category of Turkish Cypriots for whom the main source of danger has always been their own extremists. Her father, Niyazi, was a senior officer in the Nicosia municipality, but because he would not co-operate with the TMT, and opposed Rauf Denktaş' pro-Turkish politics, he was falsely charged with fraud and imprisoned for two months. Türkan, Sevgül's mother, told me of her desperate struggle to get her husband released. Sometimes when she visited the prison she took three-year-old Sevgül with her, and remembers the child's tears at seeing her father behind bars, wearing unfamiliar prison clothes. On release, Niyazi was reduced to derisory work because people rash enough to offer him employment were quickly subjected to intimidation. He had a heart ailment, and did not long survive his experience of prison. Türkan and her family continued to be watched and harassed. Her son-in-law, Kutlu Adalı, was assassinated in 1996. Sevgül, who like him is an outspoken journalist, feels this shadow over her today.

In this phase of the conflict in Cyprus, from 1960 to 1973, it is the Turkish Cypriots who were the primary victims of the conflict. In 1974 and subsequent years this would be reversed, as we shall see in Chapter 3. Of course, the gradual enclaving of the Turkish Cypriot community after the violence of 1963 meant that some Greek Cypriots, too, were obliged to move home. They could not afford to live within an increasingly inimical Turkish Cypriot enclave. But in this period the experience of uprooting was much more widespread among Turkish Cypriots.

Oya told how the village of Cihangir a few miles east of Nicosia, in which she was living as a girl of eleven, 'suddenly, in two days' was turned into an enclave along with five other nearby villages. Oya's dream of transferring to the English secondary school in Nicosia was abruptly shattered. Her mother and the other women of the village found they had new work. It was women who guarded the caches of weapons in the outbuildings, or under the soil. They were the ones who sewed sandbags, military uniforms – and Turkish flags. And as the village closed, minds closed. There was pressure on women and girls to observe tradition, to dress in a more conformist style. An old woman in the village gave Oya a Turkish prayer translated from the Arabic and told her, 'If you pray every day we may be saved'. Oya organized a little group of schoolgirls and they went out to the fields every day and prayed to Allah, 'Please save us!'

The family of Canan Öztoprak, whom we met earlier in this chapter, were among those uprooted. They left the village of Linou, just north of the Troodos mountains, when her father, who, as we saw, was a policeman in the pay of the British, was suddenly warned he was at risk of assassination by Greek Cypriots in his locality. Her mother deserted the house, leaving the washing in the sink. They took refuge in the nearby town of Lefka, a Turkish Cypriot zone. Later she went up into the hills with others from Linou and saw a column of smoke rising from their village. Their houses were burning. There would be no return to live in Linou, but later they made the trip to get their beehives, and salvaged a few belongings from the house. Canan still has some family photos from this time, charred at the edges. But the childhood recorded by these snapshots was over. For Canan this was the start of 'being a refugee'. She says, 'I have such memories of the village. I can't forget the land, the river running through it, and all the herbs that grew along it.'

For Neriman Cahit, too, 1963 meant the end of one life and the start of a new one. She was already twenty-two in that year, married, she and her husband both schoolteachers, Turkish Cypriots in a predominantly Greek Cypriot village. Neriman was pregnant, almost at term. How many times, from how many wars, have we heard this archetypal woman-in-war story, the story of the woman who gives birth in flight, beside the road, on the way to the refugee camp? There was neither doctor nor midwife in Neriman's village, so they decided she would go to her parents' home where there would be medical care. The night her labour pains began there was heavy gunfire all around. Greek Cypriot soldiers were everywhere. The neighbours had fled, the hospitals were full of wounded. Her parents went out to find a midwife, but nobody would come. Neriman was alone at home with her grandmother. The baby was breaching the perineum. 'I could feel the hair on my daughter's head,' she said. She took control of her own delivery and instructed her grandmother what to do. After the birth someone brought news that her husband back in the village had been killed. It was not in fact true, but how was she to know? 'I wouldn't give my breast to my daughter. I wanted to die, and I wanted her to die too.' Soon after, she heard of another newborn child that had been killed by a stray bullet penetrating a house. How could she protect this baby girl from the same fate? 'I put the cradle here, I put it there. I put it under the bed. Nowhere seemed safe to me.'

The experience of enclaved life was one of confinement, of closure, a narrowing down. Women, whose scope had never been wide, took it hard. Sevgül told me how her street, Necmi Avkıran Street, was cut in half by the partition line driven through Nicosia in 1963. Her district, Çağlayan, had always been a fun place to live: 'There were pubs and cinemas, and people would come in the afternoon to walk. Young girls with their mothers and boys on bikes, to see who's around.' Today, Necmi Avkıran street is not a through-road, but a *cul de sac* terminated by the Line. Sevgül remembers the soldiers arriving, placing sandbags, effecting the closure: 'All of a sudden, our street came to a dead end. All of a sudden the area died.'

Of course Greek Cypriots, too, were adversely affected by the increasing loss of mobility. They were advised to avoid Turkish Cypriot areas and on certain routes convoys were organized. Sue Lartides remembers her father's resentment of the growing restrictions on movement, whether for Turkish Cypriots or for Greek Cypriots like himself and his family. Sometimes, despite his wife's anxieties, he would drive through Turkish Cypriot villages. Sue remembers her fear when children playing in the street shouted and spat at the car with its Greek Cypriot number-plate. For Turkish Cypriots, though, the limitations on movement were much more severe. The enclaves were a kind of bird-cage of ambiguous intention, designed partly to protect the bird, partly to keep it confined. For them, when they were obliged to travel through Greek Cypriot areas, which after all were about 96 per cent of the land area of Cyprus, the experience was not merely inconveniencing, it was frightening. For Fatma Güven-Lisaniler the word 'checkpoint' recalls a haunting moment of humiliation for her father and grandfather.

> It's my grandfather's face I remember. My mum's dad. Every weekend we visited our village near Larnaca, and we needed to go through the checkpoint every time, and they'd search our car and our mum's bag and dad's pockets. Once our grandfather was visiting us, and they stopped us and looked in his pocket and found a small penknife. They said he had to stay and go to jail because he had this knife. We waited for an hour and tried to find some help, some Greek Cypriot friends. I loved my grandfather a lot and I still remember his face, him trying to control himself. Because he was an educated man, he spoke English and Greek; he had a lot of Greek friends ... He was so humiliated, and a bit angry. He didn't know where to put his hands. And because my father is deaf he couldn't do anything, so it was my mother [who dealt with the situation] which was also a kind of humiliation [for him]. My mother was trying to solve the situation herself, not to let my brother get involved, so he wouldn't try and behave like an adult, a 'man'. It's very typical, women trying to protect men.

Eventually Fatma's grandfather was released and they were permitted to travel on. But, she says, years later when she visited Israel and the Occupied Territories, this memory was the reason the checkpoints she encountered there disturbed her so much.

For Turkish Cypriots the upheaval of the 1960s meant a relative decline in both standard of living and income – relative, that is, to the past and relative to the condition of Greek Cypriots. Cypriots greatly value house ownership, and now many had to take the unthinkable step of living in rented accommodation. Women, the home-makers and often the home owners, took this loss very hard. Many middle-class people fell into poverty. Ayla Gürel's father had been a gynaeco-logist in government employment. He lost his job, borrowed money to start a private clinic, failed, and remained in debt for the remainder of his life. Sevgül's family had once been relatively prosperous, her father had had a reasonable salary as a senior municipal official, but after his imprisonment and death, Türkan, her mother, worked for fifteen years in a low-paid library job to keep her children fed. Sevgül explains her own passion for fancy clothes today by the memory of a childhood dressed in her sister's hand-me-downs, stitched by Türkan.

Ordinary working people, who had often had multiple sources of livelihood based on ownership of a small plot of land, were reduced to dependency on a labourer's wage. If it were any kind of compensa-tion, isolated as they now were, they had less opportunity than they once had to measure the gap between their own standard of living and that of Greek Cypriots. Fatma Azgın used to visit the Greek Cypriot seaside resort of Varosia, for instance, adjacent to the Turk-ish Cypriot walled city of Famagusta. It was, she remembers now, 'so flashy, you know, so interesting. A kind of Hong Kong!' But by the early 1970s a Turkish Cypriot mother was unlikely to take her children to Varosia and other such Greek Cypriot resorts for a swim and an ice-cream.

3 | Sorting, separating, sealing

Those who had worked so diligently to destroy civility and the intermingling of cultures in Cyprus achieved their goal of total separation of the two communities in 1974. It was a separation about as complete as well-organized ethnic cleansing (a little killing, a little terror, plenty of pressure and persuasion) can make it. Around 180,000 Greek Cypriots, perhaps one-third of the Greek Cypriot population of the island, were displaced from the northern reaches of Cyprus. Of these around 20,000 would be able to return to homes that remained south of the eventual Partition Line. But the remainder would be obliged to resettle in the south or migrate to other countries. Four thousand Greek Cypriots were killed and a further 12,000 wounded. Of a population of 65,000 Turkish Cypriots in the southern part of the island, all but a few hundred would move, either to the north or abroad. Approximately 1,000 were killed. It did not all happen at once. A year after the initial moves, 10,500 Greek Cypriots were still left in the north and 10,700 Turkish Cypriots in the south. A little more brutality, a little more persuasion, and over the ensuing years the Greek-speaking Orthodox Christian people remaining in the north, mainly elderly, would be reduced to fewer than 500 in two villages on the north-eastern Karpass peninsula. Around 200 Maronites, people of a different Christian tradition, also remained in the north. In the south of Cyprus by the late 1990s there were only between 300 and 400 Turkish Cypriots.[1]

The drawing of the singular Line came about this way. On 15 July 1974, as noted in the foregoing chapter, the military dictatorship of Greece launched a *coup d'état* in Cyprus, aimed at removing Makarios and his government and replacing them with an anti-communist, Greek nationalist regime. Makarios was rescued by a British helicopter, but his administration was overthrown. Grivas having died of a heart attack, the *junta* installed as President of the Republic of Cyprus, Nicos Sampson, the leader of the *coup* and 'a man with an evil reputation among Turkish Cypriots' (Dodd 1998: 30). The armed offensive continued for some days to purge the island of leftists and democrats, targeting Makarios supporters, members of the Communist Party (AKEL) and Vassos Lyssarides's Socialist Party (EDEK). EOKA-B had so far confined their attack to their own ethnic group. But, as Christopher Hitchens puts it, 'the Turkish Cypriots could not be expected to believe that Sampson was their friend; they had to ask what, if he could do this to Greeks, would he do to them? They withdrew, in large numbers into their enclaves and turned on the Turkish radio' (Hitchens 1997: 85).

Three days after the *coup* the Turkish premier, Bülent Ecevit, flew to London to test British feeling. The United Kingdom had the right, and was indeed obliged, under the Treaty of Guarantee, to take military action to defend the 1960 constitution of Cyprus in just such an event as this overthrow of the elected government. Ecevit found the British government disinclined to fulfil its duty. Turkey could also be said to have responsibilities as a Treaty guarantor, and the generals had long awaited an opportunity to intervene. The United States, this time, did not warn Turkey against sending in the military. Makarios had slipped through their fingers, so that the thing they most feared, a communist Cyprus, remained a threat. The best protection against it now was partition – a possibility US policy-makers had long been holding in reserve.[2]

On 20 July those radios to which Cypriots all over the island were anxiously clinging broadcast the news that many had dreaded, and many had longed for: Turkey had embarked on a full-scale military operation. It had started at dawn that day, with the landing of seaborne troops on the northern shore while the air force bombed and shelled Greek Cypriot positions. This attack provoked the collapse, two days later, of the dictatorship in Greece. The puppet regime in Cyprus could not survive without support from Athens. Nicos Sampson resigned, and was replaced by Glafcos Clerides, at that time the Speaker of the Greek Cypriot House of Representatives. He, like Rauf Denktaş, was a lawyer. He was considered a moderate and had experience of negotiation with the Turkish Cypriots. In Greece, the former leader Constantine Karamanlis was brought back to reconstruct the government.

The day Turkish troops landed on the island, the United Nations Security Council called for a ceasefire. The fighting, however, continued for some days more. It paused during negotiations in Geneva under British chairmanship, designed to avert outright warfare between Greece and Turkey. But Turkey showed no signs of responding to the UN resolution to withdraw its troops, and Glafcos Clerides

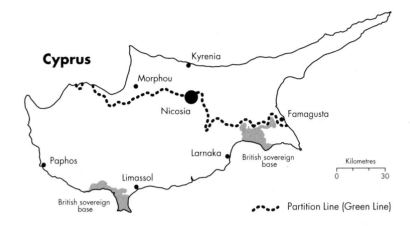

How to draw a political map of Cyprus that will not offend a great many Cypriots? For Greek Cypriots, 'The Republic of Cyprus' must span the whole island, for Turkish Cypriots this title should be located only in the south. Turkish Cypriots would call the area north of the Partition Line 'The Turkish Republic of Northern Cyprus'. Greek Cypriots would label it 'the occupied areas'.

was unwilling to accede to Rauf Denktaş's demand: a separate zone of Cyprus for Turkish Cypriots (Oberling 1982: 180).

With the collapse of the *junta*, the USA had lost its allies in Greece and was now inclined to permit its second string, Turkey, to have its head. On 14 August, Henry Kissinger, Secretary of State, issued a statement in which he made it clear the USA would not impose any sanctions against Turkish military action in Cyprus, and would look with disfavour on any British or Greek impediment to it (Hitchens 1997).[3] Nor did the Soviet Union take any step to dissuade Turkey, for it too was angling for Turkish loyalty in the context of the Cold War (Joseph 1997). Ecevit broke off negotiations and the following day the Turkish military started a second offensive in Cyprus.

The outnumbered Greek Cypriot army, strengthened by many volunteers but seriously divided and weakened by the events of July, was incapable of effective resistance. In two days, the Turkish forces occupied the east coast port of Famagusta and then pushed westwards to take control of the towns of Morphou and Lefka, before drawing a line under their operation. That line would become the Green Line as we know it today. It would deprive the government of the Republic of Cyprus, from that moment to this, of access to 37 per cent of the land area, 51 per cent of the seashore, the most productive mines and

citrus orchards and the historic coastal cities of Kyrenia and Famagusta, important sources of income from tourism.

Seeing these momentous events with gendered eyes, what is
striking is how, henceforth, the two rival masculinities in Cyprus
– Greek Cypriot and Turkish Cypriot – would have hegemony over
separate terrains. Turkish Cypriot manhood would find a new pride
in separatism, in defending its Line, in establishing its own militaris-
tic hierarchy, intermeshed in complex ways with that of Turkey. For
Turkey, too, the military success prompted a celebration not only of
redeemed nationhood but of redeemed manhood – our *mehmetçikler*,
our lads. 'The war', Vamik Volkan wrote not long afterwards, 'benefited
the Turks by giving them inner peace and a new self-esteem' (Volkan
1979: 18). But Greek Cypriot manly self-respect was badly injured and
the wounds would show themselves in the Republic's political system
for a generation.

Remembering 1974

As the history of this Turkish military action of 1974 on Cypriot
soil began to be written, the event was differently named in different
books. Those authors like Pierre Oberling (1982) and N. M. Ertekün
(1981), who were apologists for the Turks and Turkish Cypriots, called
it 'the peace operation'. Those, such as Joseph S. Joseph (1997) and
Polivios G. Poliviou (1980) who favoured the Greek and Greek Cypriot case, termed it 'the invasion'. The conflicting terminology in the
texts is matched by the divergence that marks the narratives of those
who lived through the summer of 1974 in Cyprus. It is as well to hear
about these events from individual women's memories, even though
(or precisely because) they are partial in both senses – incomplete and
'situated'. For it is not so much the facts on the ground that make
the map so difficult to redraw today, as people's beliefs and intentions,
shaped by selective recall, stories endlessly retold.

There are few Greek Cypriots today, even among those who still
favour the Greek connection and honour the blue and white flag,
who would openly justify the Cyprus *coup* of 15 July 1974. The Greek
military *junta* and its Cypriot offspring have been consigned (for
the moment) to the wastebin of history as betrayers, not saviours, of
Greek civilization. Many of the Greek Cypriot women I met had
already, as young women, been active in the left at that time. The
dictatorship had made such politics dangerous in Greece. When they

saw the armoured cars advancing on the presidential palace and the broadcasting station, they knew: the repression had come to Nicosia.

Anthoula Papadopoulou was in the city when the *coup* happened. She had been a member of AKEL since she was twenty-one, and her father too was on the left. She and her friends were used to getting away with being boldly critical of the right. 'We were insubordinate,' she said. 'Whenever we had the chance we spoke our minds openly.' Now right-wing extremists were in control of the city. She remembers realizing that political tolerance of opposition had finally died in Cyprus as it had died seven years earlier in Greece. 'The days of the *coup* were very tense because we knew people who were resisting and being picked up. We knew that people had died and were being buried at the cemetery just up the road.' She and her father, she says, 'stayed at home and smoked five packets of cigarettes a day each', while the city was under curfew and Cypriots from one side of the island to the other held their breath.

Quite a few of the women I interviewed were, like Anthoula, of an age to have been students in 1974. Several had gone to study abroad, in Athens, Ankara or further afield, and so I got a perspective of these events in Cyprus from the diaspora, as well as from within. Maria Hadjipavlou, then twenty-six, was studying in Britain at the time of the *coup*; luckily, perhaps, since she was, she knew, on the blacklist of EOKA-B. She had been actively demonstrating in London against the Greek *junta*, sending articles back for publication in a socialist paper in Cyprus. Though they did not know each other at the time, Oya Talat could be seen as Maria's opposite number. A Turkish Cypriot, also a committed leftist, she was studying in Ankara and had already been a member of the Republican Turkish Party (CTP), the main opposition to Denktaş in north Cyprus, for four years. When they heard news of the *coup* the Cypriot students gathered in the university gardens. 'We were crying', she says, 'for our country, because we feared what would come next.' Politically, these students were in a dilemma. They knew that Turkish Cypriots on the island were now at risk. But they also knew that if the Turkish military were to go in to save them, partition of Cyprus, which they deeply opposed, was inevitable.

Meanwhile, many ordinary Turks in Turkey were enthusiastic for military action over the water. Şule Aker is a Turkish woman who would later marry a Cypriot and go to live in Cyprus. Her home then was in Mersin, in southern Turkey. She says:

In Turkey everybody at that moment wanted to come to Cyprus. They thought that Greeks were killing Turks, they were being massacred, as had happened in Anatolia in the past. Some of them were ready to sail across in their own boats, they were shipping their cars. In Mersin, we were helping the soldiers, cooking and giving support. It was very important, there was such a strong feeling. To help, to fight, to save them. We thought it should have been done long ago.

It is interesting that Şule, as a young woman, had only the vaguest notion about Cyprus. When, aged twenty-three, she first met her future husband and heard he came from Lefkosa (Nicosia), she took it to be a town in Turkey. 'I didn't think it was a different place,' she says. 'We all thought Cyprus was part of Turkey. Because historically it was with Turkey for a very long time.' Meanwhile, on the island, there were many Turkish Cypriots who were only too glad that Turks such as Şule were enthusiastic for a Turkish rescue mission. They heard the rumour that troops were assembling on the south coast, but scarcely dared to believe it. Turkish intervention had been promised so often since 1963 and each time there had been disappointment.

There are many graphic memories of 20 July. People have the most precise recall of the arrival of the troops. 'It was a Saturday. It was five in the morning.' Those living on the coast near Kyrenia saw the ships approaching the shore. Those living in Nicosia saw parachutists falling from planes. They recall the shriek of sirens, and bombs falling on Greek Cypriot positions. For the Greek Cypriots this was the enactment of the scenario they had dreaded for ten years. The arrival of Turks on Cypriot soil restimulated the trauma of the Ottomans' seizure of the Christian island in 1571 CE. A very old collective memory, an image of murderous Turkmens brandishing knives, underlay the television footage of modern warfare. The Greek Cypriot population living along the northern coast experienced an onslaught by air and sea. As the Turkish tanks and armoured cars advanced to control more and more of the land area, and the planes dominated the skies, Greek Cypriot troops were outnumbered and their resistance overwhelmed. Many Greek Cypriot memoirs of those times tell of atrocities committed against them (see for instance Catselli 1975). Civilians were assassinated, many women were raped. Goods were looted from homes and shops and churches were defiled.

Sue Lartides is one of the Greek Cypriot women who recalled

for me traumatic memories of July and August 1974. Today she is a psychosynthesis counsellor, living and working in Nicosia. Then, aged twenty-one, she had just got engaged. At the moment of the Turkish landings she was staying in her family's flat near the top of a block of high-rise flats in Varosia, the Greek Cypriot suburb of Famagusta. This is her memory of the bombing raid that destroyed the nearby Salamenia Tower hotel.

> My sister was standing out on the balcony eleven storeys up, and the fighter plane had already hit the hotel but was coming round for a second hit. They had two rockets and had only thrown one. And the plane was so close that we could actually see the pilot in the cockpit. He was so close. It was like everything went into slow motion. And he saw my sister standing there. But the machine guns were pointing the other way, thank God. But I remember my fiancé just reaching out and grabbing my sister by the back of her neck, by her clothes, and hauling her in before the pilot could swing his guns round. And he came … [she broke off crying] … we were lucky.

Sue and her family on many occasions had to run down those twenty-two flights of stairs to the entrance hall to shelter from raids.

> You knew when the rockets were going to hit because of the pressure of the air. Everything changes, and everything's silent for a few seconds, and so you just wait in that silence. And those stairs, time after time, after time. And I remember the frustration if there were elderly people in front of us, because they couldn't move fast. And I wanted to jump over them, because I was so frightened. And yet, I remember my fear wasn't for me, it was for my fiancé. My fear was for my family, I didn't think of myself. It's like you don't exist. It's not your primary thought. And when the building was shelled, I remember everything falling on top of me. I remember a body on top of me.

While Greek Cypriots were in terror, most Turkish Cypriots reacted with relief and joy. Ayşe Hasan told me: 'Yes. We were pleased about it, like all the Turks. Because we had been hearing for so many years about Turkey coming to save us from the Greeks. Because since my childhood I had friends whose fathers the Greeks had shot, or fathers who had disappeared on the way to or from work.' But many Turkish Cypriots found their relief mixed with fear. The Cypriot National Guard, the Greek army contingent in Cyprus and what remained of the EOKA paramilitaries, together with able-bodied civilian men, were organizing defence. And although the main conflict was in the north where they attempted to check the Turkish advance, Greek Cypriots also occupied the Turkish Cypriot enclaves in Famagusta, Limassol, Larnaca and other towns to pre-empt uprisings (Dodd 1998). Canan Öztoprak was still living in the Turkish Cypriot enclave of Lefka, in north-eastern Cyprus, where, as recounted in Chapter 1, the family had taken refuge when they fled from their village in 1963. As the Turks advanced from the coast, Greek Cypriot forces shelled Lefka from the hills. The townspeople gathered in the cinema.

> The Greek Cypriot soldiers came there and said, 'OK, now women and children will go out and the men will stay here.' So we had to say goodbye to each other, because we didn't know what might be going to happen. They wanted us to go into the mosque, but it was already burning. Of course, the women at the front resisted to go into the mosque. The commander came and said, 'Look, everything will be fine. We will live together friendly. We won't do anything to you. The only thing is that Greeks will come and govern us. We shall belong to Greece from now on.' And he called on everyone to say 'Long Live *Enosis*!' Of course we did – they were holding guns.

The people of Lefka stayed under house arrest for the remainder of July and part of August. On 15 August the second Turkish advance began. Still they feared the Turkish military would not be able to reach Lefka town, in the far west of the island. They learned from TV that mass graves had been prepared. They believed the Greek Cypriot plan was to massacre them all. Around 6 p.m. on 16 August Canan heard a strange rumbling. The bed on which she was lying began shaking. 'Then a jeep stopped at our door. I thought, "This is the end." But the men jumped out and shouted, "Come, get out, open your doors and go and welcome the Turkish troops!" It wasn't the Greeks, it was the United Nations soldiers! And after that came the Turkish tanks. Then I understood the rumbling noise I'd been hearing.'

Displacement and flight

Immediately after the relief of the Turkish Cypriot community of Lefka, the Turks halted their action and a ceasefire was called. But the experience of those few summer weeks from 15 July to 16 August 1974 would leave a mark on the whole population. At that moment, the disruption, fear and uncertainty applied to both Greek Cypriots and Turkish Cypriots, since even the latter, the supposed beneficiaries of the Turkish intervention, felt in peril from Greek Cypriot reprisals. Many on both sides, so long as the bombardments and the hand-to-hand fighting continued, either took shelter in the dirt and dark of their own basements and coal cellars, or abandoned their homes to stay wherever they could find shelter in areas they deemed safer. Everyone who fled from home at that moment thought it was temporary. For some it was, but for many the crossing of their threshold marked a complete rupture in their lives. From then on there would always be 'before' and 'after'. The thing that made the difference was your ethnicity in relation to where on the geo-ethnic map of the island you had been living. If you were a Turkish Cypriot living north of the Partition Line or a Greek Cypriot living south of it, you were relatively lucky. You were likely to be able to keep your home, crowded though it might be for some time to come with displaced friends and strangers.

Greek Cypriots living north of the eventual Partition Line were the group to experience immediately and suddenly what today would be called 'ethnic cleansing'. With the first Turkish landings began a southward forced migration that would end with up to 180,000 displaced people. Myria Vassiliadou saw this with the eyes of a child of four, living in Nicosia. She remembers her father, a policeman, covering their little white sports car with mud to make it less visible, and driving the family south to the hills: 'We set off at four in the morning, with the headlights off. We could hardly see where we were going. We went to a house in a village in the mountains, in the south. All my mother's family were there, twenty-five of us in there, all sleeping on the floor. There was a newborn baby. But none of us were crying.' She remembers how her father went round the district with his shotgun, shooting out the street lights so Turkish planes would not detect them from the air. But the adults did not want to alarm the children: 'He told me he was doing it so nobody would see us, because they might do something wrong to us, even though we were nice people. I remember how he said that because we were nice people nothing would happen to us.'

If the Vassiliadou family had been living in Kyrenia at this time, rather than in the Greek Cypriot southern part of Nicosia, the flight Myria experienced would have had entirely different repercussions. As it was, the Line was drawn north of her house and the family would be one of those 20,000 that would eventually be able to return home. By contrast, Greek Cypriots living north of the Line in 1974, told me how, when they walked out of their homes 'in the clothes we happened to have put on that morning', 'with no more than we could carry in our two hands', 'thinking we would be back next day', it had actually been the start of their permanent migration, among 160,000 others. There would be many steps to it, all of them leading south. Many of the people from Kyrenia and the coastal villages, that first night, slept out in the mild summer air in the orange and lemon plantations. Next day they went up into the Pentadactylos mountains. Some tried to take their livestock, but in the end they had to abandon them. They joined up with people from other towns and villages in the line of the Turkish advance. Some, before they had travelled too far, dared to slip back to their homes to rescue treasured possessions. Most could not. In the first few weeks of their lives as refugees, the more fortunate were able to pile in with relatives, friends or strangers, but many spent weeks with no shelter, or were accommodated in holding centres under canvas or in public buildings.

In the first exodus, 80 per cent of Greek Cypriots crossing to the south were entirely dependent on aid in the form of food and living allowances (Oberling 1982: 90). For many it would be years, rather than months, before they would be resettled in the refugee housing estates that were hurriedly built all over the south of Cyprus, as the government began to regroup and cope with the new circumstances. The Greek Cypriot women I met who had been among the refugees told me how hard it had been to come to terms with the fact of this new identity, 'refugee'. How slowly and reluctantly they had come to acknowledge that it was beyond the power of the government of the Republic to reverse the seizure of one-third of the island and return them to their homes.

Not all the Greek Cypriots living in the north had fled immediately. Some who stayed behind did so because their husbands, fathers or sons had gone missing during the fighting and they feared that if they once left the north they might lose any chance of hearing news of them. In 2001, when I was doing my fieldwork in Cyprus, a group of these women, 'The Relatives of the Missing', had for many years been mounting a demonstration every Saturday at the checkpoint in Nicosia. They proclaim the illegality of the regime in the north and angrily demand information about their missing loved ones. I sat down with two of them, Panayiota Pavlou Solomi and Eleni Vlahou, while they told me about their lives as farming wives before 1974, and of how Panayiota's son and Eleni's husband went missing. The Turk and Turkish Cypriot forces took many prisoners. In an official exchange of 31 October 1974, 2,487 were handed back, while 3,308 Turkish Cypriots were similarly released. But some Greek Cypriot men had been transported to Turkey, where they were subjected to harsh treatment and paraded through the streets. While some of these were released between 1974 and 1976, after that date there were no returns from Turkey. Other captives, Eleni and Panayiota are almost certain, were murdered. They believe the location of the graves is known to the authorities and call for the complete truth to be told, for exhumations and DNA testing. A number of children were among the missing, and these constitute a different kind of mystery. There is a persistent myth that some were stolen by or for childless Turkish families and raised as Turks.

Panayiota told of the hard treatment she and her elderly mother and young daughter had suffered, left behind under Turkish rule: 'We were forced by the Turkish army to work from dawn to dusk in the fields in the hot weather to pick the cotton, which we were told was no longer our property but belonged to the Turkish government. We weren't allowed to enter our own fields even to gather food that was ready to eat.' Eventually, on 5 November 1976, the Turkish authorities sent tractors and trailers to move their possessions. When Panayiota said, 'I'm not leaving!' they said, 'You will go whether you like it or not.' Gradually, in many small instances such as this, those Greek Cypriots who did not meanwhile die or emigrate, eventually made the journey to the south, so that, as mentioned above, fewer than 500 Greek Cypriots today remain enclaved in the north.

The reciprocal displacement from the south of the much smaller population of Turkish Cypriots took place over a longer period and, according to the various subsequent estimates, involved 'only' between 45,000 and 60,000 people. It none the less involved a comparable experience for many individuals – a loss of homes, livelihoods and connections that would scar lives. Besides, for the many Turkish Cypriots who had earlier been obliged to leave their homes to move into enclaves, this was the second displacement within a decade. The Greek Cypriot authorities were not agitating for their removal, for they had no wish to imply any acceptance of permanent partition (Oberling 1982: 186). On the other hand, many Turkish Cypriots

urgently wished to go, despite the losses involved, both because of immediate danger to their lives and longer-term anxiety about what it
would mean to live as a now negligible minority among a profoundly
angry Greek Cypriot population. A number of atrocities committed
by Greek Cypriot extremists fuelled their fear.

I had a meeting with four widows who now live in the village of
Taşkent, on the southern foothills of the Pentadactylos, where they
were rehoused by the authorities, as a group, on arriving in the north.
They had formerly lived in the ethnically-mixed village of Tokhni,
between the south-coast cities of Limassol and Larnaca. On 15
August, the date of the second Turkish advance in the north, a gang
of EOKA-B men, led by a certain 'Andrikos', rounded up sixty-nine
of their menfolk, the youngest thirteen, the oldest seventy-four. They
drove them, with fifteen more men from neighbouring villages, to
a location where they had already prepared a burial ditch, and shot
them one by one. Of several such atrocities carried out by Greek
Cypriot extremists, this is one of the best substantiated, because a lone
survivor, hidden beneath the corpses, later escaped and was able to
name the killers and locate the grave.

In many other cases between 1963 and 1974 individuals simply
disappeared and their murderers are still unnamed. Greek Cypriot
families are demanding that the Turkish government and the TRNC
authorities account for 1,619 missing individuals, while Turkish Cypriots are calling on the government of the Republic of Cyprus to
account for 803 lost family members (Sant Cassia 2001).

A gendered experience

Several things characterized the gender-specific experience of
women during the five weeks of the *coup d'état* and the Turkish campaign in Cyprus. One was the fear, or reality, of rape. Violent conflict,
both military and communal, was nothing new in the relationship
between Turks and Greeks. As we saw in Chapter 2, in the nineteenth
and twentieth centuries there were large minorities of Orthodox
Christians in Anatolia and Muslims in territories (such as Thrace and
Crete) that were or would become part of Greece. In the violence
between these majorities and minorities, as Greece pursued its expan-
sionist project, the Ottoman Empire disintegrated and Kemal Atatürk
built the modern Turkish state, rape was endemic. These rapes haunt
the collective memory. For Greek and Greek Cypriot women, 'the

Turk' is the archetypal violator, as is 'the Greek' for Turkish and Turkish Cypriot women.

It is certain that a considerable number of rapes of Greek Cypriot women by Turkish men occurred in the wake of the landings in 1974. This is borne out by the fact that abortion was officially sanctioned soon afterwards, on account of the pregnancies that resulted. Women were, however, inhibited about talking openly of the fear of rape, especially between the generations. Older women say they had not wanted to terrorize the young ones, but that did not prevent young women whispering their fears to each other. Athena Z, who lives in south Nicosia today, said: 'It was something just we girls talked about, amongst ourselves. It was not a discussion to share with relatives or my mother, just girls.' But Sue Lartides's fiancé's mother had no inhibition about speaking the word 'rape'. Her husband's family had been refugees from Smyrna, in Turkey, during the conflict of 1922. Her mother-in-law had heard many terrible tales of what befell the Greeks. 'Hearing all this,' Sue said, 'I was petrified.' Conversely, Layık Topcan Mesutoğlu told me that Turkish Cypriot women had felt seriously at risk of violence from the deeply enraged and militant Greek Cypriot forces against whom they were as yet entirely undefended. 'I still remember how afraid I was. I was afraid the Greeks would come and rape. That was the main thing I was afraid of. I thought it was likely to happen like in the liberation war in Turkey in the Izmir area.'

A second trauma of 1974 had to do with children. It is gender-specific in the sense that women were the primary caretakers. Many mothers were separated from their children in the turmoil. Greek Cypriot refugees told me stories of children rescued and taken to safety by adult friends and relatives. It had been days, sometimes weeks, before they had been able to ascertain their safety and find them again. But there was also the anxiety about whether you could keep your children safe, keep them healthy, keep them fed during the flight to the south. Circumstances of displacement, danger and shortage were experienced by Turkish Cypriots too. Neriman's daughter, the one you will remember was born in the inter-ethnic violence of 1963, was by now eleven years old and there was a younger boy. Neriman described her persistent search for food, for milk for the children. And there was always the fear of arson, sacking, reprisals by the desperate Greek Cypriot militias. 'I was praying, for so many nights, "Please keep my children safe from the Greeks!".'

A third characteristic experience of women on both sides of the war was of having their husbands and sons go off to fight, amateur soldiers, untrained and ill-equipped, in scattered units with little effective central command. For days and weeks they did not know where they were, what had become of them, whether they would ever see them alive again. Feyziye Hulusi was one whose young son, freshly returned from abroad, did not come back from the fighting. She described to me the days and nights she spent searching for him, appealing to every acquaintance who might have word of his whereabouts, fearfully searching every hospital and every morgue in Nicosia. She remembers her growing sense of unreality as she began to realize that some informants, not wishing to strip away her last vestige of hope, were keeping from her the confirmation of her son's death. It is a story I cannot forget. As we saw, in many cases there was no such confirmation of death and, characteristically, those on both sides of the Line who campaign for information about their lost family members are women.

A further experience characteristic of women was being swept into the civil emergency services coping with the dead and wounded. Gülay Kaşer, who until then had lived a sheltered life, was overwhelmed by what she witnessed. She remembers the shock of seeing a truck in which twenty or more men were piled one on the other. The sight lives with her still. Even now she spoke of 'men', not 'corpses', because it had taken her some time, in her naivety, to realize that these were actually dead people. Not sleeping, not wounded but *dead*. She answered an appeal on the radio for nurses.

> My sister and me, we went together to the hospital. We saw so many injured people, their hands, their legs, their faces – from bombs and every kind of thing. We were trying to help them. We felt we can't go on, we can't do this work, we can't help. You have to be brave. But I was crying. And they said to me, 'You mustn't cry, because they're injured and they're in pain, and you …' [she broke off, crying even now]. I don't want to think about it.

The economic effects of the war, too, were experienced by women in a way that was gender-specific. There was, of course, a general effect: displacement ruined many families in Cyprus, and this affected both men and women. Greek Cypriots crowding into the south were the hardest hit. The displaced were ruined because they themselves lost their employment, their properties and their investments. The others were ruined because they had to share the little they had with

relatives who had been stripped of every asset. Or their own businesses failed because (like Maria Hadjipavlou's father) they felt they
had no alternative but to give credit to penniless refugees who would
never be able to repay their debts. The disaster had a huge effect on
class structure. While many of the upper class had resources on which
they could draw, inside or outside the country, many ordinary people
who were middle class, or comfortable working class, fell abruptly to
the bottom of the class structure. People who had been proudly self-
sufficient became utterly dependent on state welfare.

Relatively few married women worked in paid employment before
1974, though many used to supplement their husbands' incomes
through subsistence farming and gardening, or the production and sale
of handmade artefacts. Women who had found it normal (and correct)
to depend on the wage of their husbands, now had to contribute cash
to the household or, in the case of widows, to raise children on their
own earnings alone. They were glad to find any job and, as the economies recovered, many worked in factories for the first time. For the
women the unaccustomed labour was hard and sometimes their health
was damaged by it.

Antigoni Papadopoulou's family had been living in Morphou in
1974. Morphou was a relatively prosperous town in the north-west
of the island, in a fertile region celebrated for its oranges. The Greek
Cypriot population of the town and thirty surrounding villages was
uprooted. Antigoni would later become a politician, deeply committed to refugee rights and the project of 'return'. When I met her, her
mother and father, by now elderly, were still living in the refugee
housing estate on the outskirts of southern Nicosia in which they
had first found permanent accommodation in their exile. Antigoni's
father spends his days in the *kafeneon* frequented by men of this refugee community. Her mother, Georgia Pericleous, invited six friends
to come and meet me in her apartment. Their stories suggest that in
the north they had lived, by modern standards, simple lives, but within
their localities they had known sustainable economies. They had
raised sheep, tended orchards and planted vegetables. Antigoni translated for Georgia:

> My mother wants you to know that it was very difficult for her to
> adjust to her new life. She was very young at the time. In Morphou
> she had been a full-time housewife and mother of three children. But
> as a refugee she had to earn. She raised rabbits and chickens. Later

Georgia Pericleous was displaced from her home in Morphou in 1974 and has since lived in a Greek Cypriot refugee housing project in southern Nicosia.

< Antigoni Papadopoulou is Georgia's daughter, a Member of the House of Representatives for the Democratic Party.

When the Partition Line was opened in 2003, Georgia made a pilgrimage to visit her former home in Morphou. She was disappointed when nobody answered the door bell. (Its Turkish Cypriot inhabitant was that very day travelling south on a similar quest.) But, as Georgia gazed at the house, a former neighbour recognized her. He led her to his home and handed her this photo of herself and husband (above). He had salvaged it during the fighting and expulsions, and kept the image on his wall for twenty-nine years. 'Such a beautiful woman,' he said.

He had also rescued and saved a photo of Antigoni as a baby (above).

she found a job. It was a very hard job for women, making mattresses for beds. They had to put them on their shoulders and load them on trucks. It was very heavy, and since then she has problems with her spine and had to stop working.

These kinds of changes came as a great shock, Antigoni said. But there had been, for many women, one small compensation: holding down a job, having a wage of your own and knowing others depend on your earning power brings a new self-respect. 'In a way it made us stronger.'

Finally, perhaps the way women experienced the effects of the Partition most acutely was through loss of their homes. Women in Cyprus in those years, especially in the rural areas, still found their identity as women mainly in the maintenance of a home and in an active community life based on the neighbourhood surrounding it. They characteristically owned their homes in Cyprus, receiving a house or flat from their parents on marriage. It was rare in Cyprus (and badly regarded) to rent a house or flat. Anthropologist Peter Loizos describes the effects on the Greek Cypriot women of the northern village of Argaki, now refugees in the south.

> Almost every Argaki girl owned a dowry-house when she married, and her social standing was largely a result of its quality and contents. It was hers, and because it had often cost her and her family dearly in labour and thrift, it gave her a measure of security and independence within her marriage … Their dowry-houses gone, women were now more dependent, vulnerable, exposed, like snails without shells. (Loizos 1981: 177; see also Anthias 1992)

In the immediate aftermath of the fighting and mass population movements, women on both sides of the Line had to rebuild some semblance of home life in circumstances that had been till then quite unimaginable. Many of the refugees in the south lived for months or even years in camps. Georgette Loizou, a city girl, brought up by her Greek Cypriot parents in New York, was brought to visit her family in south Cyprus soon after the events of '74: 'I was shocked to see them living in tents, with chickens running around, children half naked. I saw this old man just lying on the ground, smoking his *nargile*. I asked my grandmother "Is he sick? Is something wrong with him?" It was her brother, my great-uncle. Now I realize that they'd lost everything. He was a rich man, and now he was living in this tent.'

In the north, there were also extensive adjustments to make in the population's housing arrangements. For a start there were the empty properties of the Greek Cypriot refugees. Coming northwards, there were the displaced Turkish Cypriots to be housed. They were assessed for 'housing points' according to their needs, and the size of the properties they had vacated. There also began to be an inward flow of Turks from Anatolia. That autumn the administration arranged for 5,000 Turkish workers to come and harvest the crops on abandoned lands. They, too, plus some Turkish war veterans, were allocated appropriate empty Greek Cypriot flats and houses.

Many Turkish Cypriots felt uneasy, set up in the jobs and houses of vanished people. It was as if, one told me, they were 'living someone else's scenario'. The authorities in the north (contrary to those in the south) wanted people to forget, not to feel themselves to be 'refugees' but rather to delight in the possession of 'free' land. Vamik Volkan has described poignantly the confusing combination of guilt and resentment Turkish Cypriots felt as they arrived from the south and were settled in the homes of vanished Greek Cypriots (Volkan 1979). Neriman Cahit had been allocated an empty Greek Cypriot home. She told me:

> In one of the gardens I saw an old woman who was dead. Like this – as if sleeping. I don't know if somebody killed her or if she died of hunger. I was shocked – to see the reality. Of death. I started to think again. Who had been living in this house [I'd been given]? Did a person die here? Or were they taken away? … And in some houses there was still laundry on the clothes line. And at a table, I think, a woman had been preparing a meal or something when she was interrupted. There was a knife. I think she'd been cutting the bread. And there was some butter there, half used. [She sighed and paused.] If you're a human being at all, unless you're a monster or a soldier or something, you feel really very upset by such things. I couldn't put it out of my mind. When I was cooking, for example, I was always thinking: 'What was the other woman doing? Where was her table? Were they sitting like us? How many children did they have?' There's nobody to ask.

§

If the events of 1974 divided the population along the line of Partition, it also, either side of that line, divided people from each other on a cross-cutting political dimension, along a continuum from

Greek Cypriot refugees from northern Cyprus organize in associations focused on the towns and regions from which they were displaced, keeping alive both memory and hope. Here the former residents of Morphou make their annual march to the Line, to demand the right to 'return'.

'compromise' to 'no concessions'. There is nothing about a woman's gender-specific experience that is liable to position her on one side or the other of this political line. I met women in both north and south Cyprus who held uncompromising views on 'the Cyprus problem', in contrast to HAD members and others campaigning for reconciliation.

In the south, refugee politics quickly became a significant factor in the Greek Cypriot system. The Clerides government, concerned that this mass of displaced and disaffected people should not cause a swing to the left, rapidly introduced a number of welfare measures including the provision of refugee housing, control of rents and rationing of food. A Pan-Cyprian Refugee Committee formed to represent the interests of the displaced. The movement did not organize on the basis of the localities in which they were now rehoused, but formed associations based on their pre-war communities, calling themselves 'Free Morphou', or 'Unvanquished Kyrenia'. They continued to hold elections to municipal authorities that were now out of reach across the line. Thus there were, and still are, two Mayors of Morphou, two Mayors of Famagusta, one in place and one in exile. It was EDEK (at one point known as KISOS), a socialist party, that was then the backbone of these radical groups and took the toughest line on dealings with the northern authorities (Loizos 1981).

There are many women active in the persistent and determined movement for 'return'. Indeed, it is within the frame of this nationalist culture that Greek Cypriot women found their main political agency (Vassiliadou 2002). Antigoni Papadopoulou, who as we saw is the daughter of refugee parents, is now a high-profile member of the House of Representatives for the Democratic Party (DIKO). She recently served a term as Mayor of Morphou, elected by 84 per cent of the voters in her constituency of exiles. Every year she is at the head of a protest march to the Line organized by the association of refugees from Morphou. She says:

> I want to keep the memories alive for the generations to come, because I think what happened to us was a tremendous violation of our basic human rights. This is something that I can't understand. The governments of civilized countries like Britain and the USA, they should bring more pressure to get implementation of the UN resolutions and the decisions of the European Court of Human Rights on Cyprus. They talk about Milosevic and Osama bin Laden being

terrorists. The terrorist in Cyprus is Mr Denktaş. He exercises a lot of pressure on his own people. I condemn these other terrorists, but what about the state terrorism of Turkey?

On the other hand, there are many Greek Cypriot women who do not allow the actions of the TRNC and the government of Turkey to derail their politics of *rapprochement*. I met some women in the south who were ready to question themselves now about Greek Cypriot policies towards the minority in the past. They shared doubts of the kind Peter Loizos heard twenty years earlier.

Why had they not heeded those leftists and assorted eccentrics who had argued that generosity to the Turkish Cypriots should be national policy? Why had Makarios not made a generous offer to the Turkish Cypriots during the five long years of the Inter-Communal Negotiations from 1968–73? … Why no 'olive branch' to the Turkish Cypriots in those years? 'What wouldn't we have given the Turks, just to stay in our properties?', they now said. (Loizos 1981: 134)

In the north there was a similar political division. Some women I spoke to had felt nothing but relief, despite the withholding of international recognition, despite the economic embargo, to find themselves at last gathered in one place after years of living in scattered enclaves. Some of them would remain supporters of Rauf Denktaş and take comfort in his uncompromising politics. They would continue to feel grateful to Turkey. On the other hand, I met many women who had from the start refused to think ill of Greek Cypriots as a group on account of the aggression carried out in their name by forces over which they had no control. They told many stories of mutual aid, of neighbours sheltering or helping each other, at the start of the trouble, before they became separated: 'We got them milk for their baby'; 'They gave us bread.' There were women who were capable of standing in the shoes of 'the other woman', even while the fighting was still going on. Sevin Uğural said:

You're sitting in the house and you hear the sound of the jets overhead. And you feel relieved. But you think: OK, I'm feeling relieved. What about the people on the other side? They must feel afraid. One sound but two different responses. I feel relieved, she feels afraid. We were hearing then about the people they killed. The mass graves. And we were very sorrowful. It's a men's game, a game they play. But you think of the women and children, living in their houses, afraid to go out. What is this? Who's winning? Both of us suffering, both of us frightened.

Overall, it took many many years for society in the south to absorb the huge numbers of refugees, to heal the divisions, to normalize political relations and, to some extent, daily life. And it took many years for the northerners to learn to live with the new emptiness. The authorities quickly hoisted the Turkish flag over every town, and put up new street signs bearing Turkish names. But the formal appropriation of property could not lay the ghosts of those who had so recently been driven from it. Neriman remembered a visit she had made to the beautiful seaside city of Kyrenia, before 1974, with her husband and children. It was then almost wholly Greek Cypriot. They had warned the children, 'Speak very quietly so they don't hear you're speaking Turkish.' After 1974 Kyrenia became a wholly Turkish Cypriot city. But when they first went there, the children continued to whisper. She told them, 'You don't need to whisper now.' But it was difficult for them, and for many others, to change the habits of a lifetime, the habits of a cautious minority. While they were whispering, with no Greek Cypriots left to hear them, down south the Greek Cypriots in question, longing for 'return', were demonstrating on the Green Line, rattling the barbed wire and shouting despairingly, 'Give us back our homes!' But they in turn went unheard by the Turkish Cypriots, because their voices could not carry across the Dead Zone.

Notes

1 The figures in this paragraph are approximate. I have drawn on several authors, including Volkan 1979, Oberling 1982, Dodd 1998, O'Malley and Craig 1999 and Brewin 2000, who in turn cite several sources, including statistics published by the United Nations and the government of the Republic of Cyprus.

2 In 1964, the US former Secretary of State, Dean Acheson, advised President Johnson to resolve the dispute between Greece and Turkey, seen as dangerously destabilizing to NATO, by partitioning Cyprus. Under the Acheson Plan, most of the island would be united with Greece, in a limited *enosis*. Autonomous cantons would be set up to accommodate the Turkish Cypriot minority, and an area of the north coast and a coastal island would be awarded to Turkey as a military base. The plan was shelved at the time but many Cypriots believe it remained a live option in the minds of US policy-makers (Hitchens 1997: 57).

3 The dubious role of the USA in the region is suggested by reports that 90 per cent of the arms used in the Turkish action of 1974 were US-supplied, while the USA had also substantially equipped the Greek military during the seven-year rule of the *junta* (O'Malley and Craig 1999: 225).

4 | Partitioned power: women and the structures

History is not memory, but divergent re-rememberings, shaped in culturally specific ways. A man lands from a parachute, a child is buried, a hand takes up a pen and signs a document. These are facts. But they are recounted with different meanings in the north and the south of Cyprus. The violent events sketched in the previous two chapters, told and retold, using words that often differ on either side of the Line ('peace operation', 'invasion') are powerfully formative of contemporary Greek Cypriot and Turkish Cypriot national identities. In fact, as we have seen, such identities barely existed before they occurred. This is the inheritance that the women of Hands Across the Divide, and others working for *rapprochement*, must deal with. Pain, anger and guilt are deep in everyone's sense of self and undermine attempts at transversal politics.

In this chapter and the next, again drawing on both interviews and secondary sources, I look at how the parallel societies developed after the barbed wire rolled out across the island. In so far as women's experience of gender and other power relations in contemporary Cyprus is similar, it is a basis for co-operation between women either side of the Line. But certain differences of positioning, as we shall see in Chapter 7, make challenging demands on mutual understanding. In the present chapter I emphasize north Cyprus rather more than south Cyprus, while in the ensuing chapter the balance is reversed. This reflects the somewhat divergent preoccupations my interviews and discussions revealed. I found women in the north particularly concerned about the political and economic stasis they were experiencing, while those in the south had more to say about social and familial change in their developing consumer culture.

In the decade following Partition, contact between the two leaderships was intermittent. The north at times demanded 'recognition before talks', which for the south necessarily meant no talks at all. But at other times there were exchanges of view, consultations, 'confidence-building measures', proximity talks and at certain times actual negotiations – mainly sponsored by the United Nations whose mandate included not only peace-keeping but also fostering a return to 'normal' conditions. 'High-level agreements' signed in 1977 and 1979 were positive moments that set a framework for later developments. The most significant disagreement impeding negotiations concerned the structure of a future state. The northern leadership insisted on recognized statehood for the north, albeit within a Cypriot confederation. The leadership of the south came to accept the idea of two federated communities but insisted on a single state.[1]

A new issue entered the negotiations in the course of the 1990s: membership of the European Union. In 1995, as serious negotiations for Cyprus's accession began, the government of the Republic embarked on the process of harmonizing its legislation with that of other member-states so as to phase itself into the anticipated enlargement process through which the Union was to expand eastwards and southwards to include certain states of the former communist bloc, plus Malta, by 2004. The EU disappointed moderates on both sides by faltering in its original view that a resolution of the Cyprus conflict should be a prerequisite of accession (Brewin 2000). In taking this position the EU put a 'strategic weapon in the hands of the south Cypriot negotiators' (Güven-Lisaniler and Rodriguez 2002: 201). Unsurprisingly, Rauf Denktaş asserted that the Republic had no right to seek EU membership for the whole island. Besides, such a step breached the 1959 Treaty of Guarantee that proscribed union with another state. To the despair of the Turkish Cypriot opposition, he refused to contemplate 'solution and entry to the EU' for the island as a whole prior to the acceptance of Turkey's often-vetoed application to join.

The presence of Turks from Turkey resident in northern Cyprus has been a perennial issue in negotiations. Greek Cypriots make the return to Turkey of 'soldiers and settlers' a key requirement in any agreement. We saw that in the period immediately following the Turkish intervention of 1974 several thousand workers were drafted from Turkey, partly to substitute for the labour power of the displaced Greek Cypriots and partly to establish 'facts on the ground' in Turkey's favour. In following years there was an inward migration of many more workers and their families from Anatolia. They came mainly from the eastern, south-eastern and Black Sea regions of Turkey, where many had been farmers (Morvaridi 1993).

The 1996 census of the TRNC records a total population in northern Cyprus of 200,587, of whom 54,650 were born in Turkey.

Individuals with TRNC citizenship total 164,460, and among these 23,924 were born in Turkey, i.e. are naturalized Turkish Cypriots (Turkish Republic of Northern Cyprus 1999: table 4).[2] Greek Cypriots doubt the veracity of these figures, and it is popularly believed in the south that the number of Turks (citizen and non-citizen together) is not far short of equalling the number of Turkish Cypriots. There is particular alarm about the disparity in fertility between Turkish Cypriots and Turks. The former typically have two children per family, the latter six or more (Morvaridi 1993: 220).

The 'settler' issue, however, is not only a point of tension between the regimes of north and south; it is a major source of political conflict in the north itself. Driven by lack of employment opportunity and disheartened by the political situation, many Turkish Cypriots have emigrated to join the large diaspora in Britain, the USA, Australia and elsewhere, thus reducing the number of Turkish Cypriots on the island. The fear of displacement of Turkish Cypriots by Turks is reflected in an article by Turkish Cypriot economist Fatma Güven-Lisaniler and colleague, who call the process 'a bloodless form of ethnic cleansing' (Güven-Lisaniler and Rodriguez 2002: 187). The opposition parties are bitterly opposed to the inward migration of Turks, believing that the granting of citizenship and other favours can be used to 'buy' votes, and that politically-inspired migration is thus a ploy of the pro-Turkey parties in north Cyprus to keep those who oppose them out of power.

Political parties in northern Cyprus

In the now autonomous north, those who held power after 1974 were naturally the same political and paramilitary people, all men, who had been prominent in the politics of the Turkish enclaves before partition. Rauf Denktaş remained their leader, and to this day his personal authority has enabled him to win one presidential election after another. Born in 1924, trained in the British legal system, he is a shrewd and dominating man, the ultimate survivor. It is hard to imagine north Cyprus without him. 'Denktaş was there when I was born, and Denktaş will be there when I die,' said one despairing young woman. This community is so small that a high proportion of politically active people know him personally. Six of the opposition women I interviewed told me of occasions when he had singled them out to wag a warning finger at them and express his 'disappointment'

On the slopes of the Pentadactylos mountains in north Cyprus, clearly visible from the other side of the Partition Line, a gigantic Turkish Cypriot flag has been painted. It is accompanied by a Turkish national flag, and some words of Kemal Atatürk, picked out in white stones that read 'How happy to say I am a Turk'.

The Museum of Barbarism in north Nicosia keeps alive memories of the murder of Turkish Cypriots by Greeks and Greek Cypriots. It is visited by coachloads of tourists, many from Turkey.

Everywhere in north Cyprus, Turkish and Turkish Cypriot flags fly side by side.

An eventual peace agreement between Greek Cypriot and Turkish Cypriot politicians and voters must resolve bitter disagreements over land and property. The sea shore of northern Cyprus is a valuable asset, as yet little exploited for tourism. The arid climate makes water a disputed resource. And there are many religious antiquities in the north that inspire passions in Greek Orthodox Christian believers.

at their 'disloyalty'. 'Come here, my little girl. What are you saying about me? I told your husband he was crazy, but you are crazier,' he admonished fifty-year old Oya, wife of Mehmet Ali Talat, both of them prominent figures in the opposition Republican Turkish Party. 'Neriman, Neriman,' he admonished the well-known poet and columnist Neriman Cahit. 'You are like a stone weighing on my head. You want me to die. Well, I will not die.' His style may be intimate and fatherly, but his power is formidable, so that the implied threat is always understood to be frighteningly real. However, not all his daughters are wayward. Because he is seen as their only utterly reliable protector against 'the Greeks', Denktaş has retained the confidence of many anxious Turkish Cypriots.

Despite the enduring dominance of Rauf Denktaş in northern Cyprus's politics, and despite the practice of Greek Cypriots to term it 'the pseudo-state', the Turkish Republic of Northern Cyprus (declared in 1983) is an electoral democracy, with a parliamentary structure.[3] Denktaş himself is an elected president. In the period of my research (early 2001 to early 2003) there were two parties that were together effectively controlling and maintaining the status quo in which north Cyprus had been frozen for a quarter of a century. The larger, in terms of votes, was the National Unity Party (UBP), the party of the Prime Minister Derviş Eroğlu. The smaller, with which Rauf Denktaş is associated, is the Democratic Party (DP), founded in 1992 by former members of the UBP.

Boycott and non-recognition left northern Cyprus no alternative to close alignment with Turkey and an important facet of Denktaş's role has been management of that relationship. The TRNC is not only heavily dependent on Turkey for funding, it is also administratively tied in with Turkish institutions so that in some respects it gives the impression of being a province of Turkey. For example, Turkish Cypriots' passports are Turkish passports, their phone numbers have the Turkish prefix, their postcode is a sub-district of the Turkish city of Mersin, and their currency is the Turkish lira. International air travellers must pass through a Turkish airport to reach north Cyprus.

More profoundly, however, in ways that are always strongly felt in north Cyprus, but are not always evident to outside eyes, it is Turkey that calls the shots. Little of significance is decided in north Cypriot politics without the agreement of the Turkish National Security Council, the profoundly masculine cabinet of ruling politicians and military top brass that effectively governs Turkey (Jung and Piccoli 2001: 95). The opposition parties claim that behind political life in north Cyprus, operating in a shady area between the politics of the ballot box and the politics of force, are the Turkish Embassy, the Turkish military and certain underground groups of men whose violent tactics and complicity in crime are variously tolerated, encouraged or commissioned by them. In both Turkey and north Cyprus, the opposition call this 'the deep state'. It is said, however, that Rauf Denktaş himself is not without influence on Turkish politics. He may be a partner more than a puppet of Turkish politicians.

The strength of the UBP and DP is closely tied to the hegemony of Turkey, particularly the Turkish military. They are known as right-wing parties. Their opposition is known as 'the left'. But these terms, in Cyprus as elsewhere, confusingly signify different positionings on two dimensions of political opinion. Right-wing means, on the one hand, conservatism on the customary business of politics: economic policy, decisions concerning infrastructure, provision of health, education and other social services. On the other it means 'taking an uncompromising line on the Cyprus problem'. Left-wing also has a dual meaning – one in relation to redistributive politics, the other in relation to nationalism, where it connotes a leaning towards flexibility on the Cyprus problem. In both north and south Cyprus, a party may be left in one dimension, right in another. In practice, the Partition of the island and the unresolved conflict it represents, dominate the political agenda and voters' attitudes in both parts of Cyprus. Domestic factors may feature in a party's manifesto, but they are a secondary factor in its electoral performance.

The main opposition parties to the pro-Turkey ruling coalition in north Cyprus at the time of my research were the centrist Communal Liberation Party (TKP) and, to its 'left', the Republican Turkish Party (CTP). The latter's constitution does in fact define it as 'socialist', but manifesto promises of social spending or reform, a concern with that 'everyday life' so relevant to women, cannot greatly influence voting behaviour. Left-wing women told me they understand well enough that, were the left to come to power, Turkey would surely close the tap on the cash flow. CTP was, however, the strongest parliamentary opposition to Rauf Denktaş and had long been a voice for reconciliation with Greek Cypriots. While the two establishment parties have taken the position that north Cyprus should not make concessions to the Republic for the sake of entering the European Union, which they view with scepticism if not hostility, the centre and left opposition have seen the EU accession moment as an opportunity to prise Cyprus from the fingers of Turkey. UBP and DP voters fear these opposition parties would 'give away too much' to get a solution. The fact that many voters do want to retain the support of Turkey is not the only reason, however, that the parties which oppose Denktaş's policies have difficulty winning voters away from the UBP and DP. The traditional 'working-class vote' cannot greatly help the left, for the division of labour in north Cyprus today means that the majority of manual labourers are Turks, many of whom do not have voting rights. Additionally, many left-leaning voters lost confidence in TKP and CTP when, at periods in the recent past, they entered coalitions with one or other of the establishment parties, sharing for a while in government. Disillusion among their supporters at the compromises they were obliged to make, and their inability to shift policy, led to a fall in their share of votes in subsequent elections.

Outside this core group of northern parties, towards the political poles, lie a number of extra-parliamentary factions that are subject to frequent splits. To the extreme right are, for instance, the National Justice Party (MAP) and the New Revival Party (YDP), which favour strong links with Turkey. To the left are the Patriotic Unity Movement (YBH) and the United Cyprus Party (BKP) which recently split from it. These are an emphatic voice for 'Cypriot' political identity, continually urging *rapprochement* and criticizing the influence of Turkey in north Cyprus. In these respects they act as a gadfly to the less consistent CTP. They have support in some trade unions, and their internal politics, were there ever an opportunity to activate them, would be socialist.

Northern women: on the political margin

Among the significant actors in the array of parties described above, women are exceedingly scarce. At the time of my research women were estimated to be around one-third of the rank and file membership of political parties, but there were no women party presidents or general secretaries, nor had there ever been since the TRNC was declared in 1983. Women, despite fielding eighty-five candidates, won only four seats in the 1999 national elections, 8 per cent of the total. There are also few women on the party executives and there has only ever been one female minister, who served for a single term. Some parties have a women's section, but their function is less to express women's opinion than to enlist women to work for the party.

Women of both left and right told me of blocks and deterrents that would be familiar to women in many other countries. First, women are impeded by their family responsibilities, because few men share the domestic load evenly. Second, they find the masculine combative style of politics alienating. Third, men do not believe in or support women; indeed, even women do not trust and vote for each other. An active woman is tolerated, Sevgül Uludağ explained, if she sticks to organizing the party's social life ('Nice day trips to Salamis'). Tolerance ends abruptly when she challenges men's authority. And finally, kicking the perennial football of 'the Cyprus problem' hither and thither strikes many women as pointless, town planner Layık Topcan Mesutoğlu told me. Why bother to engage in a political process in which 'women's issues and environmental issues are the least important topics on the agenda'?

Only the Republican Turkish Party (CTP) has been the site of anything that could be termed a sustained struggle by women for a share in decision-making. Since it is the largest left-wing party and a consistent parliamentary voice for *rapprochement*, it is worth looking in closer detail at their experience. Oya Talat has been active in the CTP since 1977 and today is an executive committee member. Her husband, Mehmet Ali Talat, is currently party president. They met in the early 1970s, soon after the party was formed, when both were students in Ankara and already involved in left-wing politics. Looking back on the Cyprus of the 1970s and '80s, Oya reflects on how women's contribution was neglected by the male activists: 'Women feel themselves very close to politics, just as men do. We were going everywhere. We were doing propaganda, writing, organizing demonstrations, putting slogans on the walls. We were afraid of nothing. But we didn't have the status. When it comes to decision-making, women are on the outside.'

One possible vehicle for bringing women in from the cold was the Patriotic Women's Union (PWU), established in 1975, not as a women's section of the party, but as a closely associated NGO. Today, this is the largest of the party political women's organizations in the north, and Oya is its president. But there has always been a tension within the PWU between the impulse to use it as a recruiting mechanism for the party and the wish of some women to use it as a means for expressing women's interests and promoting their needs. In 1988 some women waged a successful campaign to introduce a 'quota' for women in the decision-making bodies of the party. But not all women, either in the party or the PWU, supported quotas, and a later campaign to increase the quota from 10 per cent to 30 per cent did not succeed.

Perhaps the biggest obstacle to women making the political contribution of which they are capable is the marriage relationship. At the grassroots, many female party members are members only because their husbands are. They are seldom active on their own account, deferring to male opinion, careful not to emasculate their menfolk. 'The men are happy to have their wives beside them, so long as they're not competing. What we need', says Oya, with a grimace, 'is more women who don't have a husband active in the party!'

Meral Akıncı told me of the route she has taken through these quicksands. The wife of Mustafa Akıncı, former leader of the Communal Liberation Party (TKP), she is a well-respected psychologist, and was in fact the earliest professional psychologist in north Cyprus. She insists on being known as Meral Akıncı rather than 'Mrs Akıncı' and has chosen to express her passionate concern with women's empowerment not through the party but through Kayad, the community association she founded. She is at pains to keep Kayad entirely unassociated with the TKP, in contrast to the Patriotic Women's Union which, she believes, despite its formal separate identity, is essentially part of the CTP. The point is, however, that both Oya and Meral, in their different ways, have had to fight against a prevailing tendency for the wives of important men to be seen as appendages of their husbands.

Oya herself explained carefully to me the long struggle she has had with herself and with the movers and shakers in the party, concerning her role in the CTP. Prior to one general election, she made herself available for candidacy, but failed to get the nomination. She would have been the first-ever woman candidate – a step too far, perhaps, for the party. At one time she expressed the wish to contest the seat of mayor in the municipal elections. But at that time the party was tasting its moment of power, in coalition with the DP, and her husband, Mehmet Ali, was Minister of Education. She was told that if she fought the election and lost, it would damage his reputation. 'But this is me,' she felt like insisting. 'It's not him, I'm not just his wife.' Feeling the pressure, she prudently stepped down, though she continued to feel aggrieved about it for some years afterwards. In any case, the danger foreseen by the party apparatus was probably not 'supposing she loses' so much as 'supposing she wins'. For later, when Mehmet Ali became its president, the party would express concerns about his wife holding any significant office in the party. Mehmet Ali and Oya have done their best to find a way through this thorny thicket where familial gender relations intersect with those of party politics. At no moment has Oya given her hopes of personal achievement priority over her commitment to the political programme. She is not at all bitter, merely reflective. But her story is important, because of what it says about the difficulties that may stand in other women's way.

The political system in the south: women's perspective

Political life in the south is less polarized than in the TRNC and, with Greece in the European Union and Cyprus about to be, neither country feels the need for the interventionist relationship that existed in the past and that still exists in the case of Turkey and the TRNC. But many women in the Republic of Cyprus are similarly disillusioned with the parties that eternally fail to produce a solution to the Cyprus problem while using vigilance against the 'enemy' as good reason to keep the lid on demands for social change. The Republic of Cyprus has a presidential system of government in which the elected president of the Republic forms a government of ministers from his own party and its allies. At the start of my research period Glafcos Clerides was president and the government was an alliance of his own party, Democratic Rally (DISY), and the Movement of United Democrats (EDI). DISY is often termed the 'establishment' party, conservative in the sense of being the party of business. It is also deemed right-wing in terms of the Cyprus problem, combining a commitment to inter-communal negotiations with a sustained refusal to compromise. Under Clerides's leadership it has tried, not entirely successfully, to shed the undesirable reputation it acquired after 1974, when it took in the politically homeless EOKA-B nationalist extremists. The United Democrats, DISY's parliamentary ally on the Cyprus question, is a relatively new party, formed in 1994, defining itself as centre-right. Its founder, George Vassiliou, had served as an independent president of Cyprus (1988–93). Many Greek Cypriot bi-communalists vote for EDI because they prioritize EU accession and a solution: bi-communal, bi-zonal and federal.

In February 2003, Tassos Papadopoulos displaced Glafcos Clerides as president of the Republic. In the government he subsequently formed, DISY and EDI lost their pre-eminence, to be replaced by the former opposition trio, AKEL, EDEK and DIKO. The largest of the three is AKEL, the Progressive Party of the Working People. Once Soviet-aligned, it remains formally a communist party, is strongly aligned to the trade unions and shows a concern with social issues. It is not, however, consistently left-wing in terms of the Cyprus problem, and can at times seem as rejectionist as more right-wing parties. AKEL's electoral dominance among the Greek Cypriot working class and intellectuals has tended to impede the growth of a socialist party, though the United Democratic Centre Union (EDEK, formerly KISOS) employs socialist discourse and has an honourable reputation won through having borne, with AKEL, the brunt of the Greek *junta's* viciousness in early 1970s. The third of the newly influential group of parties is Papadopoulos's own party, DIKO, the Democratic Party. It is 'rejectionist', that is to say uncompromising, on the Cyprus problem. Its former leader, Spyros Kyprianou, was president of the Republic from 1977 to 1988, during which time peace negotiations slowed to a crawl. Refugees are calculated to be one-third of the population in the south. With their untarnished vision of 'going home' to the land from which they were expelled, they are voters all parties must woo. DIKO, however, comes closest to being their voice in parliament, and they pursue a line that is deeply resistant to any compromise that might default on restitution and return.

Women's participation in the parliament of the Republic is fractionally better than in the TRNC: they have six seats in the House of Representatives, 9 per cent of the total. There is one woman among the eleven ministers in the present government of Tassos Papadopoulos (she is Minister of Health). Women are 16 per cent of elected local councillors (Nearchou-Ellinas 2001). I met and interviewed women who play a significant role in each of the five major parties of the Republic, and women who want no part in them. The 'joiners', whatever their party, told of struggles to get women and women's issues taken seriously and to get a 20 per cent quota for women adopted (four of the big five have conceded it, AKEL being the exception). They say there is a dire shortage of good and willing women candidates to fill the lists, perhaps because women have had little reason till now to believe the parties would respect or reward their contribution, or adopt the policies that matter to them.

The most positive experience of any 'joiner' is perhaps that of Androula Vassiliou. A lawyer, and wife of George Vassiliou, leader of EDI, she is currently the party's only MP. She appears to have skirted the hazards of 'couple politics' and achieved respect inside and outside the party, while finding space for her women-friendly agenda. To his credit, her husband, when embarking on the contest for a second term as the country's president, famously announced to the media, 'Androula and I have decided ... ' to take this step. Sniggers were heard in this macho political scene, but the gesture was not lost on women.

Women criticize the system for a number of flaws that together have the effect of keeping the majority, men as well as women, from getting anywhere close to the levers of power. The first is the system of 'influence' that sullies political life. Cyprus is infected with the clientilism that has been endemic in Greek politics (Close 2002: 7). Katie Clerides is the daughter of former President Glafcos Clerides. She has been an MP for DISY, and is a member of the party's Political Bureau. She is respected by women both inside and outside the party for her persistence in placing 'unpopular' women's issues, such as sexual harassment and pensions, on the party agenda. Despite her insider status, she is clear-eyed about this problem of clientilism.

> A voter will vote for a party because they agree with its philosophy. None the less they are liable to feel that having given their vote to that party, the party and its candidates owe them a favour ... The close family connections in Cypriot life, that you always support each other, gets transferred into the political realm. So people expect you to put in a good word for them when, let's say, they go for a job interview.

A second flaw, patriarchalism, is something the Greek Cypriot political system also shares with Greece, which, as David Close writes, 'diverged even from the rest of southern Europe in the extent of men's grip on authority ... men [have] continued to dominate the leading positions in political parties and in every major occupation group, professional organisation or political institution' (Close 2002: 218). Politics in the south of Cyprus, women of several different parties told me, is a masculine power game played by men 'in it for their own glory'. Finally, the system tends to elitism. If you are not of the right social class (readable from many subtle signs) and preferably connected to a reputed political dynasty, you are swimming against the tide. Thus, though there is no equivalent here to the deformations felt in northern politics due to the influence of Turkey, politics is none the less an alienating and inaccessible sphere for ordinary Greek Cypriot women.

I asked Maria Hadjipavlou, as a political scientist at the University of Cyprus, to put her mind to the question of women and power. Are women completely powerless, even in the structures of the state? She believes we must think in terms of different kinds of power, particularly 'the distinction some feminists have made between "power over" (power as domination) and "power to" (power as capacity)'. In Cyprus (and she meant north as well as south) women live in a field of power that is of the first kind, and in it they are subordinated. What is more, they internalize that subordination so that they live it in every aspect of their lives. Unlike some women, she believes that introducing quotas for women in the parties and in parliament is not a bad starting point for getting a grip on power. After all, 'politics is power! I mean, it has a lot of power to affect our lives, either in the private or the public sphere.' Introducing quotas for women in parties and in representative bodies can be a way to get women closer to power. But what matters is that, being there, we change policy agendas, shifting power from the 'dominance' mode and making 'spaces for women (and men for that matter) in which to develop our creativity, irrespective of gender. To develop our own capacities.' As women we would then be able to clarify and state our differences from men, but without being put down or excluded for them.

As it is, political power in Cyprus manifests no such aim. The two political systems of south and north are expressions, not critiques, of the male-dominated gender order. Each is fixated on the Partition, the injustices that fire the passions in their grassroots constituencies and the calculations that keep peace seemingly for ever out of reach. The still unresolved state of war between the south and the north overshadows all else in the twin political systems. It shapes the style of politics. Each side must be strong, unrelenting, and give the impression of being ready at any point to fight – to guard the Line or to sweep it away and take control of the whole island. It is what Cynthia Enloe (1993: 15) calls 'the gendered culture of danger', an environment that prioritizes masculine qualities in politicians.

Parallel economies: women's status

It is no distance at all between the two Nicosias. It takes me about fifteen minutes to walk across the Green Line from the Institute where I lodge in the south to, say, Fatma Azgın's house in the north, even if I dawdle on the way to pick her some of the wild flowers that flourish in the dead zone. But in some respects, in those days before the 'opening', the two Nicosias seemed to me to be on different planets, and the realities of one world were not easily grasped when living in the other. The most dramatic difference was an economic one. The north is a relatively less prosperous, speedy and growth-oriented world than the south. Its natural beauty is unspoiled – the plus side of a lack of investment in buildings and infrastructure. The south, in what is termed its economic miracle, turned the loss of a third of the Republic's resources in 1974 to phenomenal growth. Its cities therefore offer citizens some metropolitan facilities northerners lack – but they include McDonald's hamburger outlets and other in-cursions of Western capital that not all Greek Cypriots feel are a gain.

The condition of the economy of northern Cyprus is inseparably linked to the political system. Because of its unrecognized status, the TRNC receives no international aid. The Turkish exchequer sub-sidizes the island, and invests heavily in infrastructure. But the nature of the economic relationship with Turkey is criticized by the left. They say Turkey has failed to invest in local skills and productive capacity, deliberately creating a condition of stasis and dependence, perhaps to diminish Cypriot cultural autonomy and self-esteem. (Turks can be stung by Turkish Cypriots' pride in a certain relative modernity and European sophistication.) Despite being the only state that does not impose the international trade embargo on the TRNC, the 'motherland' (as the right-wing call it) has appeared more concerned to protect its own producers than to open up to Cyp-riot goods. As a result of such factors, the per capita gross domestic product of the north is only one-third that of the south. There is an observable difference in standard of living between that of an afflu-ent elite, controlling the distribution of Turkey's input, and that of the majority of Turkish Cypriots who live within the narrow confines imposed by modest wages and pensions paid in a currency that has little value outside the island. Some migrant labourers from Turkey, besides, live near the poverty line.

Among the less well-off, women are disproportionately represented.

A recent study by Fatma Güven-Lisaniler (2003 forthcoming) based
on published statistics and an independent sample survey, shows considerable economic gender inequality in north Cyprus. Although they
pass through primary and secondary education in equal numbers, little
more than half as many girls as boys continue to higher education
(ibid: table 39). Only 40 per cent of women of working age, as against
70 per cent of men, participate in the labour force (table 3). There is
considerable segregation of women into particular employment sectors and relatively few reach management grades (table 6). Three times
as many economically active men as women are employers, and twice
as many are self-employed (table 9). Women spend twice as many
hours per week as do men in unpaid household tasks (table 22). Taken
together such disparities result in a substantial earnings differential between the sexes at every educational level (figure 7). Traditional gender
roles, with pressure on men to perform as breadwinners, women as
home-makers, are one cause of these inequalities. They especially, but
not only, affect women who have migrated from Turkey, a large proportion of whom live in rural areas, and who experience more poverty
and disadvantage than women born in north Cyprus (table 21).[4]

The constitution of the TRNC contains a non-discrimina-
tion clause. Yet discrimination in employment is rife. Both sexes are
affected by 'cronyism'. Members of the ruling coalition, whichever
parties it happens to be, ensure job opportunities and preferment for
their political supporters. It is widely understood that an incautiously
voiced opinion or a rashly cast vote may damage your career prospects, or those of your family members. Left-wing women in particular told me one story after another of promotions withheld. Derya
Beyatlı, for instance, was fired from her university teaching job for
refusing to regrade failed students who were the sons and daughters
of important political and military men. Gülay Kaşer spent her working life in the municipal authority, retiring where she had begun
twenty years before, on the bottom rung. She does not doubt that
being an active member of the left-wing YBH had something to do
with it. 'Honestly, Cynthia,' she said, 'I am a hard worker. I always
finish a job. But they don't care how you work. That's not the thing.'

It is not, however, only when they are supporters of the opposi-
tion or trade union activists that women are shunted on to the sidings.
Discrimination on grounds of sex, too, is routine in northern Cyprus.
This is clear from the experience of even conservative women.

I interviewed Latife Birgen, a highly educated woman who worked consistently for almost two decades in various supportive roles in President Denktaş's office and the Ministry for Foreign Affairs. She reflected thoughtfully on her career. 'I got no promotion in so many years,' she said. 'And yet I was a person who was told she could do the work of four men.' Others who witnessed her substantial contribution to the UBP in the years following Partition are convinced that, had she not been a woman, she would have been made a government minister. Ayşe Hasan is another example. Her loyalty to the authorities is in no doubt, since she has held a local political post in a mainstream party. She combines this political work with the direction of her own company. But what jolted her into setting up in business on her own account was her experience as a bank employee. After some years she saw clearly that it was going to be well nigh impossible, as a woman, to get promotion to bank manager. Two other women told similar stories of a glass ceiling in the private sector that prevents women reaching the top.

There is as yet no national office for women's rights in the administration of northern Cyprus, though one is in the planning stages. Meanwhile, all the mechanisms of sex discrimination, direct and indirect, subtle and shamelessly crude, combine to exclude women from responsibility and authority in the workplace. Women of the civil service trade union ÇAĞ-SEN told me how employers regard any man, whatever his lack of qualifications, as preferable to any woman, however well qualified. Employers say to the woman candidate, 'If you're single, you're bound to get married and leave. If you're married, you're sure to get pregnant and go on maternity leave for months. Either way we don't want you.'

I had the opportunity to interview a number of women teachers and administrative personnel at the Eastern Mediterranean University. Biran Mertan was one of them. She had been influential in founding a Centre for Women's Studies there. In an article in the first issue of its journal, *Kadın/Woman*, she analysed the male dominance of the university (Mertan 2000). In the year 2000 women were 75 per cent of base-line lecturers yet held only 17 per cent of professorial posts. Of the thirteen most senior positions in the university, only one was filled by a woman. In general, women were underrepresented among academic staff (41 per cent) and overrepresented among manual workers in EMU (66 per cent). Biran had recently resigned as director of the centre, in some disappointment. On International Women's Day 2003 she wrote to the Rector to point out to him that the percentage of decision-making positions in EMU held by women, far from improving, had declined between 2000 and 2003 from 17.4 per cent to 12.9 per cent.

Ayla Gürel, a lecturer in engineering at EMU, explains these statistics as a product of male bonding. 'The men just prefer to appoint someone from their boys' network. They're more comfortable with their own kind. Say, if there's a racket going on, they're not going to be able to include a woman in it so easily. So they gang up, you know, they play the boys' game.' But Biran feels women too often groom men for success: 'Say two students get married. They both finish their Masters. The woman is likely to say to the man, "Go on, you do your PhD. I'll look after the baby." We have this kind of mentality.'

In the year 2000, an already tough economic situation became dramatically worse. Irresponsible administration and personal greed brought about the collapse of a number of banks operating in north Cyprus. An estimated 50,000 people lost their savings. Although compensation later mitigated the disaster, per capita income fell by 40 per cent in four months. The currency was subsequently devalued, halving once again the worth of earnings and savings. Thousands of people were forced to default on their housing loans.

Neşe Veçhioğlu is a dressmaker in Famagusta, with her own tiny workshop and shopfront. She told me how this crisis had affected her family. Her regular customers could no longer afford her sewing services, sales of wedding dresses and other garments had slumped. Two older family members had put their retirement money in a bank. Now they had lost it all. Her adult son and daughter, whom she and her husband, a building worker, had seen through university, were now unemployed, and with no job prospects she feared they would emigrate. She said, 'The poor are poor. But a lot of the rich have become poor too, and their factories have closed. There's no money around any more.' Although the bourgeoisie had been shaken by the crisis, however, the class gap remained, and in 2001 it was still possible to see conspicuous wealth. When Ayşe Hasan, whom we met above, left her bank job, she set up her own business and became something very rare among Turkish Cypriot women – a highly successful entrepreneur. She lives in a large and finely appointed house in a prosperous residential area on a hillside overlooking the sea.

The economy in south Cyprus contrasts dramatically with that in the north. A downturn had affected this economy, too, in the period when I was carrying out this research. But its effects were not immediately apparent to a casual observer. Its cities burst at the seams with prestigious hotels, the shiny glass-and-steel offices of banks and airlines, glitzy boutiques and pulsating tourist resorts. There are numberless construction sites and the traffic seizes up at rush hour. Few people doubted that the economy would pick up and the trajectory of growth would continue. Of greater concern to many of the women I spoke with is the direction in which prosperity is taking them. With 25,000 offshore banking enterprises, 'Cyprus has established itself as the successor to Beirut as an unregulated centre of capitalist enterprise in the Mediterranean' (Brewin 2000: 149). Consumerism rules, women told me. There are gross inequalities. Money-laundering and other kinds of white-collar crime proliferate. And I could see for myself that ugly constructions are everywhere invading natural environments.

As we saw in Chapter 2, one effect of the 1974 war was to bring many more women into the labour market. It has been suggested that their contribution both in paid labour and 'their unpaid services in their homes' substantially contributed to the 'economic miracle' of that decade (Stavrou 1997: 77). Certainly, as the south has modernized, women have come closer on many counts to the average for Western Europe. They are more economically integrated than in the north: women are approximately 50 per cent of the population and 40 per cent of the labour force. Nevertheless, women's average earnings are only 71 per cent of men's (Republic of Cyprus 2000: table 18). This is partly due to the fact that their share of better-paying and higher-status jobs is meagre. 'The majority of Cypriot working women are particularly likely to be subject to male authority. Very few women are at the top of hierarchies, even in jobs that are predominantly female' (Stavrou 1997: 69). The brunt of unemployment is borne by women who have lost their traditional jobs in manufacturing. And the many thousands of super-exploited and insecure Asian migrant workers in the south include a high proportion of women.

The process of preparing for entry to the EU has stimulated official attention to women and sex equality. The government has established a National Machinery for Women's Rights, in the Ministry of Justice. Its Plan of Action includes reforms to expand women's rights

The part of Nicosia that lies in Greek Cypriot south Cyprus, with its glossy shopping malls, boutiques and cafés, is a thriving centre of modernity and consumerism.

in labour and family law and in relation to domestic violence. The NMWR's principal officer, Maro Varnavidou, is working towards the 'mainstreaming' of a gender perspective into the work of all government departments (Republic of Cyprus 2001). Myria Vassiliadou points out, however, that the impetus towards European accession is not due in any measure to enthusiasm for European legislative norms on sex equality. Quite the contrary, it is driven by 'patriarchy and nationalism' (Vassiliadou 2002: 477). The EU has given women a language in which to assert their rights, but implementation is another matter. As in the rest of Europe, women in Cyprus are still far from equal with men.

Militarized masculinity: every mother's son

So we see that, while Partition has generated certain differences between the two political and economic systems it brought into being, they are not dissimilar as gender orders. In Cyprus it is men who constitute the power that straddles the Line, maintains it, and administers ethnic differentiation and separation. Politics and business life are stamped with masculine cultures. To this of course we have to add the military factor, in which again the two societies are similar. I climbed one day to the ruins of the Palace of Vouni, not far from Morphou. The Phoenicians built it in the fifth century BCE, to dominate and control nearby Soli, which was pro-Greek. It put in perspective the many fenced enclosures I had passed along the road, with their armed guards and 'forbidden' signs. It reminded me that this island has been more or less a garrison island throughout history, with troops billeted from here and there. And I understood the doubt I heard so many women express that they would ever be rid of soldiery and weapons.

There are six armies in Cyprus. The United Nations peacekeeping force, UNFICYP, has something over one thousand soldiers whose task is to patrol the Line and prevent outbreaks of ethnic violence along it; watch over the well-being of the small minorities either side; and work for a return to 'normality' in ethnic relations on the island. The British have two military bases in the south, covering 99 square miles, with an unknown number of personnel. This territory is legally not Cypriot at all, since under the Treaty of Establishment of 1960, sovereignty rests with the United Kingdom. The bases operate high-technology intelligence devices scanning the Middle East and, as we

have seen, are crucial assets for NATO and inevitably involve Cyprus
in international tensions and dangers.

In the south of Cyprus there is a force of around 950 Greeks, permitted under the Treaty of Alliance of 1960. They work closely with
the 10,000-strong Greek Cypriot National Guard, the Republic's
own army. In 1993 the two states agreed that Cyprus would be part
of one Greek unified defence space, and the orange and white flag of
Cyprus and the blue and white flag of Greece fly together over their
military establishments (Brewin 2000: 144). By far the largest army on
the island, however, is that of Turkey. Turkey had been permitted 650
soldiers under the Treaty of Alliance. But in the course of the military intervention of 1974 the number massively increased, and today
there are thought to be 35,000 Turks stationed on the island. Turkey
disposes, in the homeland, of the second largest army in Europe, a fact
which makes these outlyers particularly fearsome. Furthermore, it is
the Turkish commander of the military forces in Cyprus who is head
of the police and fire brigade (Constantinou and Papadakis 2001).

In one sense, all politicians in both north and south Cyprus are
'military men' because the entire male population, bar a few ethnic
and religious categories deemed unreliable (such as Catholics and
Turkish Cypriots in the south), are conscripted into military service.
Women are not required to serve in either military. In the north, political and military power are even more closely and menacingly intertwined, with the Turkish military supervising, from the wings, many
aspects of political life and civil society. Conversely, the low presence
of women in the upper echelons of political and economic life in
Cyprus is felt by many to be due to the emphasis on national defence
and the gladiatorial politics it tends to privilege.

Militarism, as an ideology and a culture, wherever it occurs, scores
the gender line particularly deep. Where in a relatively unmilitarized
society the heroic man might be a statesman or even a writer (Dudink
2002), the heroic masculinity of a militarized society is unquestionably the soldier and the ideal value of manhood is courage. As men
are trained for military service they must forcefully eject every trace
of the feminine in their nature – a coward is 'nothing but' a woman.
Conversely, militarism is bad news for women's social standing. In a
state in which full citizenship is associated, whether constitutionally or
metaphorically, with military service, and where, as in Cyprus, women
are not conscripted into the military, women are bound to be seen as

incomplete citizens. And among the values and beliefs that make up militarist ideology are clear prescriptions for gender. The ideal military masculinity, crucially important for the sustained militarization of a society, implies a particular form of femininity. Cynthia Enloe's detailed research has demonstrated how deeply militarization penetrates even a peacetime society and how entwined with it are women's lives. A wife and mother must believe that the most important thing is that 'her' soldier does his military job the best he possibly can. She should feel that in helping him, right down to washing his clothes, she is doing her patriotic duty for nation and state. She has to pick up willingly all the familial tasks he neglects by being called to duty. She has to be tolerant of his bonding rituals with his fellow soldiers, however alcoholic and misogynist they may be. She must be specially understanding when he is under stress and she may even have to tolerate domestic violence (Enloe 2000).

In the case of Cyprus we saw how in the 1950s and 1960s men were caught up in violent nationalist movements. Women were characteristically home-bound in this period, as seemed natural and proper, but they were practically supportive of their paramilitary men (Anthias 1989). 'In those days,' Gediz Inan reminded me, 'everybody was a volunteer. It was in every house, it was our father, our brother. You loved them.' Several women commented to me that those times had left a legacy in present-day gender relations. Today, however, I sense a tension in relation to the military. Many young men dislike the obligation to serve, and ridicule the army's routines. Yet I heard of no conscientious objectors and there is certainly no political movement of refusal as there is, for instance, in Israel. For women, too, it seems difficult to take an open stand against militarism. So long as there is no peace agreement, national security still feels in peril. How can women complain that state budgets tend to prioritize military expenditure over the social spending from which their everyday lives would benefit? How can they take issue if their children's schooling stresses military values? How can a woman protest at the presence of a gun in the cupboard under the stairs when it might turn out to be her children's last defence against the 'Greeks' or 'Turks' from the other side of the Line?

In the short run, however, many women are preoccupied less by protecting their children from the enemy than protecting them from the army. Compulsory military service is twenty-four months in the north, twenty-six months in the south. In the north it is easier to evade — you can defer it during higher education and even buy your way out if you have several thousand pounds saved up. In the south, boys are conscripted immediately after secondary school, when they are very impressionable. Women are divided on the effects of service on their sons. All fear for their safety for, besides the threat of war, bullying is prevalent and suicides occur. But some feel young men emerge all the better for their enforced militarization, more independent, more mature. On the other hand, many women are deeply preoccupied with the way it inculcates racism and hatred for 'the others'. Sue Lartides said:

> [In our family] we don't advocate any kind of violence! I mean, we don't step on ants if they get in our way, you know! And I saw my seventeen-year-old go into the army, a child! And each time he came out, he was a bit harder, and a bit more aggressive, and a bit more hatred had been fed into him about the other seventeen-year-old children on the other side of the Green Line, that he was being taught how to wound or kill … I can't even find the words for it!

She felt an overwhelming anger at her helplessness. The child in relation to the mother has suddenly become a man in relation to the state. The mother has given years of her life to do motherhood well. At a stroke she loses control, as the life and well-being of her child is subject to the power of the state.

§

The foregoing account shows women living parallel lives in adjacent societies, whose gender orders are both systems of male dominance. These feuding brother patriarchies are not identical. Limitations on economic change, together with Turkish migration, have maintained a degree of patriarchal rural traditionalism in areas of the north and even a revival of Islamic religious observance in a society noted for its secularity. Capitalist modernity has brought new consumerist trends and subcultures to the south and opened it more to foreign, especially North American, cultural influence. (We shall see more of these differences in the following chapter.) In both regions, however, the patriarchal gender line drawn historically between men and women, glimpsed in Chapter 2, persists today and, though under challenge, retains much of its authority. Women are contesting political power, but remain on the margins, their issues rarely addressed, obliged to com-

pete with men in the prevailing masculine mode of politics that they
find distasteful and disadvantaging. More women have been coming
into employment, and seeking opportunities in business and the pro-
fessions, but unchanged domestic responsibilities and inadequate state
support, combined with vertical and horizontal lines of exclusion
maintained by those, mainly men, who control access to opportunity,
result in women having less disposable income of their own and fewer
prospects of economic autonomy.

Neither militarism nor nationalism is conducive to women's equality and autonomy. In Cyprus these twin mind-sets are still firmly in
place, everlastingly legitimated by the unresolved war, the unsigned
peace. Rebecca Bryant shows how the nationalisms that contest for
power in Cyprus are not identical. Greek Cypriot nationalism, like
Greek nationalism, is primordialist. Its inspirational metaphor is Greek
'spirit', the pure Greek Christian soul, inseparable from freedom.
Turkish nationalism, relatively recently shaped by Atatürk, is more
adaptive. Its inspirational metaphor is 'blood'. Turkish blood shed
in war encapsulates the Turkish Cypriot community's links to the
land. But in both cases, Bryant argues, the symbolism is gendered.
Greek Cypriot nationalist discourse evokes the purity and chastity
of the land as body of the nation, equated with femininity (Greece
the mother, Cyprus the maiden). In Turkish Cypriot nationalism the
blood soaking into the land is virile, fertilizing the feminine land
(Bryant 2002).

An emphatic prescription for gender relations is at the heart of
nationalist ideology, as of militarist ideology. Nationalists have a very
clear idea what a proper man and a proper woman are like and they
are usually energetic in shaping them up. In most nationalisms, and
those of Cyprus are no exception, the ideal gender order is characterized by an authoritative and protective male head of household.
Women for their part are by no means undervalued. They are represented as particularly important to the nation, the ones who reproduce the two things most vital for its continuance: children, and the
collective culture. Often 'woman' is used as a symbol of the nation
(Anthias and Yuval-Davis 1989); but being a symbol never bodes well
for the flesh and blood woman.

Contemporary Cyprus, then, as women describe it, appears to be
an interesting example of the mutual constitution of an ethnic order
(binary nationalisms) and a gender order (modernizing patriarchy),

both shaped by, and shaping, a capitalist economic order with its class structure. These in turn are reinforced by, and help sustain, the militarization of the island and its cultures. Some women are deep into the patriarchal bargain, playing their part to the full in sustaining the hierarchical gender order in exchange for things they value, including security, a reassuring sense of belonging, the respect they gain as mothers. On the other hand, it is clear that some women do not subscribe to these linked ideologies. This small minority, stepping out of line, rejecting proper femininity, is a subversive and creative influence. The gender order, however, can survive a few women defectors. It is the reproduction of proper masculinity that is the bottom line for patriarchy. And, in Cyprus as elsewhere, few men as yet are refuseniks.

Notes

1 For detailed accounts of the many mediations and negotiations between the Greek Cypriot and Turkish Cypriot leaderships from 1964 to date see Polyviou 1980, Ertekün 1981, Groom 1993 and Dodd 1998.

2 Mete Hatay, basing his estimate on a study of updated census reports and voter registration cards, suggests that in the year 2000 there were approximately 50,000 Turks with TRNC citizenship, of whom 30,000 were born in Turkey and 20,000 were born in Cyprus of mainland Turkish parentage (Bahcheli 2003).

3 I give reasons for my own choice of terms in note 4 of the Introduction.

4 For women's status in the immediately preceding period, see Women's Research Centre (1995).

5 | Binary logic: marriage, sex and bodies

Türkan Uludağ was born in 1917 to a Turkish Cypriot farming family in a village in the Famagusta district. In those days, girl babies were not very welcome news. Türkan tells me her father was so angry when he knew his wife had given birth to a girl that he stormed off to the coffee shop and for three days the baby remained unnamed while he refused to acknowledge her. But Türkan survived and thrived. Photographs over page show her at various stages in her life. The one that interests me particularly was taken in 1923 and shows the children clustered round the father who is wearing a fez. The picture is notable for the absence of Türkan's mother. Since the visiting photographer was a man, it was not felt seemly that she should emerge from the house to appear in the family portrait.

The patriarchal principle, expressed in the seclusion of women in the home, the pride in sons and the lesser value ascribed to girls, also characterized Greek Orthodox culture in Cyprus at this period. There are many accounts of the traditional Greek Cypriot family as it existed in the first half of the twentieth century, its similarities to and differences from other Mediterranean family forms. They stress the importance of honour (in Greek, *filotimo*). Floya Anthias describes this as a specifically male concept, 'denoting self-respect, masculinity and conformity to the standards of male behaviour'. For a woman the equivalent term, *timi*, denoted sexual innocence, obedience and domesticity. A man's honour was most vulnerable to the sexual behaviour of the women of his family, for it depended on their purity. Control of women and girls by the head of the family was therefore of paramount importance (Anthias 1992: 82). Traditional practice in both Greek Cypriot and Turkish Cypriot families in the past, however, was for marriages to be contracted by arrangement. The union was negotiated between the respective parents, though the young might have a degree of veto over their proposals. It was considered important for the new wife quickly to fall pregnant, to prove her husband's virility, fulfil her destined role of motherhood and, of course, to produce a son to continue the male line (Anthias 1992).

From the 1930s a new factor entered into both Greek and Turkish Cypriot marriage relations in Cyprus: the 'dowry-house'. It became the practice for parents to provide a house or flat and furniture for their daughter on marriage. Usually it was built near or as part of the family home. It is still very common for women in Cyprus to be assisted by their families to own their own flat or house, and siblings and parents are often found living in proximity. Such matrilocality and female property ownership are widely seen by ethnographers as strengthening a woman's hand in a society that is otherwise male dominant. But Anthias points out that the practice denies a woman personal, human value. It makes her a marketable commodity and strengthens parental power, making her dependent on the economic status of her father. She is also morally bound by the investment her parents have made in her to care for them in old age (Anthias 1992; Vassiliadou forthcoming).

The live question for today's young women is how much of these traditions lives on in their own families of origin and in Cypriot society at large, to constrain their autonomy and limit their choices. We saw in the previous chapter how a woman tends to be evaluated, and granted or refused respect and opportunity, according to the family whose name she carries. Whose daughter or wife a woman is makes a difference to her chances in politics, enterprise or employment. The family as an institution still has a very strong hold in Cyprus, north and south. The reinforcement of the family by religious authorities is particularly strong in the case of the Greek Orthodox hierarchy, a bulwark of conservatism and patriarchy in south Cyprus. In recent research Myria Vassiliadou found it a dominant influence on the lives of urban women in Cyprus, even when these women are non-religious and/or non-practising (Vassiliadou forthcoming). In the north, the Turkish Cypriots have long tended to non-observance. They are the most secular community on the island. Their culture was shaped by the modernizing revolution of Kemal Atatürk in the 1920s and '30s, which promoted a feminine identity closer to that of Western Europe. Among migrants from Turkey, however, the imams retain more sway. Some Turkish Cypriots are dismayed to see a great many new mosques being built with money from Turkey and the influential Islamic Foundation Evkaf. Though this mosque construction is more a political than a religious act, the sight of minarets rising in the villages seems to them to threaten a return to a distant past.

The modernizing economy, demanding women's participation as producers and consumers, has shaken the ground under both the

Türkan Uludağ (above) today and (right) as a child standing in front of her father, with siblings. Her mother is absent here because it was considered improper for her to emerge from the house to pose for the visiting male photographer.

Türkan (centre of the front row above) with
her school class, 1933.

As wife and mother, 1953.

As an 'air raid precaution' volunteer
in the second World War.

religious authorities and the patriarchal family. Many women I spoke with, regardless of age, had found themselves at some point contesting their parents' authority in order to take control of their own lives. In both parts of Cyprus today, girls are getting as much education as boys and they aspire to support themselves by their own earnings. Familial constraints thus appear outrageous to young women. A sociology student told me: 'You have to make your revolution.' All the same, it is very rare indeed for the young to turn their back on the family. Even renegades stay in touch with their parents. As Georgette Loizou put it: 'It's hard to find a Cypriot who doesn't have lunch with their extended family on Sundays.' So the reality typically experienced by a woman today is a struggle to combine a genuinely felt honour and love for her parents and husband with a passionately desired control over her own life.

Moira Killoran's research in north Cyprus explores the poignant story of two women choosing different, ultimately self-damaging, strategies to achieve autonomy within the constraints of marriage. One uses deceit, a double life. The other openly uses the humorous and proud 'I'm a bad Muslim!' tag – a culturally sanctioned part of self-representation within secular left-wing society in the north. She finds, however, that this is only sanctioned for a man. A woman dicing with convention in this way forfeits her virtue – and possibly her husband (Killoran 1998).

I have found it difficult, throughout this book, to know where Cyprus ends and the rest of the world begins. Women tell me, 'This is how it is here', and very often I feel a spark of recognition and think, 'Yes, and this is how it is in England too'. A wealth of feminist research and analysis from many countries shows women in transition between tradition and Westernized modernity. In Cyprus, compared, say, with England, the transition has been accelerated, and the tensions gen-erated are necessarily higher. So what I express of women's experience in Cyprus is not intended to suggest that it is unique, or that it reflects all Cypriot women's realities. Simply, it is a meaningful experience to some women in Cyprus, and we may examine it for reasons why some women want a women's movement for change, and for pointers to the direction it would logically take.

What is at stake in this struggle between the younger and older generations of women (for grandmothers are a notable force in this) is fundamentally the maintenance of the line that differentiates two genders. As Jill Julius Matthews writes: 'All the component parts of our world are geared to distinguish between female and male and to offer different possibilities and choices' (Matthews 1984: 5). The inter-generational struggle many young women launch today is about whether and how the dichotomy male/female will be reproduced, proper complementarity between masculinity and femininity be ensured, and women's dependence on men retained.

Marriage and the single woman

In all this, marriage remains the key issue. For a Greek Cypriot woman, not finding a husband is still considered by the older generation to be a disaster that threatens social marginalization. Interviews I had with Katarina K and her mother Anna K brought these generational changes to life for me. They are Greek Cypriots and live in a village not far from the Line. Katarina, twenty-five, speaks English with a recognizably English accent, acquired, like her British passport, by having lived in England until she was eight and again more recently when she returned for a postgraduate degree course. Her mother Anna was born in 1950 to a working-class rural family. For her generation there were no such opportunities for education and travel. Looking back, she still feels sad about how her father had eyes only for his son. She recalls, as a frank injustice, the power he had in the family. Anna left school at twelve and started working alongside her mother in the fields for a cash wage. She remembers: 'Together we earned £60 in three months' potato picking. My father took it all. He didn't even give me £5 to get something for myself, not even a dress. I only had two dresses.' He told her he needed the money to build a dowry-house for her older sister.

Most of her life Anna has been a factory machinist. As a young woman she went to England to join her sister and brother-in-law in their fish-and-chip shop in the Midlands. She married a man in whom she had little interest, and gave birth to a child after nine months. She describes the tough life that, like many other economic migrants, the family endured for years before eventually returning to her Cypriot village. She wants her daughter's life to be different.

I would never say to Katarina to marry a man she did not love. I always thought about my mother first. I didn't do anything for myself and that has turned back against me, so I want my daughter to do things for herself. I want her to do the things that she wants to do regardless of what I think. I will agree with her because I trust her. When I was engaged it was very different. I told my sister I didn't think we were going to be happy. Sometimes I hurt now because I knew from the beginning that it was not a love marriage.

All the same, Katarina feels pressure from other members of her family and even her friends:

> I am at that age now … They openly ask me all the time, and it's so frustrating. They say: 'So, Katarina, when are you going to get married? Are you looking for a guy to marry? Are you going out with anyone? Are you serious with anyone? You're not that young any more. You know, you've finished with your studies, it's high time you settled down.' It's very common, very common – it's like in your face the whole time … Everybody's under pressure.

The pressure comes not only from the older generation but also from peers. 'So long as you are on your own,' Katarina says, 'you're *less* in young people's eyes … The minute you have a partner, whether it's a fiancé or a boyfriend or whatever, your value goes up … It's celebratory and it gets you, like, more respect and, you know, adds to your value.'

I asked Katarina whether there were any attempts being made to 'marry her off'.

> Yes! Oh, yes! That's going on – matchmaking. It's not like the way it used to be with my mum where they decide who she's going to marry and send her over and finish. I do have a choice … But it would be, 'This woman phoned and she's thought of this guy who she thinks would be suitable for you' or '[so and so] thinks her son is looking to settle down and they thought you were a nice girl, and maybe they'd talk to him'.

Katarina is shocked at this notion of blind dates with men – 'basically I don't know them, I've never talked to them'. It is clear she will choose her own partner. I pointed out the contrast between her own situation and the powerlessness her mother had experienced, but she said fiercely: 'Yes, but whatever is her story is also mine. It is my background too. I carry it with me. It's always in the corner of your mind, "Here I am at University in the UK because of what my parents went through".' I asked her if the gratitude she had to feel was in itself a burden. 'Exactly that. My mother doesn't, but my father makes me feel as if I should be grateful. You owe him and feel obliged. Even if they don't say it, you know it.'

A similar mother/daughter interview I conducted in the north gave me the sense that Turkish Cypriot and Greek Cypriot cultures are rather similar in these familial norms and the contemporary challenge to them. If there is a divergence of practice it seems to be between the village and the city. In the capital, especially in the more dynamic south side, women are more quickly gaining the freedoms of a metropolitan lifestyle. Nevertheless, even in Nicosia I came across women whose lives exemplified the price you pay for failing (or re-fusing) to find a husband, and, even worse, for leaving the shelter of the parental home and living as an autonomous single woman.

Gülay Kaşer, fifty-one, lives in Taşkınköy, on the northern edge of Nicosia. She is highly unusual in being a single woman who is satis-fied and proud to live alone, unmarried, in her own hard-earned house. She is a spare and energetic person, so it is no surprise that for years she was a folk dancer. Now, having taken early retirement from her office job, she volunteers for the Folkloric Centre. Looking back, she says of herself: 'I was just a girl brought up to get married, nothing else. But I was discussing myself with me. Who am I? What do I want from life, really?' So, when her father proposed engaging her, aged thirteen, to a Turkish soldier (the appeal of a military son-in-law), she said, 'No, it's too early. Wait till I leave school.' But her father took a cue from her response and never again pressed the issue of marriage. And Gülay never did meet a man who seemed right for her. Some, who came close, felt dubious about their own status around her trans-parent strength and determination. Gülay guesses they thought, 'This is a woman we can't carry. She's going to carry us. It's better to stay away.' Ten years ago she acquired a home of her own and moved out of her parents' house. She relishes this independence: 'Living alone, it's wonderful. I can have many friends, I can do anything I want. I don't have to be home at a certain time. I can help anyone, everyone. I have spare time and if my house is untidy, I don't care. If it needs cleaning or something, I can clean it in my own time or a cleaning lady can do it for me.' All the same, acquaintances give her grief over her choice. Because she does not seem to need a man, some wonder if she might be a lesbian. Others, watching the coming and going of friends and political colleagues at her house, suspect her of 'seeing men'. No other woman of her acquaintance lives alone in this way.

In a memorable image, Jill Matthews wrote: 'Walls of necessity were built around the institution of marriage and the rest of the landscape was blasted so that no feminine living could be had from it' (Matthews 1984: 113). She was writing about Australia in the early twentieth century, but there is something of this within many European cultures even now. Cyprus is one where the pressure to marry continues to be strong. Men who do not marry also suffer for it, for different reasons and in different ways. But 'compulsory' wedlock, whereby women have validity only as part of a couple, is a serious limitation on a woman's personhood because of the unequal nature of the marital relationship, in which the woman is the subaltern partner. Here is patriarchy in almost classic form, men reaping their patriarchal dividend. For there is no doubt we must, as Bob Connell insists, regard not only men-in-the-state and men-as-capitalists but also men-in-marriage, *husbands*, as a 'power': 'It flies in the face of conventional political analysis, but it makes sense. In a patriarchal gender order, husbands' interests in their wives' sexual and domestic services are institutionalized on a society-wide basis. This is a power to which state agencies have repeatedly accommodated' (Connell 2002: 104).

This may seem a hard judgment on men, especially when it comes down to individual men, known and loved; but we are talking here about a long-lived system that is proving hard to shift. And it is not only the male head of the household who sustains it. The extended family as a whole enacts patriarchalism, and often the woman is the force that achieves its functioning, notwithstanding the drunken or absent husband, the pressures of consumer individualism, the rebellious young bringing back foreign ways from study abroad. Often enough mother and daughter honour the implicit deals of the patriarchal bargain without a word being spoken. The daughter knows her mother worries about her 'not being settled', and suffers for the pain she causes her.

The quality of partnerships

Once married, women who have been used to paid employment often continue to work today, and, in Cyprus as elsewhere, this raises new expectations of men's participation in housework and childcare. Myria Vassiliadou's research among contemporary women in south

Cyprus, however, suggests there has been little change in the relationship between husband and wife in response to new circumstances (Vassiliadou forthcoming). I have found no comparable study of women in northern Cyprus, but women there talked in similar vein to those I interviewed in the south. Ayla Gürel, for instance, lives in the north of Cyprus and when I met her she was teaching engineering at the Eastern Mediterranean University. When in her twenties she had met a man, married him, inadvertently become pregnant, and given birth while still working for her PhD. She had not been ready for this change.

> After having given birth, I had three months to prepare for the qualifying exam! It was very unrealistic. I didn't even have a washing machine, and there weren't these disposable nappies in those days. I had to wash the nappies by hand, and it was terribly time-consuming. In those days I didn't know how to minimize the crippling effect of these things on my life. I simply had no time to study, and I failed. I went to Ankara [for the exam] and I simply failed. I came back thinking, 'That was my first significant failure.' I remember telling my husband, you know, 'You really have to help me a little bit more in the house because I don't think I can handle this.' And he said, 'Well, I'm afraid, that's your own problem.' I didn't hold it against him at the time. But I didn't realize how deeply it had affected me.

So Ayla took the main responsibility for their son, and when after two years she went back to Ankara to do her PhD she had him with her all the time. About the marriage she was now deeply ambivalent, alienated in it yet uncertain of being able to survive without it. She became deeply depressed, pulling through only by making the decision to seek a divorce. But it was against her husband's will, and when he sued for custody of their son, the judge awarded it to him.

The distance of husbands from cooking, cleaning and caring is reinforced, I was told, by the perception in Cyprus (as in many other countries) that to do such work is humiliating for a man. Other men dislike seeing a man, metaphorically, 'wearing an apron'. They chide him jokingly but with serious intent, because he has allowed himself to be reduced to the status of women and raises the spectre of the emasculation of all men. Another marriage I came across in north Cyprus shows that a different outcome, though it takes an improbable amount of foresight and a very strong will, is just possible.

Fatma Güven teaches at the same northern university as Ayla. She deferred marriage 'undesirably' long – she was thirty-three when she married. Even so I am not quite sure where she got the clear-sightedness and nerve to make her requirements so plain, both to herself and her prospective partner. We were talking about women's domestic relationships with their husbands. Fatma exclaimed, 'They always use this word, "help". Not "share". They say, "My husband is very good, he *helps* me." I hate that!' When she had been introduced (by a friend, in matchmaking mode) to a man who pleased her, she approached marriage somewhat as a contract: 'Before marriage I put my points, "Look," I said, "I'm an active woman and I want to continue to be. I'm a member of this and that; I'll be out two nights a week doing this and that" … and he agreed.' She also laid the groundwork for a marriage that did not involve enclosure or possessiveness. She said to Izmet: 'I want to tell you everything about me, my education, my PhD, my other activities. I want you to know that I have a lot of male friends and women friends. I visit their houses, I am close with a lot of men in a friendly way. Are you ready to accept all this?'

Having started this way, Fatma scarcely needed to negotiate shared childcare. Izmet himself was not totally convinced they should 'bring another child into this world'. But when Fatma said she would like one,

> he made the decision that it would be a common responsibility to always share; it was his decision … When Mehmet was only six months old I went to Malta; when he reached one and a half I went to America for a fortnight. Izmet was the one who looked after Mehmet. Both our mothers rang up and said to him 'Come, I'll take care of him', but he said no. Now we have a girl who takes care of Mehmet in the day, from eight until six, but it's for *both* of us.

Since getting married in the first place has such continuing importance in Cyprus, it follows that slipping the bonds is highly problematic. On divorce a woman forefeits the mature acceptability of the married woman. She does not fall back to the juvenile status of the spinster, but she becomes an anomaly of a different kind, and, as in many cultures, is seen as a threat to other marriages. Magda Zenon is an interesting example of a divorcee who is also a single parent. She was born to Greek Cypriot parents living in South Africa and speaks English with a South African accent. She is sturdy and forthright, a defender of the underdog, and was a student activist against apartheid. Today she is proud of being a single parent to six-year-old Angelo, her adopted son, with whom she has made a home in south Nicosia. To be a single parent is not yet respectable, even in the city. Magda, typically, has turned it into a political act by organizing with other single parents in an NGO.

Magda had met her husband while on holiday in Greece. Soon after, she left South Africa to live with him there. He clearly fell very much in love with her, and she enjoyed the affection of this expressive and emotional person. 'He'd tell you he loves you. He'd bring out a lot of things. It was what I needed then and I found it quite refreshing. Temporarily.' She succumbed to his pressure to marry. They tried unsuccessfully to conceive; they underwent fertility treatment but that failed. It was then that they set about the adoption process and were eventually successful in adopting the tiny, maltreated, newborn Angelo. And in motherhood Magda found something that she had not found in marriage. She also realized that 'for those fifteen years of my marriage I'd lost me. The advocate of justice in me was lost. I didn't find a way to express it. And divorcing him brought me back. In fact, my sister said "welcome back".' I asked her in what way she had meant it. 'In terms of liveliness, in terms of being assertive, and being positive, and not subservient. My son brought me to life.'

Magda now lives in south Cyprus with Angelo, who also spends time in Greece with his adoptive father. She is annoyed when people pity her for being divorced: 'You get a lot of sympathy that I find quite pukey! I don't feel sorry for myself. I'm better for being divorced … For fifteen years I was in a marriage that suppressed me … Then I realized that this wasn't life. I was actually doing a disservice to myself. I was accepting situations that shouldn't be acceptable for anyone … [Now] I'm answerable to no one. I wanna go, I go!'

Body politics: elusive intimacy

In both south and north, women told me there are many important areas of lived experience that are not much spoken about, even between friends, much less in the family. It is not so very different from the time when (as we saw in Chapter 3) women could hardly voice the word 'rape', though the danger of rape at that time was never far from their minds. I organized parallel round table discussions on 'body politics', during which the specificities of desire, orgasm,

intimacy and sexual choice were necessarily aired. Two generations
of women were involved. In both north and south, some women said
afterwards: 'We just don't normally talk about those things, even with
each other.' Those who disagreed with this observation tended to be
women who had lived a good part of their lives outside Cyprus.

In the round tables and in interview women told of many taboos.
You fear falling pregnant, but do not talk, or even think, until the
worst happens, about how you will get an abortion. You do not talk
about HIV/AIDS and, since men refuse to use a condom, you just
take risks. There is an obsession among women with weight and
keep-fit, but eating disorders are not suspected or discussed. Everyone knows that domestic violence is prevalent, particularly inflicted
on women by male partners, but the front door is kept tightly shut
to hide it from view. You know there is prostitution involving both
local and immigrant women, but rather than eliciting concern for
women who may suffer abuse or lack rights, prostitutes are seen as
a threat. This is the way the partition line between the sexes is laid
down: it distinguishes you from 'the other', the man, but, in making
heterosexual coupledom the obligatory condition, it also separates
women from each other. Greek Cypriot students I talked to, aged
around twenty, spoke of having quite bad relations with other girls,
mainly due to jealousy over boys. It is a small society, especially in the
north, 'a tightly knit world of gossip and social constraints, particularly
for women', 'an open prison' (Killoran 1998: 184). In such a world,
women do not 'look after' each other.

Katarina K said of women in Cyprus that she believes they feel
continually watched and judged for their bodies and the clothes with
which they cover them. 'I've met women from all over the world,
and I've never seen a culture giving so much emphasis to every detail
of the body.' The many silences that cover up the real bodily experience are in dramatic contrast to the in-your-face images of women
that smile and sulk from every hoarding, TV commercial and shop
window. Sexualized, romanticized, women are all around, enticing
you to buy. As everywhere, the commodification of women puts
actual women in a perilous double-bind, feeling their own bodies
must match the seductiveness of the representations. Women do
emphatically dress 'up', in Cyprus, particularly in the south. It is felt
necessary to dress 'properly' (hair-do, make-up, skirt, heeled shoes)
for almost any social occasion. Casual untidiness feels inept and rude.

Many young women dress, like their counterparts in Western European countries, in skimpy and revealing clothes. Carrying these new ways even into the parental home and on to the village street, however, where traditional views of women's comportment may still be current, creates tensions. Both the contradictory message for men this represents, and the dismay it causes elders, puts relationships under strain. It sometimes seems as though women are moving from one version of femininity that they did not choose to another, dictated by the market, that they did not really choose either.

I found myself thinking again of John Berger's book *Ways of Seeing*, published in 1972. It did much to make us aware of how men look, photograph and paint, and more often than not it is women they look at and portray. He wrote: '*men act* and *women appear*. Men look at women. Women watch themselves being looked at. This determines not only most relations between men and women but also the relation of women to themselves' (Berger 1972: 47). The trouble is, the gaze directed continually at women's bodies, by both women and men, does not merely objectify women like moths pinned out and displayed in a case; it carries with it a strong dose of morality, one of its intentions apparently being to drive a wedge between women's bodies and their unruly minds.

Salome G is especially interesting on this. As a child, she was rather small, conventionally pretty and, most significant of all, fair-haired. This classically feminine look was cherished and admired by her Greek Cypriot family who considered fairness 'European' and equated darkness with the 'East'. For good and for bad, these distinctive looks have always been a factor in her identity, both her sense of self and the identity she is ascribed by those who see her. Salome emerged from school, she says, 'tiny and skinny' but clever and 'good'. She turned out to have a sharp, inquiring intellect, and went to study in England, where one of her teachers became an impressive female role model, with her Doc Martens boots and Mohican haircut, raising the consciousness of many students about sexual harassment and other stormy topics. When Salome had to go back to Cyprus, 'the little girl who had come home and was expected to marry right away', she heard the voice of her teacher reminding her the world was her own and she could do what she liked with it. And this she has tried to live up to. Today, she is a successful feminist academic, but she has continually met with the problem that looking sexy is considered incompatible with being a serious, intelligent and political person. Of her appearance she says: 'I've had to be so aware of how people see me, and so careful with it. Especially careful of how women will react to me … It has affected me in good ways, in that people don't ignore me. But in my work it's affected me in every negative way possible … You can't read Marx, be interested in peace issues and wear platform shoes.'

The second effect of the morality in the gaze is policing women into (heterosexual but chaste and subordinated) femininity. This means avoiding androgynous clothes that might speak of mannishness, but at the same time not being seduced by the fashion market into wearing those feminine-sexy clothes in the wrong place – at work, for instance. Of two friends working in the education system, one told me she had been forbidden to wear jeans in school, while the other told me how she and other teachers had been reprimanded for wearing tight skirts or clothes deemed to be too skin-hugging.

Fatma Güven's story of her work experience in a north Cypriot industrialists' association is a wonderful example of what can happen to a woman when she steps into a man's working role. Aged twenty-five, this well-qualified economist answered a job advertisement and was, to the surprise and dismay of some of its members, appointed general secretary of this association of important entrepreneurs. She experienced all the expected put-downs. Her reports were ignored, they treated her as 'the secretary' rather than the 'General Secretary', and she was expected to be the office ornament. The issue of dress caught her in a serious contradiction. At first she went to work in trousers, her preferred day wear. The president made it clear he did not like this. So she compromised by going home and changing into a dress each Tuesday evening in preparation for the executive board meeting, over which he presided. But of course, she was in a no-win situation. On the one hand the trousers were clearly too similar to men's own attire, appearing presumptuous, as if Fatma considered herself their equal. The trousers heightened the contradiction of having Fatma there among them, the only person of frankly the wrong sex. At the same time, when she wore a dress and pleased them by looking feminine, it sealed their perceptions of her as a non-member of the team. 'At these meetings they wanted to talk about women, about these new nightclubs. They kept saying, "Oh, Fatma is here!", until finally they said "Fatma, close your ears". They'd talk about which nightclubs had better girls, and tell ghastly jokes. After the meeting they would all go off to a nightclub.'

Where these men positioned women, the other side of the gender line from themselves, was in one of three categories: secretary, wife or whore. How could one of this sex be the general secretary of their association? 'What they wanted', said Fatma, 'was a male General Secretary, who could do the same as them.'

Another issue women talked about in the 'sex and the body' round tables was how marriage relates to sexuality in Cyprus. The women who participated in the round tables felt that men, in Cypriot cultures, do not necessarily think of sexual pleasure in connection with marriage but as something you find outside marriage with prostitutes or lovers. Wives are for motherhood. They spoke of knowing several married men who had Eastern European mistresses, 'blondies' as they are called. The important question remains, therefore, what intimacy and sexual pleasure do women actually find in their marriages? This is something, they said, that is very rarely spoken of, even among women. In our discussions on this theme even young women with young partners felt that most men do not understand women's bodies and most do not really aspire to give women pleasure. Properly, even now, as in the traditional patriarchal family, women's own desires should be suppressed. Certainly among older couples, a sexual woman is felt to be a demanding woman. Our conversation had a lot of resonance with Andreas Onofriou's study of young people 'in a climate where marriage is characterised as the national sport of Cypriots. Young women seem to invest in men for happiness, security and autonomy, and female desire remains an unexplored space' (Onofriou 2002: 30).

At the round table in south Cyprus, Magda was present, and also Vera L. Magda told us how she had had only one relationship in which the sex was good. Even then it had been short-lived. 'Three really good months that touched my soul,' she said. 'It's something at least. But in forty-four years? That's sad!' But she is convinced this is a common experience and few marriages afford satisfying sexual relationships for women. Maybe it was this that inspired Vera to tell us in such an honest and moving way about her feelings about her body. Vera has been married for twenty-five years, and she and her husband have a teenage son and daughter. Of her family of origin she said, 'Being in my mother's environment silenced my tendency to be sexual. I mean, to express my sexuality.' Her marriage had been a love affair at the start, but it turned out to be unfulfilling.

There were times that my body was talking to me, in the sense that I needed an erotic partner. I felt that I needed maybe more *density* in my relationship. And [pause] – not getting that, I felt rejected, or somehow suppressed … At times I tried to speak it out, but it was perceived by my husband as my needs speaking, my physical needs, my biological needs, or my *madness*, or whatever.

Vera L suggested to her husband that they go together to see a marriage guidance counsellor. 'But he said, "I don't have a problem. You have a problem – so you go!" ' She laughed wryly. 'So I ended up going to therapy alone!'

It is perhaps not surprising that it should be Vera who has this special awareness about her relationship to her own body, because what is most striking about her, to those who know her, is her wonderful bodily persona. She is a celebrated actress, whose powerful presence gives other people an almost physical pleasure wherever she performs. She says:

My body gives me a lot of trouble! But at the same time, I'm happy with what it is. I enjoy it. I enjoy all of it. I enjoy looking at it in the mirror, I enjoy dressing it up. [She laughs.] I was reborn through the births I gave. It's a fantastic feeling and I wish I could have it again. But not being married and having a husband. Just having anybody's child, just for the opportunity to give birth again … that final push!

All this reminded me of Shulamith Firestone, writing in the 1970s: 'Love, perhaps even more than child-bearing, is the pivot of women's oppression today.' Why is there such silence on the subject? It is because, she says, 'women and love are underpinnings. Examine them and you threaten the very structure of culture' (Firestone 1979: 121).

One topic that did not enter readily into our round table discussions on sex and the body was alternatives to heterosexuality. Many women may feel a strong desire and need to find a partner and share a home with him and, like Vera L, within the relationship make a continuing bid for satisfaction. The chances are, however, that not a few women, if they lived in a society that made it acceptable, would look for intimacy and sexual pleasure with another woman. The circumstances of Cyprus make this an all but unthinkable option.

Many of the women with whom I raised the topic of homosexuality, however, were open to discussing it. It had been noticed, for instance, that when a few brave Greek Cypriot parliamentarians finally, in the summer of 2000, managed to get gay rights legislation adopted by the House of Representatives (and it took a ruling of the European Court of Justice to defeat the fierce opposition), it was only *male* homosexuality that was at issue. Lesbians in Cyprus are invisible (Vassiliadou 2003). There seem to be no well-known lesbian performers, actors or singers. When I raised the matter I was told: 'They all go abroad where they can express themselves. You should look in the diaspora.' Andreas Onofriou, in his research on gendered subjectivities among Cypriot students, was unable to find a single case he could identify as a lesbian currently living in Cyprus. He ended up writing of 'the not-yet lesbian subject'. While he interviewed women who spoke of same-sex fantasies, their stories, he says 'remain in the private realm among friends and rarely get into the public sphere' (Onofriou 2002: 213). It seems, therefore, that in this as in other respects the patriarchal gender order in Cyprus is rather successfully surviving the challenge of modernization and its own in-built contradictions. Marriage is still socially extremely important, and sex in its visible and sanctioned mode is still subject to what Adrienne Rich has called 'compulsory heterosexuality' (Rich 1980).

The other woman

The existence of the Green Line, impeding any interaction between Greek and Turkish Cypriots, means that Greek Cypriot and Turkish Cypriot women have not been called on to deal with *each other* as their own feminine/ethnic 'others'. There is no sexual rivalry between the women of the two communities for the same reason there is little friendship: they have seldom been in a position to meet. There are, however, painfully racialized relationships today between Cypriot women (Turkish and Greek) and other 'other' women.

It is the practice for Cypriot women, especially those who work in demanding jobs or are economically well off due to their own or their husbands' circumstances, to employ domestic servants. On the other hand, working-class Cypriot women are disinclined to work as domestic servants today because they can get employment in other fields where the pay and prospects are better. In the north, it is often Turkish immigrant women who are employed as domestic servants.

And in the south, in the last fifteen years, many Asian immigrants have begun to get permits to work in Cyprus. They come mainly from Sri Lanka, Thailand and the Philippines and they do unskilled labour in agriculture, industry and services. It is from among the women of the Asian community that Greek Cypriot women tend to draw their domestic workers today. Some of them live in the family home. Some are professionally qualified women (midwives, teachers) who have left home to earn the extra money needed to take pressure off a husband's wage, perhaps to send a child to university. Local employment regulations will not permit them to use their qualifications, so they work instead in unskilled jobs. They are a new phenomenon in global migration (Lutz 2002).

Some of the complexity of relations between Greek Cypriot and Asian domestic workers is explored in the research of Sondra Sainsbury (2003). Many migrant workers feel they made a good choice in coming to Cyprus. Many employers are warm towards them and there is mutual learning. However, Sainsbury also details instances of bad treatment. In a meeting I had with immigrant women, hosted by the Immigrant Support Action Group, I too was told of many cases of bad treatment. Some employers are autocratic, and treat their Asian servants inhumanely. The women I met explained that the man of the family has ultimate power over the domestic worker, but the wife is the one who manages her work. When relationships are abrasive, the unpleasantness is often with the wife. The domestic worker must answer even to children. Joyce explained that there is a distinct hierarchy that goes: man, woman, boy child, girl child, servant. And Rebecca chipped in: 'Don't forget the dog. Dog comes below girl and above domestic!' The Immigrant Support Action Group hears of many instances of abuse. They helped Rebecca bring charges against a man, a friend of her employer, who raped her. The police refused to prosecute. Wanting justice, she took out a civil case, and resisted considerable pressure by the family to settle out of court. When sexual harassment occurs, the authorities tend to suppose that the woman has invited sexual attention. Many Greek Cypriot women hesitate to employ a live-in domestic for fear she might seduce the husband or son.

Asian women, however, being dark-skinned, are not thought by Cypriot men to be attractive – though this does not stop some men treating them as casually 'available'. There is another wave of migrants arriving in Cyprus today: women from Eastern Europe and the former Soviet republics, an estimated 1,500 in the south and a further 400 in the north, who are given short-term entry permits to work in nightclubs and bars. Research among such women in the north, who come mainly from Ukraine and Moldova, suggests they find their work through specialist agencies, coerced only by economic necessity (Rodriguez et al. 2003). Madeline Garlick, however, whose work for the United Nations peace-keeping force, UNFICYP, gives her a unique vantage point, says that Cyprus is undoubtedly an arrival and transit point for women forcibly trafficked by an international male mafia. Those who stay and work in Cyprus, though they are termed 'artistes', are in fact employed by nightclub managers as sex-workers, on terms that amount to indentured servitude (Rodriguez et al. 2003). In Turkey and north Cyprus these newcomers are known as 'Natashas' (Gülçür and Ilkkaracan 2002). Being relatively 'blonde' and tall (features that are popularly fetishized in Cyprus), they are exploited to appeal to the better-off and more 'discriminating' Cypriot client and the weekend-break sex-tourists flying in from Turkey, while Turkish prostitutes serve less affluent men. There also turns out to be a value-differential between north and south. When the Line opened in April 2003 newspapers reported that business quickly doubled for sex clubs in the north as Greek Cypriot men discovered they could 'buy a woman' for one-fifth of her price in the south (*Cyprus Weekly* 2003b).

While it is probably only a minority of Cypriot men who buy commodified sex, the new trade has generated a sense of anxiety. Some local women believe the Eastern European 'artistes' to be adventuresses coming in search of a well-off and compliant husband or patron. They meet Cypriot men in bars and clubs, or make contact with them through the internet. I heard several stories of Cypriot women whose men had left them for a 'Natasha'. It appears to be a replay of the days when tourism was first getting under way and Cypriot men made out with 'tall, blonde' Scandinavian holidaymakers. An argument sometimes heard is that introducing such genes to the population will improve Cypriot stock. The same is not said of Asian genes, yet this does not deter Cypriot men from seeking casual sex with Asian women. The latter say they feel perennially vulnerable on the street. They take taxis to protect themselves. But Joyce, a Filipina, was propositioned by the taxi driver even on her way to our meeting.

Greek and Turkish Cypriot women therefore are caught up in a rather damaging set of sexualized and racialized relations with 'other' women. The gender order, despite rapid economic development and globalization, is in some respects showing little change with regard to sexual politics. It permits women's sexuality to be expressed only in heterosexual monogamous marriage, while endorsing men's pro-miscuity. Even there, women's sexual and emotional needs are denied – and they are sometimes subjected to violence. Sex for men outside marriage, even if formally frowned on, is permitted and provided for. Meantime, we see shifts in the gender order occurring through the arrival of two new groups of women who are entering into new racialized relationships with the Cypriot family. A relationship that women might, as individuals, want to be one of friendship, is de-formed by the inequalities of class and the contradictions inherent in the family structure based on obligatory, unequal, heterosexual marriage. As Cypriot women have entered employment, and their menfolk have failed to pick up their share of domestic responsibilities, they have resolved the housework problem by (as Nicoletta Charal-ambides, of ISAG, put it) 'climbing on the back of the Filipina or Sri Lankan domestic'. But as Cypriot women have become less docile and more demanding of freedom, rights and a sharing of family res-ponsibilities, they have become less attractive to their husbands and more vulnerable to competition from Eastern European women, professionalizing their sexuality to clamber out of economic need.

The gender line: disputed tactics

I asked Maria Hadjipavlou whether she thought men were losing any of their power in Cyprus today. She did not see any fundamental change.

> We're still in a patriarchy here, it's still defining our norms, how to behave, how to dress, how to please, how to be respected and we still play very secondary roles. I don't think that women are getting a proper education. One which would allow us to acquire a sense of self and of separateness. We're still not autonomous selves, we're defined in relation to men. Men are our reference points. You never step back and say: who am I, irrespective of that?

In a round table on power, in north Cyprus, women noted how often in a roomful of men 'you speak without being heard'. Individu-ally, a few women are paid attention. Gülden Plümer Küçük said: 'If you have a strong professional identity it is easier to be proud and strong as a woman in Cyprus. That's the only way for a woman to be heard.' Mostly, the women in the north felt the same as Yiota Afxentiou, a psychologist in the south, who describes a huge frustration among women, even those who have achieved a great deal in their field, and especially those who push for change. 'I feel as if I'm all the time banging my head against the wall!'

In the preceding chapter and this one we have addressed two particular structures of male power, the institutions of state, enterprise and the military; and the institutions of heterosexual marriage and the family. We have seen the dividend that accrues to men as a sex through their control of both. And here they clearly are, buttressing the wall against which Yiota bangs her head. She goes on: 'It's all for men. It's constructed for the pleasure of men – sex, power, everything! I find myself in a society that doesn't support me as a woman … And nothing is changing. The same people who created this situation [i.e. the Partition] are still here.'

Despite this, there is little sign of a feminist movement in Cyprus – and I use the word here in the sense of a collective and active opposition to patriarchal gender relations. Myria Vassiliadou, in her research on urban middle-class women in the south, found that individually women exhibit a great deal of gender consciousness, but that there is a notable lack of feminist activism or mobilization of women on any issue other than the ethnic conflict (Vassiliadou 2001). The passivity, she believes, partly derives from the past. In interview she talked about her disappointment in the absence of a feminist movement: 'I had hoped for that. It would make room for me and for all the women who don't fit in. It would make room for alternative ways of talking. It would make me feel supported in the way I do things.'

Moira Killoran's research in north Cyprus suggests that when an individual woman, especially a married woman, tries to reshape herself in line with a 'modern, Western, feminist identity' she pays a heavy price (Killoran 1998). In my conversations with women I detected three additional reasons for the absence of a movement to challenge the gender order. First and foremost was the Partition. 'You have to choose the most urgent question. What is that? The Cyprus problem. It's burning us all up' (Gülden). Second, 'identity politics were never on the agenda of the left in Cyprus' (Myria Georgiou). And third, although Cypriot society is highly mobile, the air lanes are busy and airwaves busier, it is somehow isolated from world movements. 'We haven't connected our condition here to the bigger picture of what is going on in many other parts of the world' (Maria H). As a result, women are more prepared to act as individuals, tackling the situation in their own families, than collectively as women. For example, 'What I want is equality – and *in my house it is so*' (Bahire). Men have ana-thematized 'feminism', so that it has become very costly for women to identify with it. Leyla X, for instance, sometimes chooses to act simply as a human being, in a way that challenges the line drawn between men and women. But, she says, 'Most of the men, when I declare my ideas, say, "Oh, I know – you're a *feminist!*"' And Anthoula says: 'In Cyprus, if you tell people you're a feminist, it's almost like saying a swear word.' (Note that there are voices here from both south and north.)

There is a particular way that gender-conscious and dissatisfied women sometimes prefer to conceptualize and organize around dis-advantage. It employs the concept of human rights. Mine Yücel and Derya Beyatlı are friends, both in their twenties and both members of Hands Across the Divide, and they articulate very clearly a poli-tical philosophy they have evolved together. Derya says: 'I always thought of myself as a feminist, a very active feminist, when I was in the university. Then I started looking at it from another viewpoint, that maybe working on human rights altogether would be better than working specifically for women's rights.' And Mine, too, says: 'I don't consider myself a feminist because I don't believe in dividing people into subgroups when we can call them human beings.'

What these statements do is highlight the important differences and similarities we have already noted that exist in the effects of 'othering' in ethno-national relations and gender relations. I still have a mental picture of Mine, in an incident she recounted, trying to ignore, nullify, the Green Line. One day she arranged with a friend in the south that they would go to a certain place in the Line, on the Nicosia city ramparts, where you are separated from the other side by only a few yards and a drop of some thirty or forty feet. As it hap-pened, there were no border guards in the vicinity, so for a while they were able to shout their messages to each other. She noticed, on the other side of the fence, the Greek Cypriot bystanders looking at her friend, 'kind of blaming her for being friendly, for looking at me. It's not legal, there's a sign saying you're not to talk or respond to anyone who calls you. But none of them actually looked at me, because I was invisible to them. For the other side we don't exist.'

It is because of the brutality of the Line – the ethno-national Partition – that Derya and Mine are reluctant to countenance the recognition of any other line, such as a line drawn by women that might seem to emphasize their difference from men. But other women, like Maria Hadjipavlou, also a HAD member, would say that a line has already been drawn between men and women, not over centuries but millennia, establishing separation, complementarity and inequality. It is not feminists who invent it. There are of course women's movements, essentializing, self-righteous and reactionary (and some, alarmingly, even call themselves feminist), that reinforce the gender line, claiming superiority for women. But that is not the feminism, it seems to me, that Cypriot feminists either side of the Green Line are talking about. I have heard them argue for a movement among women to raise consciousness about the gender line and the hierarchy it inscribes, and to evolve strategies for transgressing it and eventually removing it.

Men have mainly been the ones to draw the gender line, though women (as we have seen) have in the main co-operated, having had little choice but to strike their bargain with the patriarchal powers. Women are the ones now who want to challenge the gender order. Notionally, such a challenge implies winning men's partnership in eradicating sexism as a mind-set, in institutions and in individual behaviour. That is the strategic perspective. The trouble is that while individual men suffer greatly within the oppressive and hierarchical structures of patriarchy, its transformation into a gender-equal order would cost men as a whole their patriarchal dividend – not only considerable monetary benefits, but also authority, respect, sexual and other services, safety and housing, access to institutional power and the very considerable relative control they have over their own lives and those of women (Connell 2002). Since few men are prepared to lend their efforts to theorizing and practising such a struggle, it is not surprising if women feel they can rely on no one but themselves.

However, though the feminist strategy of line-challenging may be clear, this tactical question of how it is best actually to deal with a line of partition (whether an ethno-national or gender line) is quite reasonably in dispute and subject to testing. We must leave the question unresolved at this point. We shall see in Chapter 7 how, within the group Hands Across the Divide, one of the most hotly disputed issues was whether having meetings as southerners and as northerners alone (i.e. mono-communal meetings) helped or hindered their efforts to imagine the Green Line away and work as a unitary organization, prefiguring unification. And we shall see that another theme runs in counterpoint to this debate: uncertainty within the group as to HAD's purpose and potential as a project in which women organize and act alone.

6 | Challenging the Line: women's activism

In Chapter 4 we saw how women in both parts of Cyprus have been sidelined in the formal political system as well as disadvantaged in the workplace, and how a certain kind of masculinity either side of the Line has been privileged by the militarism and nationalism that are both a cause and an effect of Partition. In this chapter we shall see, however, that some women have found an outlet for their creativity and energy in the voluntary sphere of civil society. The term 'civil society' needs some explanation. I use the expression here in the way it is popularly employed in Cyprus today, giving it a meaning considerably narrower than most academic and theoretical usage. In Cyprus, both south and north, as in Eastern European and many other local contexts, civil society is taken to mean simply *the sphere of non-profit voluntary association* between and apart from the state, the political system, economic activity and the family.[1] What the term probably brings to mind for most people is 'non-governmental organizations'(NGOs). As we shall see, however, when political parties in Cyprus, especially oppositional parties, engage with other organizations in social movements, as distinct from their parliamentary activity, they are included within civil society. So too are representatives of businesses when, as distinct from enterprise itself, they organize together in 'chambers' of commerce or industry. Certain concerns of the family, too, such as domestic violence and single parenting, when they take expression in voluntary associations, are popularly included within Cypriot 'civil society'.

The sphere of free association

This arena of voluntary association in Cyprus north and south has been relatively sleepy, developing only slowly throughout the 1980s and '90s to reflect changing needs and interests among the two populations. Like the state, the political sphere and the economic world, civil society as a whole was, and remains, male-dominated. To have a place in decision-making and to get their own issues on the agenda, women, it seems, need their own organizations. And in civil society, in contrast to the formal political system, gender separatism is possible, and tolerated.

In south Cyprus, Greek Cypriot civil society appears to have lagged behind the dramatic pace of economic development. Viewing non-governmental activism here at the turn of the millennium, Gisela Welz comments on its poverty, putting it down to 'the clientilistic underpinnings of social institutions' (Welz 2001: 23). Within this not very flourishing sector, however, women are key actors in a number of long-standing NGOs. I found women were giving their energies to, broadly speaking, three kinds of organization.

The first was a set of nationalistic NGOs (mixed-sex, but with a predominance of women) that are less concerned with the present than the past ('what was taken from us by the Turks') and the future ('what we demand from the Turks'). Thus, the Organization of Relatives of Undeclared Prisoners and Missing Persons of Cyprus keeps alive the memory of the Greek Cypriots missing since 1974. Its members are the mirror-image of the Organization of Martyrs' Families and War Wounded in the north, demanding the return of those they believe are still alive and information about those who were killed. There are also numerous associations of refugees, organized on a territorial basis, such as Free Morphou and Unvanquished Kyrenia, mentioned earlier. Though these involve both sexes, many of their prominent activists are women and there is a Federation of Women's Refugee Associations. In terms of gender identity, however, they are traditionalist and familial. When I asked Eleni Vlahou of Relatives of the Missing why it was always women, not men, demonstrating on a Saturday morning, she answered in one word: 'Mothers!'

Secondly, many Greek Cypriot women are energetic trade unionists. Some political parties and trade unions have set up women's sections, or inspired women's NGOs. These have two missions: first, to mobilize women in support of the parent organization; second, to advance women's rights and gender equality. They tend to hierarchy, bureaucracy and formality of procedure. One of the most prominent, Protoporia Women's Association, established in 1978, is related to the conservative party DISY. It describes its aims and objectives as 'the promotion of equality between men and women, co-operation and friendship between women all over the world, the search for solutions to problems of youth, and awareness of and participation in all important aspects of Cyprus Life'. Lia Efstratiou-Georgiades, a practising lawyer, has been its president since 1985.

Protoporia's counterpart on the left is the Pancyprian Federation of Women's Organizations (POGO) founded in 1950. Associated with the Communist Party, AKEL, it reflects the party's national, regional and district structure, linking 15,000 members in numerous local groups. Its analysis of the woman question invokes 'unity', 'solidarity' and 'progress'. Thus, a central issue is 'the common struggle with Turkish Cypriot women for a solution of the Cyprus problem and the reunification of the island'. POGO's general secretary, Christina Demetriades, describes women's disadvantage as indissolubly linked to class disadvantage. 'We cannot say that women form a class. But women form the majority of the population and so are the victims of the largest part of the exploitation,' she told me. Women's rights are thus 'not an issue only for women, but an issue for the whole society'.

The other main political parties also have women's organizations. DIKO has its GODIK and EDEK its Women's Socialist Movement. DISY's women's organization is termed GODISY and that of EDI is GOED (you can go dizzy in civil society with acronyms). Together with POGO and Protoporia they sit on the thirteen-member Council of the National Machinery for Women's Rights (NMWR). Maro Varnavidou, the principal officer of the NMWR, told me, however, of what she feels to be a healthy growth of a third kind of women's NGO: single-issue women's groups. She named associations concerned with family-planning and domestic violence, single parents, a group representing professional and business women and a housewives' organization. Recently a Women's Cooperative Bank has been established to help women set up in business. These are a useful development, Maro feels, with their independence from political parties and their specific fields of knowledge.

In north Cyprus the oldest surviving women's NGO is the Turkish Cypriot Women's Association (TCWA), formed even before independence, and historically close to the Turkish Cypriot establishment. Eighty-year-old Feyziye Hulusi, whom we met in Chapter 2, has long been active in the TCWA and is currently president of its Kyrenia branch. She described to me its humanitarian purpose and charitable activities. The NGO had clearly been an important vehicle for this energetic and competent woman, as no doubt for many others. A more recent 'establishment' women's organization, formed in 1975, is the Council of Turkish Cypriot Women (CTCW). It owes its existence and its mission to Latife Birgen, who put into its development the energy and talent that, as we saw, was undervalued in the political system. Unsurprisingly, the focus she chose for the CTCW was women's rights and women's empowerment. A third organization, the Turkish Cypriot Working Women's Association (TCWWA), is positioned further to the right wing of civil society, but a fourth, and more politically ambiguous, women's NGO is the Turkish Cypriot Association of University Women (TCAUW), formed in 1991. Its aim is to empower women in all sectors of society, but is partly prompted by a higher education system where (as we saw was the case in EMU) women get little if they do not look after each other's interests. The TCAUW has recently undergone a change of leadership, shifting the association towards a 'more professional system involving delegation of power'. The new president, Gülden Plümer Küçük, has her own business. Despite family connections to the political establishment she has avoided party politics. She says of herself that, in wanting to achieve something through and for the TCAUW, she is 'not an extremist', rather 'trying to keep a balance'.

I described in Chapter 4 the Patriotic Women's Union, an important progressive women's organization, linked by its political philosophy to the opposition Republican Turkish Party, in which Oya Talat has been a moving force. Several trade unions too are important elements of the opposition to the northern regime. Despite the many active rank and file women in the labour movement, it is top-heavy with men. Women make up only 10.8 per cent of union executive committees (Güven-Lisaniler and Uğural 2002). A refreshing exception that deserves special mention is the small union ÇAĞ-SEN, that broke from another union on the issue of union democracy in 1992 and is unusual in being independent of any political party. Its members are outspoken in persuit of a united Cyprus. More than half the members are women, mainly employees of government and municipal offices. What makes ÇAĞ-SEN unique, however, is that both its president and general secretary are women, and 'even the male members understand women's position' and support gender-conscious policies. The president, Cemaliye Volkan, a HAD member, is an effective trade unionist who has the liking of women as well as the respect of men. One of her members explained to me just how difficult it is for a woman to reach such a senior position in the union movement: 'Male domination in Cyprus isn't exactly a matter of women's husbands saying outright "you can't go there, you can't do that". Yes, she can go and do her Master's degree. She can go to aerobics classes. But when it comes to participation in the union, because it's so connected to "the Cyprus problem", they don't want her to spend time in *that*.' It is important to note, therefore, that Cemaliye evades political reprisals by being safely pensioned out of paid employment. Being unmarried she is free of marital constraints. Her members say she devotes twenty-four hours a day to the union.

Questioning ethnic separatism

The term civil society has a ring about it of 'civility' and good manners. But, no less than the political and economic spheres, it is a site of unruliness and struggle (Keane 1998). Non-governmental organizations are every bit as likely to pursue nationalist extremism as charitable works or progressive social change. In the TRNC the ferocity of the voluntary sphere increased dramatically from the year 2000. At the time of the bank scandal and ensuing economic crisis, the political parties CTP and YBH, with a number of trade unions and other voluntary groups in civil society, formed a social movement called the 41 Organizations. From the end of 2001, when the leaders began a new round of talks under pressure of the Republic's imminent accession to the European Union, the 41 Organizations alliance mobilized street demonstrations for an immediate solution to the Cyprus problem and against the country's subordination to the Turkish deep state. They took their principal slogan as an organizational title, calling themselves the 'This Country is Ours Platform'. Many women are involved in this upsurge of activity in civil society, but the prominent personalities are male and as yet there are no signs in it of a critical gender politics. Of the forty-one organizations only three are women's groups.

Turkey and pro-Turkish forces in north Cyprus appear to have felt threatened by the popular support for the 41 Organizations and by the pressure of the European Union accession process which was bringing a renewal of peace negotiations. In May 2001 a new non-governmental organization, the National People's Movement (UHH) appeared on the scene. Its creation is understood to have been prompted personally by Rauf Denktaş. It was to be the embodiment of his trusted silent majority, those whose love for the Turkish 'motherland' was unshaken, who were not taken in by the slogans of the irresponsible 'minority' in the 41 Organizations. That it is housed in a Turkish military facility clinches the evidence, in the view of the left, that UHH is the deep state's intervention in civil society. It organizes briefings in villages and towns and uses the media to warn the masses about the many 'internal enemies' of the TRNC and Turkey.[2] Its key personalities are men, with women apparently playing a traditional supporting role.

There was anxiety lest the new left activism provoke the Turkish deep state to violence. The memory of Kutlu Adalı's murder in 1996 was still live, and it was known that the Turkish Grey Wolves suspected of the assassination still had a presence on the island. Left-wing readers carefully scanned the right-wing press, particularly *Kıbrıslı* and *Volkan*, media which they see as fronts for Turkish forces. Their tone was becoming increasingly vituperative, pointing a slanderous finger at anyone opposed to Denktaş's Turkish connection, groups and individuals favoured by the UN, the EU or Western embassies, or 'soft' on reconciliation with Greek Cypriots. Conversely, the critical *Avrupa* (renamed *Afrika*) has been raided and fined many times by the authorities, and firebombed by unidentified assailants. In July 2002 its editor Sener Levent and another journalist were arrested and sentenced to six months' imprisonment for critizing Rauf Denktaş.[3] This incident, too, brought the 41 Organizations on to the street in a demonstration estimated at 15,000 strong. State harassment of journalists continued in 2002 and 2003.

The upsurge of opposition activism in the north won a modest response in the south. Some pro-*rapprochement* individuals and groups felt that the movement of Turkish Cypriots had not been adequately supported in the south, because 'the necessary culture of understanding and co-existence, as well as the will for attaining such principles, have not yet been developed within the Greek Cypriot community'. These words are taken from the founding declaration of a Greek Cypriot umbrella organization, established in February 2002, called the Citizens' Movement for Re-unification and Co-existence. Under the slogan 'Ahead for a Common Country', it organized street actions at the time of the Denktaş/Clerides talks in December 2001 and January 2002. The movement is alert to issues raised by the northern Platform and has organized occasional meetings with its opposite numbers in the buffer zone village of Pyla.[4] Again, though committed women are involved in the Citizens' Movement, its executive committee, and spokespeople, and more than two-thirds of the co-ordinating committee are male. Among the forty affiliated NGOs, only four are women's groups.

Many of the individuals active in the This Country is Ours Platform and the Citizens' Movement for Re-unification and Co-existence are those who had been involved for a decade or more in bi-communal activity. In the decade immediately following Partition there was very little contact across the Line at the level of civil society. A rather extraordinary exception is that, from 1979, prompted by a crisis in the sewerage system, there has been co-operation between urban planning teams in north and south Nicosia. There was a little more contact in the second decade. Around 1982 a Cyprus Turkish Peace Committee was set up in the north, matched by a Cyprus Peace Council in the south. Externally mediated activity began in 1984 with a conflict resolution workshop for a small number of invited participants organized in Harvard by Professor Herbert Kelman. From 1986, POGO and the Patriotic Women's Union began a long-standing co-operation involving exchange visits and joint activities on inter-national women's day.

From 1991, however, there was a remarkable flowering of exter-nally sponsored and mediated bi-communal activity. In that year a United States conflict resolution practitioner, Louise Diamond, co-founder of the Institute for Multi-Track Diplomacy (IMTD), came to Cyprus and made contacts with a view to ongoing work. A group of ten participants was established either side of the Line, with a deliberately wide political span. Indeed, in the north at first the right- and left-wing participants felt politically unready to join Louise Diamond's conflict management workshops as a single group. Official permission was obtained for the first unified and bi-communal work-shop in late 1992. The following summer a significant step was a ten-day workshop for ten-plus-ten participants in Oxford, UK.

Many of the people who became involved with Louise Diamond's initiative in this period had never had an opportunity to meet anyone from across the Line. Thus, 'in the first round of dialogue, people were asked to listen to one another speak about whatever was important to them about the Cyprus situation'. She helped people commit to staying with the process, 'to keep themselves going through the many hard places in rebuilding broken relationships' (Diamond and Fisher 1995). Bi-communal conflict resolution activity soon became more institutionalized. The US Fulbright Commission had had a presence in Cyprus since 1963 and maintained offices in both south and north. Now it raised funds to enable it to support a sustained programme of activity. The principal source of support was USAID, confirming the common belief that Fulbright sponsorship of bi-communalism enacts US policy.

The bid submitted by Diamond's Institute for Multi-Track Diplomacy in partnership with two other United States NGOs won the contract. Working under the name of the Cyprus Consortium, with a local partner structure, the Conflict Resolution Steering Committee, the IMTD organized a series of activities for both women and men between 1994 and 1997. In retrospect, this can be seen as the highpoint of bi-communalism in Cyprus. Louise Diamond's personal mediation was replaced by that of a succession of (male) Fulbright scholars acting as 'field practitioners'. Activities took place in the buffer zone, mainly at the UN-administered Ledra Palace, a former hotel. English was the working language. Certain core principles of bi-communal activity in Cyprus began to firm up. One was 'deep dialogue', by which was meant careful listening, understanding different experiences and acknowledging different points of view. There was agreement on the importance of mutual respect; that each participant would speak only as an individual, not as a representative of others; all that was said and done was to remain confidential; and decision would be by consensus.

Of particular importance was initial training for men and women project leaders, which developed into a nine-month programme called 'training the trainers' through which fifteen-plus-fifteen participants became a permanent team of educators. They moved on to work with no fewer than twenty-five autonomous groups, some with more than a hundred members, meeting regularly in the buffer zone. In all, an estimated 3,000 people were involved. There were groups involving lawyers and business people, cultural groups and, most successful of all, youth groups (Wolleh 2001). Several of the women we have already met in earlier chapters, and of whom we shall see more in the context of Hands Across the Divide, came through this process. To name just some of them, Sevgül Uludağ, from the north, prompted the Bi-communal Women's Group in 1995, while Fatma Azgın took her interactive management skills into the Bi-communal Educators' Group, a group for university students, and another for potential young political leaders. From the south, Katie Economidou was a key figure in the Citizens' Group which in turn had many offspring, including a very successful Bi-communal Choir. Along with Youth Encounters for Peace, the choir is unique in flourishing even in the discouraging circumstances of today. Maria Hadjipavlou, who had attended Kelman's Harvard workshop back in the 1980s, was active from the start in the Fulbright process and has done much to theorize it, reflecting on it in several analytical articles (Hadjipavlou-Trigeorgis 2001a, 2001b, 2002 and forthcoming).

The programme described above worked best when participants were individuals without elite status in the two communities. It worked less well when political personalities participated, especially if close to their respective establishments. They tended to be seen, or see themselves, as representatives of their organizations and feared things they said, through the transmission of the US mediators, might have an effect on the official negotiating process. Partly for this reason the Fulbright Commission, sometimes in partnership with other external institutions, simultaneously ran separate bi-communal group activities, many of them off-island.[5]

The year 1997, however, was a turning point, marking an abrupt decline in bi-communal activity. In 1996 relations between the two sides had deteriorated badly due to two incidents. In the first, Greek Cypriot bikers broke into the buffer zone and one was beaten to death by Turkish and Turkish Cypriot counter-demonstrators. In the second, a Greek Cypriot man was shot by soldiers as he climbed a mast to pull down a Turkish flag (Dodd 1998). The resulting bad feeling seriously interrupted the official co-operation needed for meetings in the buffer zone to be possible. Then, in December 1997, a European Union summit meeting in Luxembourg announced the inclusion of the Republic of Cyprus in the anticipated enlargement process, while dashing the hopes of Turkey. Rauf Denktaş closed down on permissions for cross-communal contact in a freeze that was lifted only after the Helsinki summit of December 1999 took the decision to treat Turkey as a 'normal state' and potentially welcome its accession to the EU at some future date (Brewin 2000).

The golden age of bi-communalism, however, was over. Increasingly, Greek Cypriots, almost all of whom in any case refused on principle to submit to the TRNC's official procedure for crossing the Line, began to feel that even entering the buffer zone amounted to legitimizing the status quo. Permission from the northern authorities for Turkish Cypriots to cross the Line were never a certainty. New Fulbright bi-communal activities occurred, as and when circumstances permitted, including many one-off specialist meetings (liver anaesthesiology, historic sites conservation, environmental pollution) and a successful series of 'co-villager' encounters, events linking Turkish Cypriot and Greek Cypriot people who had lived in the same village before Partition. But from early 2001 there was a clampdown on access to the Ledra Palace, so that most contact was relegated to the much less accessible buffer zone village of Pyla, where meeting space is limited.

Women and bi-communalism

The place of women and gender issues in bi-communalism is an interesting question. The Institute for Multi-Track Diplomacy and the Fulbright Commission do not seem to have had any explicit policy on the inclusion of women. Although gender balance appears to have been the usual practice, it was not required. A comprehensive report on the trainers' programme states that 'the parity between men and women mirrors *the internal values of the founders of the groups*' (my italics). And it notes that 'in the North more women are organised than in the south, and sometimes they felt noticeably hindered by the principle of equal numbers' (Wolleh 2001: 21). More significantly there appears to have been no *gender analysis* built into the programme – thus gender relations were not seen by its American organizers or the local steering committee as integrally related to ethnic relations, shaped by them and shaping of them. It was certainly not considered that a transformation of ethnic relations on the island might be bound up with a transformation of gender relations. Benjamin Broome, the Fulbright field practitioner who ran the trainers' programme, reflected in writing on the possible bearing of his US ethnic identification and American methods on his facilitation work (Broome 1997). But there is no evidence that he or other facilitators were similarly reflective about the effect of their masculine identity.

In actual fact, women were drawn in considerable numbers to bi-communal activities and played a full part. But some commented to me that gender interactions were not well addressed in the groups. Maria Hadjipavlou recounted an occasion when they had been distressingly ignored.

> We were at an advanced workshop at Ledra Palace. By then people had really developed, you know, their thinking and so on ... And we were talking about something really emotional and very deep. There

was a deep wound there, you know? And I wanted to communicate my point, how I was feeling it. And I stopped, because it was really very emotional. And I remember on each side of me there were men, and one of them patted me on the shoulder, 'Oh, don't take it seriously.' And he addressed the whole group – he said: 'She's a woman, she's always so emotional.' And discarded completely what I was saying, dismissed it!

Maria left the room to deal with her feelings alone. Later she came back to the group and invited reflection on what had taken place. She said, 'Surely we should talk about how we experienced this intervention. This means we have some work to do on how we experience the authority of each other, and gender too.' But while she got some support from other women present, the male facilitator dismissed what had happened and stressed the importance of 'getting back to work'.

There were some women-only activities both within the Fulbright schema and outside it. Important among the former was the Bi-communal Women's Group, already mentioned. Within this some good working relationships were forged and have endured. I heard Maria report to a meeting in Strasbourg how 'both groups [i.e. Turkish Cypriot and Greek Cypriot] viewed the patriarchal structure of social organization as well as the absence of women from decision-making bodies and the peace process as big obstacles to the well-functioning of true, representative democracy in Cyprus'. They went on to generate 'a women's map of shared interests ... as well as a vision for their homeland' (Hadjipavlou-Trigeorgis 2001a: 9).

Another significant women's initiative was that launched by Simone Susskind, a well-connected person in the 'European' environment. This took place over two and a half years from 1997 and involved one meeting in Brussels, at the prestigious Egmont Palace, followed by a second in London. Susskind's strategy was to use contact between significant women of south and north to make a political breakthrough in the Cyprus deadlock. She planned to bring into being a 'Cyprus Link' organization, comparable to the well-known Jerusalem Link, between Israeli women and women in the Occupied Palestinian Territories. She invited twenty-five women from each side of the Line, including representatives of both left- and right-wing NGOs. First-hand reports I received of the 'Brussels Group', as it was called, suggest that it was a valuable experience for the women who took part. But there was considerable internal tension between the participants, not so much on lines of ethnicity as because the political spectrum among them was unrealistically wide. Many were linked to, and felt they must be answerable to, political organizations of the left and the right. Although some participants continued to meet for a while in Pyla on return, the group fell apart over the structure of the prospective organization, reproducing very much the positions of their respective political establishments.[6]

Overall, I sense, women have gained a great deal from bi-communal experiences. Perhaps 1,500 women have participated at one time or another. I heard especially positive views from those who have gone on to be active today in Hands Across the Divide. Mine Yücel, for instance, a young participant in the north, found herself more or less by chance at a meeting between Cypriot students in the USA, organized by Fulbright. This meeting with Greek Cypriots turned her head around: 'My idea of Cyprus was that the Greeks are bad and that Turkey saved us, and so we don't want to talk to the Greeks any more ... I mean, you grow up with this big idea and it stays with you maybe for ever – if you're not lucky.' The encounter made her realize for the first time how the concept of human rights she had been learning about in the USA applied to Cyprus. And Fatma Azgın, a generation older than Mine, who went through the entire Fulbright training programme, looks back now and says:

It was like love, a love affair, when I first started to discover it, you know. It came to me as very attractive, so many things ... We discovered ourselves, we asked so many questions, we learnt how we can communicate with each other, we talked for hours and hours. Most people were saying after the meetings how it had absolutely changed things in their lives – discovering people and having the chance to visit the Greek side of our country.

Katie Economidou in the south said:

At first I wasn't interested. I thought, I don't want to talk to 'Turks'. But I will go to see how the methodologies of conflict management are applied. And I stayed, and took all the training that was offered ... A lot of times I feel tired and disappointed. I see there's no end to this, no change, and it's so difficult to deal with other people in groups. But still I'm in that direction.

Maria Hadjipavlou explained her long commitment to the process by saying: 'I believe in dialogue. I believe it is only through face-to-face contact we can heal these deep psychological wounds which are turned into politics ... Because I thought – neither of us can do this alone, neither them nor us. We are in this together.'

So for many women the sense of belonging to a bi-communal movement became part of their sense of self. 'Bi-communalist' was becoming an identity, a qualifier to Greek Cypriot or Turkish Cypriot. But I did meet many women, who had only dipped a toe in, or had not participated at all, who either felt bi-communal activities were 'harmless but ineffectual' or were seriously critical of what had become 'an industry'. They say: it is exclusive, cliquey and has created a bi-communal elite among the English-speaking urban middle class. People are in it for the jaunts abroad. It's a political show, not genuine. It's stuck in a rut, going nowhere. It's been a launch pad for competitive and individualist women, who have kept the opportunities to themselves. It's 'lovey-dovey', exaggerated, 'showing off you have so many friends on the other side'. It's all stage-managed; they are 'Denktaş stooges' or 'Clerides clones'. Or (entirely to the contrary) they are traitors to their side, they undermine the national cause. Or, it is manipulated by the internationals, who are in it for their own ends.

Going for a fresh formula

It has been important to sketch this history of bi-communalism for the purpose of understanding how Hands Across the Divide came about and what are its antecedents. It was not an accident that an organization resulted from the *Divided Societies* seminar of March 2001, described in the Introduction. Kate Economidou and Sevgül Uludağ had for some time, on occasions when they met up abroad, shared a dream of building a women's structure that could span the Green Line. It was their diagnosis that earlier women's bi-communal activities had failed to survive the downturn of the late 1990s precisely because they had had no durable organizational structure. In their minds, the seminar would be a tool for bringing such a thing into being. Thus it was unusual among bi-communal events in being neither an institutional initiative nor a foreign one, but rather the brainchild of individual Cypriot women who subsequently sought UK government funding and engaged the practical support of the British Council. Unlike a Fulbright-style project, no one this time was acting in the role of mediator. I was enlisted, by women who knew my writing and my commitment to feminist anti-militarism, to chair the event. As I wrote earlier, I was never seen, or saw myself, as 'doing conflict resolution'. The seminar broke new ground too in the political background of the women most actively involved in it. In the south they were women almost all without strong party affiliations, and few had experience in women's organizations. In the north, they were almost all outspoken supporters of the opposition – though they did not see themselves in any sense as 'representing' particular parties. Several had formed their friendships in a relatively feminist and non-institutionalized tendency that had emerged in civil society in the north since the late 1980s.

In 1988 a group of individual northern women, Oya and Sevgül among them, had come together in something they called the Women's Movement for Peace and a Federal Solution (WMPFS). They sought, but failed to find, Greek Cypriot partners south of the Line, to join them in a cross-community push for peace. So, mono-communally, they did some street actions, distributing leaflets and olive branches. Although it continued to exist in name, the dynamism of the WMPFS soon drained away, partly due to differences over the style of organization. Some preferred a feminist refusal of hierarchy, with rotating leadership; others, rooted in the older traditions of party politics, considered continuity and centralization more practical. Around 1991, however, a handful of feminist women, mainly writers, came together as the Women's Research Centre. Again Sevgül was in-volved, and also the teacher and writer Neriman Cahit, who is known to us from earlier chapters. In the way feminist pioneers everywhere have to do, they set about creating a better understanding and accept-ance of the concept of gender. Up to 350 women passed through their gender workshops. The WRC had a lot to say about women in the political system and about domestic violence.

The United Nations' fourth World Conference on Women, held in Beijing in 1995, inspired activism among women in Cyprus as it did all around the world. Women's groups quite differently positioned on the political spectrum sent representatives to Beijing. On return those from the north tried to sustain this span of interests in an alliance they called the Women's Platform. It involved, from the left, the WRC, the PWU and what remained of the ailing WMPFS. From the right were the establishment TCWA and the University Women (TCAUW).

Over several years the Platform organized many seminars and workshops, with a view to changing consciousness. Among their concrete achievements was mobilizing lawyers and members of parliament to bring about legislative amendment to the archaic and repressive Family Law of 1951. In effect, they organized a remarkable anti-patriarchal offensive, winning among other gains: a raising of the minimum age of marriage; divorce by mutual consent; provision for the marriage between Turkish Cypriot women and men of other religions; the right of women to keep their original family name on marriage; and the right of women, on divorce, to an equal share of property acquired during the marriage. They also succeeded in having the TRNC administration adopt CEDAW, the UN convention on sex discrimination.

However, the Women's Platform did not long survive the attentions of the deep state. Sevgül Uludağ recalls how the Turkish ambassador's wife engineered some right-wing 'entryism' that eventually paralysed it. 'We would have been willing to work with them,' she says, 'but these women were not coming to work. They came to stop us working.' In 1999 some of them tried to organize afresh, with what they called the Women's Civil Initiative for Peace (WCIP). Again the founding statement was signed by Oya, for the PWU, and Sevgül for the WRC. It was specifically directed to a 'solution', calling for women to have an active role in the peace process to make sure that women's needs would be satisfied in any settlement.

That these left-wing Turkish Cypriot women's organizations have involved only a handful of familiar names may seem sad – but it is also unsurprising. North Cyprus is a small society in which the individual who steps out of line is highly visible. The penalties for opposing the Turkish connection do not involve imprisonment or punitive violence, but they are certainly socially damaging. Women prepared to stand up and be counted as 'traitors' are inevitably rather few. What is heartening, and hardly to be expected, is the persistence of such a small cast of actors. In order to become actively bi-communal, however, they needed, and failed to find in the Republic of Cyprus, autonomous, activist women's organizations like themselves, simultaneously left-wing, feminist, not tied to a particular political party and looking for *rapprochement*. Feminism, however, does have a slender foothold in the south, in women's and gender studies in the University of Cyprus and Intercollege, where Marie Hadjipavlou and Myria Vassiliadou respectively have been innovators. There were also indi-

vidual southern women, Katie Economidou among them, whom the
northern women had been encountering both in the local Fulbright
programme of the 1990s and in internationally sponsored activity
overseas. It is from among these individuals, and from altogether fresh
faces, that our *Divided Societies* seminar drew its southern participants.
Rather few came from the usual cast of established NGOs associated
with political parties and trade unions, for the invitation had been
worded to attract individuals rather than 'representatives'.

Hands Across the Divide

The March 2001 *Divided Societies* seminar, then, had been conceived
from the outset by its initiators as directed towards starting a new
women's cross-Line organization. In the final session of the seminar a
number of decisions were made. A group would form to look into the
possibilities of founding a single formal non-governmental organization with membership in both parts of Cyprus, even if this meant
basing it off-island. Second, e-mail would be the main means of communication. Within days of the seminar Sevgül had set up a list-serve
with the e-addresses of all who had expressed a wish to sign up to it.
An organizational life of a kind began then and there, in cyberspace.

A third decision pitched the incipient organization directly towards
political action. There would be an international campaign mobilizing
support for what was felt to be the basic human freedom of which
Cypriots were deprived by the Line: normal movement and communication on the island. A connected theme was the European Union.
The time was fast approaching when the Republic of Cyprus would
accede. Without a peace agreement between the Republic and the
TRNC, the north would be left adrift, still unrecognized and em-
bargoed, in the Eastern Mediterranean. Many Turkish Cypriot women
at the seminar were stressing the urgency of seizing the moment. They
warned the southerners: if there is no solution before accession, many
more of us will emigrate; we are an endangered species; helping us is
in your interests too, because you will soon have no Turkish Cypriot
partners left in the north. Working groups were set up to further the
thinking on these two issues.

During April and May, a number of 'mono-communal' meetings were organized by the co-ordinators of these groups, north and
south. Effort was also put in to getting a cross-Line meeting. After the
minor political scandal surrounding the seminar (as described in the

Introduction), permissions for crossings at the Ledra Palace check-point were systematically refused to HAD. It was not until mid-June, three months after the seminar, that the first get-together could be arranged, at the alternative buffer zone venue of Pyla village. By now, some of the momentum had been lost in circular talk. Difference on a number of dimensions was holding things back.

Some women wanted openly political action on the peace agenda. They shared a feeling expressed by Bahire Korel: 'The main thing that brought us together is "Cyprus",' she said, 'so I think we have to do something on that immediately.' She wanted HAD to 'shout that we don't want these military in our country. We are Cypriots. *We* must make the decisions, not Greece or Turkey.' But other members were canvassing more social and creative projects, activities that would help HAD engage with a wider range of women and build towards a genuine, whole-island, Cypriot women's movement. Among the ideas floated were: a collective quilt; a handicrafts exhibition; a children's story book; a cookbook; a sheet covered with paint footprints with names and villages; a women's festival; a women's march to the Ledra Palace with candles and songs of peace. At the seminar Tina Adami-dou had heard the Irish speakers tell of a lace-making project that had linked women of Northern Ireland and the Republic of Ireland. She had already edited a book of poetry and short stories from north and south Cyprus (it was called *Weeping Island*). Now she had this 'dream of different types of embroidery from all around the island and join-ing them all together in one big, bright, thing ... Something where you can get the grassroots interested in doing something, like. The old people in the villages.'

Neriman, though, may well have spoken for many members when she said, 'I can't choose one or the other – I want *both* kinds of thing!' Above all she just wanted action. And this issue of 'talk or action' was a rather different cross-cutting divergence. For women who had not been part of the bi-communal movement of the 1990s, this was the first time to meet 'the other' in any depth. What they dearly wished for was to take it slow, exchange experiences and work gently towards an understanding of each other's sense of self, their positionings and values. Quite a high proportion of the southern group were of this 'talk first' turn of mind. Sofia Georgiou, for instance, said: 'I don't think we can jump to action ... I don't feel that commitment. I don't feel safe in the group yet.' But some northerners too tended that way.

By contrast, the more experienced bi-communalists, although they welcomed the fresh faces, were impatient. 'Sharing our experiences', 'finding our commonalities', these had been the currency of Louise Diamond and the Fulbright Commission. What they wanted above all for HAD was that it would be the first cross-Line project to involve open, joint, concerted political action. Fatma Azgın, for years a bi-communal trainer, said: 'I joined this group as an *action* project … With EU accession, it is so urgent to get a political solution. Let's get to know each other *through* the action.'

The truth is, too, that differences of agenda on a north/south axis were beginning to emerge, some of which I explore in Chapter 7. Everyone agreed with Tina in feeling, 'I don't want this to be a them-and-us group. I want it to be that we think with one mind and speak with one voice.' But this was somewhat idealistic, since they had so far not achieved the quality of engagement with each other needed to get beyond mutual affection and clarify the political affinities and differences arising from their embeddedness in two societies with an unresolved conflict. On the question of campaigning for a freeing-up of communication, it soon became clear that finding a wording for this that did not trigger bad feelings on one side or the other required more discussion and thought. Freedom of 'movement', for instance, could sound like an innocent desire to be able, say, to drive a car the length and breadth of the island (and who did not long for this?). Alternatively, it could sound like a threatening reassertion of that old demand of refugees to 'move back into our former homes'.

On the question of the European Union, the working group was thinking of different ways they could get women's voice heard, with gender-specific reasons they could stress for negotiating a peace agreement. But 'the EU' too was turning out to mean two rather different things. Those in the south, who need not doubt they would be joining the EU within a few years, were interested in learning more about how the EU worked and particularly what gains might be expected for women, given the EU's well-known advocacy of gender equality. For the north, the EU was instrumental – they saw the anticipated moment of the Republic's accession as providing leverage on their politicians to sign an accord. It was 'solution' they were after, single-mindedly. After the June meeting at Pyla, work on the 'freedom' campaign was dropped indefinitely, and on the EU issue did not revive for some months.

Over the summer, back in London, I was doing two things. First, at the request of the women in Cyprus, I made contact with a number of Cypriot diaspora women already known to HAD women. Some had worked together organizing a bi-communal Cypriot women's conference in the UK a couple of years previously. We began to meet, partly as a support group to HAD, but also to explore what our own London agenda might be. Secondly, I raised funding for a two-year project.[7] The grants covered a supplement to my pension and my administrative and travel costs so that I could work with HAD and do the research on which this book is based. It also included resources to support HAD's own projects. I went back to Cyprus, six months after the seminar, in September 2001, and began to feel my way into the dual life of being a HAD member, sharing in the daily activity of the group, while also, as a researcher, gathering information through individual interviews and group discussions. It was a complicated situation to be in, and every day brought difficult decisions. How to work and act, and simultaneously listen and record? Whether to intervene when the action seems to require it, though you are intellectually interested to see what happens if you do not?

I went first to the south of Cyprus, where I found the women demoralized. There had been a scheduled meeting in Pyla at which members from the north had failed to show up. All kinds of personal emergencies can occur in individual lives, and it only takes a few coincidences for this kind of disappointment to set in. But something more serious had occurred besides. Sevgül had been subjected to a vicious, personalized and directly threatening attack in *Kıbrıslı* newspaper. Another dissident had been car-bombed. In this climate, some northern women were understandably reluctant to cross into the buffer zone at Pyla, where the police check your computer records. But when women in the south had wanted to speak out publicly in defence of Sevgül, they had been told to hold back – anything they said would play into the hands of those in the deep state who were saying bi-communalists were lackeys of the Greek Cypriots and the internationals. It seemed HAD in the north was calling out for help to southern members, yet what they could or should do, they felt, was not made clear to them.

Many women in the south were at the point of giving up on HAD. But they asked me to use my ability as a foreigner to cross to the north for a few hours, to check out the feelings of Sevgül and others. This I did, bringing back positive messages. They asked me to propose to the southern women two practical projects to carry the group forwards. First, they should cease for a while to rely on getting to meet in Pyla. In the meantime, Sevgül proposed we seek funding for a meeting of several days, for everyone, off-island. Here would be the opportunity not only to exchange ideas in depth but even to agree a constitution and establish the longed-for NGO, under UK law. Second, why not raise funding for a website, to give HAD a uni-fied and public persona. With the agreement of the south I drafted two project proposals, one to the UK High Commission for a four-day meeting for twenty women in London; the other, to a different funding source, for the website. Both projects were adopted by HAD, subsequently submitted and eventually funded.

In November, we were jolted out of our concern with relational issues by a surprising turn of events. It was announced that the polit-ical leaders, Rauf Denktaş and Glafcos Clerides, would meet in the buffer zone for 'a talk' on 5 December 2001. This would be their first face-to-face encounter for four years. Even more startling, on 26 December Clerides would cross the Line to dine with his long-time rival. The two halves of HAD responded to this news at a dif-ferent pace. The northern women already had the framework of the Women's Civic Initiative for Peace, well experienced with action, on which to fall back. They quickly went out on the streets of Nicosia in the early morning rush-hour with placards reading 'Enough! Agree! Solve it! Sign it! And let's go into the European Union together'. They also joined a demonstration organized by the 41 Organiza-tions near the site of the leaders' meeting. The northern women were disappointed that the southern group did not do the same on their side of the Line. But at this moment they were preoccupied lobby-ing, on behalf of HAD, an EU woman minister visiting the south. And anyway some were feeling aggrieved with the northern group: 'You've failed to respond to our initiatives all through the autumn – now you expect us to jump up and respond to yours.'

However, at the political leaders' dinner date a concerted action was achieved as separate HAD groups, south and north, dispatched and received Clerides's official car with similar demonstrations wel-coming the visit and featuring the release of white doves. A letter to the two leaders on HAD headed notepaper was transmitted through the good offices of the United Nations. After their initial contact, the two men committed themselves to a regular weekly meeting to explore anew the possibility of seizing the EU opportunity to make a peace agreement that would bring Cyprus under a unitary, if federated, state structure. The northern women, desperate for the talks to succeed, demonstrated on the streets with even more outspoken placards: 'Sign or resign', 'Reunite the island or we will do it', they were saying.

When, in February, the time came for the women to fly to London for the planned workshop, the mood in HAD was high, in the feeling that something had been achieved as a unity. We held our meeting in the Cypriot Community Centre in north London, well known for its bi-communalism. Our meetings were highly emotional. The women were open with each other. They tackled issues laden with human meaning. They wept. In this the women's talks could not have been in greater contrast to those of the two leaders going on in Cyprus at the same time – wary, technical and calculating. However, the purpose and nature of HAD looked different to different members. The northern women, particularly Sevgül and Fatma, passionately appealed at the London workshop to everyone in HAD to sacrifice other issues to the singleminded pursuit of the EU opportunity before the June deadline. But the division was only partially a 'north/south thing'. There were differences along other dimensions, too, not least concerning process and style. From the start, almost a year previously, HAD had shed or lost potential members due to personal and political differences. Now, in London, there were women on the point of withdrawing. Even today there are divergent views on the rights and wrongs involved and these will be explored further in Chapter 7.

For all the tension and the drama, however, the opportunity for socializing over several days and nights in London generated a good deal of warmth and humour. And on the final day of the meeting agreement was achieved on a constitution, later adopted at an inaugural meeting in Pyla which also elected officers. A London postal address was established for the new NGO, an account opened in a London bank, and the new association signed up to the British umbrella NGOs, the National Association of Women's Organizations and the National Council of Voluntary Organizations.

There was weary but genuine satisfaction in this achievement. The press statement issued on the return to Cyprus proclaimed it 'a first': no other formally constituted Cypriot association until now

Hands Across the Divide (top left) tell political leader Rauf
Denktaş 'Enough!' and urge him to agree and sign a peace
agreement to enable citizens of south and north Cyprus
to enter the European Union together. Both sides of the
Partition Line, Hands Across the Divide went on the street
(above) to welcome the renewed negotiations between
Greek Cypriot and Turkish Cypriot political leaders.

had transcended bi-communality to be unitary. The constitution provided for three 'membership regions'. The Republic and the TRNC
were not named as separate entities, nor were Turkish Cypriot and
Greek Cypriots identified by ethnicity. Simply, members would reside
either north of the Line, south of it or overseas. This permitted several
London women, including me, to be among those signing the constitution as inaugural members of HAD. This was not Greek Cypriots
and Turkish Cypriots in alliance across the Line, but a transcending of
Partition.

Some weeks after their return to Cyprus, HAD engaged Marie
Mulholland, an experienced feminist activist who had been involved
in getting women's interests taken into account in the peace process
in Northern Ireland, to spend two weeks working intensively with
the group. She went first to the north, then to the south and finally
they held a workshop together at Pyla, where Marie helped them to
talk through the group's aims and intentions and to think their way
to workable strategies. Marie's perception of HAD was that it had
achieved many things in its short life but seriously lacked a 'centre'. It
had so far skimped on the difficult process of putting heads together
to work out what real political agreement existed between them and
where they diverged. She also believed that their actions so far, though
boldly political, had been rhetorical – demands that were probably
unachievable, for a future that, even among themselves, they had not
yet filled with a content. As she left, the group committed itself to
working out a set of shared values and goals, as women, for the kind of
changes they wanted peace to bring.

A couple of months later Marie Mulholland was involved with
HAD again. The Bruno Kreisky Forum for International Dialogue
had been approached and had agreed to host a two-day meeting in
Vienna between HAD and the Women's Initiative for Peace (WIN-
PEACE), an alliance of women from Greece and Turkey. Marie
steered the meeting through some rocky moments as Turks and
Turkish Cypriots discovered the political gap between them on
'the Cyprus issue'. But the seven-woman HAD team came back to
Nicosia feeling that experiencing this demanding dialogue – voicing
to WINPEACE the support they needed and expected, as Cypriots,
from peace-minded allies in the women's movements of Greece and
Turkey – had made them feel, as never before, that they really were
the unitary and coherent body they had set out to become fifteen

months before. Maria Hadjipavlou reported to members who had not been able to be there, 'the Vienna meeting was very intense, rewarding and opened up meaningful dialogue and many new possibilities … the journey is on!'

While the women had been doing their diplomacy, the two leaders and their teams (100 per cent male) had been meeting under UN auspices to see if they might pull together a solution before the deadline of June set by the European Union. June came, and they had failed. The EU set a new deadline, the Copenhagen summit of 12 December. The talks continued, behind doors that remained closed. Civil society in the north was losing patience. There was anger in the left-wing media, there were demonstrations against Rauf Denktaş for his failure to deliver an agreement. Hands Across the Divide, in late September, drafted a letter to Kofi Annan, Secretary General of the United Nations, in Greek, Turkish and English. Women in HAD T-shirts were photographed posting these letters in north and south Nicosia, Barcelona, London, Austria and New York and won some media coverage.

Just before the Copenhagen summit, the UN slapped a draft peace agreement on the table, the 'Annan plan'. A stunned population studied its small print. It involved the north giving back substantial tracts of land and property, but far less than southern refugees were demanding. Could they live with this compromise? Many Turks and Turkish Cypriots would have to be uprooted – more ethnic cleansing? The Copenhagen meeting came and went, and once again the Cypriot leaders missed the opportunity. The Republic was definitively accepted for membership of the EU with effect from 2004. Yet another 'final deadline', 16 April 2003, was set for a settlement that could bring both parts of Cyprus into Europe together. This Country is Ours Platform brought very large numbers of people on to the streets demanding compromise from Denktaş. The BBC estimated 'as many as 50,000, more than a quarter of the population'.[8] The right also mobilized very large counter-demonstrations. In the south, the pro-solution elements of civil society were less militant, and there were contrary voices warning 'no sell out'. The Citizens' Movement called for demonstrations in support of the northern protests – but the numbers ready to turn out, never more than a few hundred, were disappointing to HAD.

HAD supported a hunger strike in the north. In a parallel action in

Eleftheria Square in south Nicosia the women collected messages for peace and issued white ribbons to the public. The northern women sent Denktaş some henna[9] to apply to his private parts; an arcane Turkish gesture of enmity and scorn, apparently. The puzzled women in the south speculated about its origin at some length. It seemed the mutual impact of sexual politics and ethno-national politics was about to become painfully clear – to one man at least. And, who knows, maybe the henna trick worked. For it was not very long after, on 21 April 2003, that the women heard the extraordinary, the unbelievable, announcement that the TRNC would open the barrier at the Ledra Palace checkpoint.

Notes

1 Different theoreticians at different periods have variously defined civil society as including in addition: the basic unit of the family; business enterprise (the market); political parties; and the juridical structure. See for instance Keane 1998 and Fine and Rai 1997.

2 Internet: <www.yenicag-ne.com/ybhyouth/report.htm>, 03.09.2001.

3 Helena Smith, 'Denktash under fire after Cypriot journalists jailed', *Guardian*, 12 August 2002.

4 Internet:<www.tech4peace.org/nqcontent.cfm?a_id=1252>, 03.01.2003.

5 Other external actors promoting bi-communal contact have been the US Embassy, which has its own Bi-communal Support Programme and officer; the British Council and UK High Commission in Cyprus, the Czech and Slovak embassies, and various governments, universities and institutes in Sweden, Norway, Germany, Austria, the UK and other countries. Trade unions have met bi-communally, and there is also a group of business people who see economic advantages in a solution.

6 Other women's bi-communal activities have included several attendances by a Cypriot group at the Women Waging Peace workshops organized by Swanee Hunt of Hunt Associates and the Harvard School of Management in Boston; and participation in Empowerment of Women workshops on Domestic Violence and for Businesswomen, at George Washington University also in the USA. In addition, Simone Susskind revived her project in 2003.

7 The funders are listed in the Acknowledgements.

8 British Broadcasting Corporation on line. *BBC News World Edition*, 14 January 2003 <http://news.bbc.co.uk/2/hi/europe/2656211.stm>

9 Henna is a natural dye used by Turkish and other women to colour skin or hair for personal adornment. It has complex symbolic meanings.

7 | Transversal politics: problems of practice

I was in Famagusta, the famous old maritime city whose harbour looks across the eastern Mediterranean towards Syria. I walked along the sand in front of the Palm Beach Hotel. The Line meets the waves here, at a tangled mesh fence, filled in with battered sheets of corrugated iron. As you look southwards through the fence along the lovely curving shore line, it takes a moment or two to realize that for as far as you can see, a mile or more, is a developed, modern coastal resort without a living soul in it. I counted at least fifty blocks of what were once hotels and flats, up to fourteen storeys high, the render on their walls crumbling away around the bullet holes. Their windows, the glass long since shattered, are eyeless sockets staring seawards. Before 1974 this was Varosia, the Greek Cypriot part of Famagusta. It could have been in one of these high-rise blocks that Sue Lartides had that close encounter with a Turkish fighter plane. Back from the seafront, deep in eucalyptus and palm, cactus and tall grasses, are villas, each one the subject of a dream of 'return' in the mind of some Greek Cypriot family. The only movement here is that of birds, flycatchers making their acrobatic sorties from the rusty reinforcing rods that project from the ruins.

In 2001 and 2002, when the Line was as impermeable and forbidding as it had ever been, I asked women to tell me how they saw it, what it meant to them. Zehra Nalbantoğlu lives not far from here, in Famagusta itself, a city made lively by thousands of university students. A Turkish Cypriot, she knows Varosia by its Turkish name, Maraş.

> I think we just accept that we aren't allowed to go there. We don't question it. We think there's something there that's not good for you. Maraş is frozen, like a sleeping beauty that's been there a hundred years. There *is* great beauty there – still the flowers grow, no matter what happens, and the trees continue to open with their freshness. But everything tells you that what's gone on is wrong! There's no shining, no happiness, no positive energy coming. There's something covered up and buried in the unconscious.

Zehra is in her early thirties. The students she teaches are mainly in their twenties. Then, before the mass rallies and the opening of

2003, she said that young people in the north seldom questioned the existence of the Line: 'They accept it as it is. I have no memories of "a time before", even in my dreams. I can't say, like some people, "When I was eight I had this Greek friend". What we see is just news from the newspaper, and it's just like reading a story.'

In Chapter 3 we saw how northerners, all but a very few, were relieved when the Line was drawn in 1974. And it is probable that a majority, even today, would not wish to see it entirely erased. Ayşe Hasan, for instance, says: 'I'm used to it, I grew up seeing it, so it doesn't really disturb me. I just disregard it … I mean, it does make me feel safer because I know the Greeks can't get over to this side. If it wasn't there, I wouldn't trust the Greeks not to travel over here and – you know, [it would be] like it used to be.' But this is a view from the right, of that part of the population that does not want their southward defences weakened, seeing their security as dependent on Turkey. Zehra, on the contrary, is on the left, and a member of Hands Across the Divide. So is Bahire, a generation older, who sees Turkey and the Turks, not Greek Cypriots, as the main problem. Bahire's hatred of the Line is intense: 'Sometimes I want to cry. It's a small island, my island, and it's divided into two so we are penned in, just like sheep or dogs, it's like a fence. [CC: You never felt protected by it?] No, how can a wall protect you? Our ideas could protect us, if we could learn how to be human beings.'

Bahire believes that the Line is no longer necessary for the safety of Turkish Cypriots, if it ever was. With the women in Hands Across the Divide, and a growing number of other northerners, she refuses to accept the logic of Partition and actively addresses it. But there is a wide gap between the option of maintaining the Line as con/federal border and removing it altogether in the interests of reunification, and northern HAD members are not necessarily of one mind on which is preferable.

On the other side, in the south, it would be difficult to find anyone who, like Ayşe, accepts that the Line of separation between the two parts of Cyprus has been a sensible safety precaution. Athena Z, like Ayşe, is in her forties. She resembles her, too, in being unenthusiastic about *rapprochement*. When she sees the Line and brings to mind those Turks who staked it out she feels 'hatred. I hate them.' Then she sighed. 'When I say that, I mean I hate what they've done to us. And I'm one of the lucky ones. If I look across to the other side I don't see my house. Imagine someone who does! They look across and see their house, only a hundred metres away, and they can't get there.'

Most Greek Cypriots share Athena's feeling – the Line is theft, the Line is outrage – and there have been women, ever since 1974, who have demonstrated against it. Women Walk Home was a group that carried out high-profile direct actions at the Line involving thousands of women in 1975, 1987 and 1989. Helen Soteriou remembers: 'We had the idea that you had to cross the Line, a real sacrificial thing, something you might be shot for, you had to be prepared to make the sacrifice for.' When they got to the fence, though, 'The reality of the Partition came home to us then. We were facing hundreds of yards of wire barricades and beyond that the mines. And it became clear to us then that we were not going home. Not then, and maybe for a long time.' The refugee organizations share this rage at the Line. But the southern women who have joined Hands Across the Divide have a more modulated concern with it. They believe it is wrong and resent the injustice it embodies, but they do not invest quite so much of themselves in 'getting our homes back'. They acknowledge that many people in the north had reason to feel safer, thirty years ago, for having obtained a space of their own.

Katie Economidou is one of these. From the moment her thinking was turned around on the Cyprus question, she has worked tirelessly for *rapprochement* and sees people like herself as a mistrusted minority in both south and north. She is one of those who have taken 'bi-communalist' as a personal, oppressed, identity. For a while, the Line itself obsessed her. She would go out at night and walk along it, looking for holes. She would watch the cats to see which route they took. She joined every bi-communal opportunity that was offered. 'I think I can't be away from the buffer zone for more than a month. It's like a psychosis.' What the women of Hands Across the Divide, north and south, share is that they do not ignore the Line, but neither do they simply want to tear it down. They share a commitment to *deal with it*. Dealing with it has meant on the one hand a material struggle to find legal ways of crossing it, on foot if necessary, to shout or whisper through it, or fly (at great expense) around it. On the other hand, it has meant a mental struggle, a project of imagination, to transcend the Line, to wish away its constraints by sheer willpower.

Many disagreements arose in the group as they tried to build a solid unitary organization. In this chapter we shall see, in relation to four 'problems of practice', the interplay of difference in those three factors of transversal politics identified in Chapter 1: identity, positioning and values. We shall see that their relation to each other's relation to history and culture, to ethno-national *identity* and belonging, was sometimes misjudged. Differences of *position*, the details of their respective situations, also caused tension. There were collective inequalities: relative security, relative freedom to travel abroad, relative prosperity. There were individual inequalities such as academic status or facility with English. *Values* on the whole were shared. It was taken for granted that everyone believed in the importance of dialogue, respect for women, an ethic of care. But that is just it: values were too often taken for granted, remaining inexplicit. A fundamental requirement in negotiating such differences is good group process. This, as we shall see, was acquired in a stumbling fashion. There were serious difficulties in the group of the kind commonly ascribed to 'personality problems', but these I believe are common in organizations. They can usually be seen on closer examination to be the result of faulty process, and this is how I have treated them. Gaining an adequate process was seriously impeded by the tyrannical limitations the Line itself imposed on the group.

Problem 1. How to communicate?

The Partition of Cyprus has been an extraordinarily complete barrier to communication. Not only has the fence been difficult to penetrate and the two crossing points rigorously policed, with all movement subject to a forbidding bureaucracy, but other forms of contact have been frustrated too. Even if the recent opening of the Line is not cancelled, it will take a long while for normal communication to be reinstated. Cypriots have long grown used to the fact that letters with an address in the 'wrong' part of Cyprus are often 'lost' in the post. Even if they get out of the country, they must pass through the biased scrutiny of postal services in Greece and Turkey, and so are unlikely to arrive. Phone calls to or from north Cyprus have been possible only via Turkey, cannot be dialled without operator intervention and are charged at exorbitant rates. There is a limited United Nations phone facility, if you can manage to make it work for you, but people have been reluctant to use it because lines are tapped by the political authorities. Who wants to be noticed habitually phoning the enemy and put on file as a security risk? Communicating across the Line has thus been a perennial struggle. This is precisely why in the past foreign mediators like the Fulbright Commission were a necessary element of bi-communal projects.

HAD had chosen to go it alone, and without external sponsorship it proved impossible to fix regular bi-communal meetings. There was disagreement in the group, however, about the legitimacy of meeting mono-communally; it amounted to a contradiction between, on the one hand, practical considerations of 'getting work done' and, on the other, the dream of transcending bi-communalism to become one organization. Sevgül and Rita among others spoke against mono-communal meetings. If they wanted to build a common country they must begin by building a group identity. To meet as distinct groups either side of the Line would be to recognize the Partition and play into the ideology of separatism. It would 'steal the magic' out of the project of unity. There was also a practical risk that collective positions would harden either side of the Line, and consensus would then be more difficult to find. Tina could understand this. She too wanted to 'think as a Cypriot'. And Georgette told me: 'I had that same idea, that if you're not 100 per cent bi-communal, all of the time, then you're not bi-communal at all.' But both she and Tina came to agree with the majority who felt that mono-communal meetings were a necessity. She said: 'Now what I believe is that we have to do all of the work at the same time or else none of it is possible.' And Magda, too, felt strongly that each 'side' must work at its own pace. She wanted to see their group in the south hold their own meetings, not because they were thinking like separatists, but precisely to lobby the government effectively on behalf of their sisters in the north. This was not a north–south divergence, for some in the north agreed with her. Neriman, for instance, had no identity card and so at first could not cross into Pyla. Nor does she have a computer. If there were to be no mono-communal meetings she would effectively be out of the circle altogether. That Sevgül's fears were not unfounded, however, was brought home to me by Katie, who at one moment was in despair because, instead of the dialogue she had longed for, 'we seem to be caught up in two unconnected monologues'. Eventually everyone was driven to realize that it was going to be just impracticable (and from a security point of view inadvisable) to trek down to Pyla very often, and in the meantime it was simply impossible to progress any of their projects without getting together in mono-communal meetings to discuss and work on them.

This hesitancy about how best to meet was one of the things (though not the only one) that held HAD back in its first nine months of life. It took the new programme of talks between Denktaş and Clerides, and the prospect of HAD's own London meeting, to kick us into action towards the end of 2001. Even after this, however, it proved difficult to get the whole group down to Pyla on anything like a regular basis. Towards the end of 2002 Sevgül suggested a new approach: instead of feeling aggrieved when the whole membership fails to commit to meetings in Pyla, let's activate the 'management committee' provided for in the constitution. Let this smaller group, who after all have been elected and authorized, take responsibility for keeping up the momentum of face-to-face meetings, while everyone else joins them when they feel able to get to Pyla.

From the start, a great deal of hope had been placed on e-mail. Indeed, Fatma Azgın, jaded by a decade in which she felt she virtually lived in the buffer zone, had only joined HAD because it seemed e-mail could allow this group, this time, to do without endless meetings. But e-mail was a mixed blessing. On the one hand it seemed to be just what was needed – bouncing messages from satellites in space is an almost instantaneous, almost secure, means of communication across the Line. On the other hand it often ruins the very relationships it enables, so that I sometimes felt it was a poisoned gift bestowed on this infant project by some bad fairy. I believe it may be useful to spell out the particular difficulties we encountered in HAD, because more and more women's groups are struggling with similar problems and we may be able to learn from each other.

The first and perhaps the most basic problem was that not everyone in HAD was 'on line'. Today, having access to a computer and an e-mail account has to be seen as a positioning of relative power. When a group begins to depend on e-mail as its main medium of intra-group communication, those members who do not have computers quickly become peripheral. Any group relying only on e-mail is bound to draw its membership from a rather narrow slice of humanity, and a Cypriot bi-communal one is further challenged in this respect because only English speakers can engage (very few Cypriots speak both Greek and Turkish). In the case of HAD, well-meaning efforts were made to keep in touch with non-e-mailers by phone, but they inevitably missed out on details and remained much less 'visible' to the group than those whose names appeared frequently at the foot of messages. Even among those who were on e-mail, however, there were marked differences between those who logged on and replied to messages routinely each day and those who went to their screens irregularly, or depended on using someone else to field and forward their correspondence. So HAD developed as an organization which, although it did not, does not, think of itself as a hierarchy, is none the less structured by the twin usage of e-mail and English so that some are at the core, others a little more distanced, some quite marginal and some who might otherwise very much like to take part simply do not join at all.

Something that often deters reluctant e-users is overload. HAD at its moments of peak activity over the last two years was generating up to twenty messages a day. It might take an hour just to read them all and reply to some. From time to time members of HAD complained about individuals writing to other individuals using the HAD group address, unnecessarily filling up everyone's in-boxes. At a certain point members' birthday dates were added to the member telephone list, and from that moment greetings messages would pour in to each woman on or around her birthday. In theory these could all have been addressed by individuals to individuals. On the other hand, sending them around via the e-list built up a valuable sense of caring, belonging and shared pleasures that, as women, we valued.

Perhaps the main peril to the group in e-communication was the scope for misunderstanding. Long-running and at times angry disagreements were generated around matters that a face-to-face meeting could have quickly resolved. It is so easy, late at night, tired at the end of a long day, to throw in a two-line message thoughtlessly worded. It is too late to recall it if you think better of it in the light of day. Those who receive it cannot read the look in your eyes or interpret your body language. There is nothing to soften the impact. Something meant as a joke will read as deadly serious. One little ambiguity and within hours there will be two or three tetchy replies. Sarcasm is fatal. Mistrust, hurt, bad humour all escape from Pandora's Box and it can take weeks to recapture them.

This kind of problem was increased in HAD by virtue of the fact that there was a marked difference of positioning among the members regarding the written word. A professional journalist (and there are several in HAD) who spends hours at the keyboard each day and is used to writing fast and powerfully, will take an e-initiative more speedily than, say, a social worker or therapist who is slower to get to the keyboard, more cautious about using words and whose professionalism is invested in carefully thought-through interpersonal relations. When upsets occurred, as they frequently did, over some incautious phrase, there were two kinds of response. Some women at some moments would prioritize 'love/generosity', and send out a wave of conciliatory messages. Others at other moments would prioritize 'honesty/transparency' and respond confrontationally. At times, neither of these perfectly legitimate approaches seemed the right move for resolving differences or achieving decisions.

Another difficulty in an e-list is knowing how to interpret silences. When members did not join in the e-conversation on a given topic, what did it mean? That they had no point of view to contribute? That they assumed their agreement to be understood? That they had a disagreement they were withholding? Or simply that they had gone on holiday? There was much discussion, especially in the early days of HAD, about 'commitment'. Some of those who were very active on the list felt uneasy about those who contributed rarely, taking this to mean a lack of commitment to the group. But the silent ones felt: surely if we have said we want to be members of this group, our word should be good enough? Do we have to prove ourselves by chipping in some comment every three days? But (the 'double but' that always signals a contradiction) it was understandable if members discussing sensitive political topics had an uneasy sense of being overheard by silent listeners.

After HAD's inaugural meeting in February 2002, the benefits e-mail brought to the organization, relative to the perils it entailed, began to be more evident. At this meeting women were elected to the positions listed in the constitution, and one of these posts was that of an e-moderator. At this point more serious thought began to be given to group process, including not only the facilitation of e-interactions, but also the chairing of meetings and procedures for making decisions – such as the always contentious matter of choosing representatives to attend events abroad. One of the serious difficulties encountered by HAD in using e-mail was that of concluding discussions and coming to a decision. Without an agreed procedure, the tendency was (as in most e-lists) for she who spoke loudest, longest or last to get her way. The e-moderator now issued proposals for courteous conduct of discussion and, most importantly, introduced the notion of placing time limits on pursuit of a given issue, and enabling an e-vote in order eventually to terminate it. A separate e-address was set up called 'ballots' to which members were to reply by a given date. The voting choices could vary from one issue to the next. For instance, an array of options might be: I agree to the proposed activity and will take part; I agree to the proposed activity but cannot take part; I disagree but am prepared to accept a majority decision; I disagree and wish to block this proposal.

A similar system could be used to select preferred dates for meetings. The group began to learn fast from procedural mistakes. Members who were disappointed to have missed sharing in some decision learned to keep more in touch in future. One crisis occurred when the required 50 per cent-plus-one 'yes' vote ('Are you *for* this action?') was not achieved because women, for various reasons, were failing to read their e-mail. Next time, so that the proposal would not fall by default, the question was pitched for a 'no' ('Are you *against* this action?'). Members quickly familiarized themselves with the expecta-tions inherent in the methodology. It seemed a moment of success when the e-moderator, based in south Cyprus, was able to go away for a few days in the middle of a crucial decision process, and simply hand over to a substitute moderator, an overseas HAD member living in New York at the time, who saw it well completed.

Problem 2. Whom to include?

The issue of membership has been another critical matter for many women's NGOs, particularly those that organize transversally across ethno-national identity groups and even more those among them that have an avowed political intention. In this respect, the experience of HAD may be a useful contribution to collective experience. We saw above that immediately following the *Divided Societies* seminar Sevgül, probably the most e-connected person present, quickly registered the e-address <cypriotwomensgroup> and fed in the names of those who had signed up to be included. She was technically the list 'owner', with the facility to subscribe and unsubscribe members.

In the first couple of months it became clear that there was a nucleus of active members who stayed in touch and attended meet-ings, and an outer band of non-attenders. At first Sevgül, in role, would phone uncommunicative members (in the north at least) to discern their intentions and tell them the dates of meetings. This was clearly an exhausting process that could not continue. She suggested removing from the list anyone who did not attend bi-communal meetings and thereby prove 'commitment'. The active group, however, were disunited on whether 'no show' and 'silence' should be considered blameworthy. Women had many sound reasons for being unable to attend weekend meetings in Pyla. There were work commitments, family commitments. Some northerners might not feel able to afford the political profile it gave them to be seen crossing the checkpoint regularly. Anyway, 'silence' too could be read in more than one way. It did not necessarily mean lack of interest. Some women at the start were not confident they would be understood. Sofia Georgiou was a consistent attender at meetings, but did not often feel ready to speak in them. She therefore felt some loyalty to those other 'silent' members who had now been excluded from the new list. She said: 'Everybody contributes in their own way. Some will speak and some won't speak. Sometimes you need time to take things in. It doesn't mean you're not participating. I know what's going on.'

Fireworks had already been flying through cyberspace for some weeks on this matter of inclusion/exclusion when the whole question became more urgent: *security* became an issue. There had been some vicious (and unpleasantly sexualized) comment by a columnist in a newspaper in the south about three HAD members, Tina Adamidou, Magda Zenon and Netha Kreouzos, all outspoken bi-communal journalists. Sevgül, up north, had written a passionate article hitting back at the *Sunday Mail* on their behalf.

> It's hard to be a woman and an activist on both sides of Cyprus. To be a woman and smart at the same time is confusing to the fascists. They cannot accept it. For them a woman has to be a part of the system … an ornamental plant, an object that satisfies their rising hormones, or a mother … The whole system stands on supremacy–inferiority, in other words 'power'. Differentiation is feeding the system. Equality is like a nightmare to them.

The *Mail* in the south then published an article that included information that could only have been acquired through access to the <cypriotwomensgroup> e-list. It was almost certain that no hacking had been involved, so it was feared a member had leaked information to the media. If the list were indeed insecure, how much did it matter? North/south differences of political environment, but also the different positioning of individuals, were bound to affect the answer.

The women in the south were living in a volatile society. Some outspoken nationalists opposed to any compromise on the Cyprus problem would occasionally burst into view and generate an unpleasant atmosphere. Writers such as Tina, Magda and Netha were particularly exposed, but long-term bi-communalists like Katie Economidou and Maria Hadjipavlou too were often represented as 'traitors' to the nation. All the same, the regimes of the Republic and the TRNC differ in the degree of threat experienced by political nonconformists. In the north, the presence of the Turkish deep state is continually sensed. We have seen that there are occasional incidents of actual violence against those who openly oppose Turkish hegemony, and there is a drip of sinister comment in the right-wing newspapers in which bi-communalists are named, their visits abroad listed and threats issued. Sevgül was frequently singled out for this kind of treatment, her name sometimes appearing in two-inch-high headlines. Her understandable preference was therefore for an e-list of women who inspired trust because they were known personally to each other from their attendance at bi-communal meetings at Pyla. The names on the original e-list from the *Divided Societies* seminar, between seventy and eighty in all, included staff of the UK High Commission, the British Council and the US Embassy. Sevgül said to me in interview: 'We don't know who's watching ... I have to feel comfortable when I write, that the media isn't watching me. It's not that I have secrets, but they can take your words and you don't know how they'll use them.'

Members were divided, though (and not on a south/north basis), as to whether the best strategy was openness or secrecy. Neşe Yaşın is an unusual individual, not only because she is a celebrated poet in the Turkish language, but because she is a Turkish Cypriot who decided to come and live in the south and work for peace by personally symbolizing communication across the Line. She felt it best to be realistic.

Yes. Somebody's listening. These e-mail lists are like that. I mean, you should think you are speaking in a public place. My way of dealing with things is to be open, to be outspoken and not to fear. I have done this all my life and I have suffered from it, but this is my decision. I can't expect this from everybody – they may have different worries. But in my experience you're more secure when you're open ... It should be really crystal clear what you say, what you do and what you are. You win respect from your enemies and they have to check their behaviour.

Women of Hands Across the Divide.

In these early days of HAD's life there was as yet no formal procedure for taking decisions. Consequently, the few who felt most strongly about this issue acted on the impulse to create a new, less inclusive, working list of known active members. The new list was called <handsacrossthedivide>. The <cypriotwomensgroup> list remained in existence for circulation of information of more general relevance. Probably the majority of those who were not transferred to the inner list had had no great interest in the group's activities. But the way the shift was handled did dismay some members who felt puzzled, and then excluded, when the information on the larger list just dried up without explanation. Netha, in the south, who was on the cusp between one list and the other (at first taken off, later readmitted) told me she felt the process had been undemocratic. It might have been acceptable had the inner list been an elected executive of the bigger membership. But where was their mandate? The inner group, she felt, had run off from the rest. Olga Demetriou agreed: 'The security risks are well understood. But even so, I think the <cypriotwomensgroup> could have been allowed to develop more inclusively. The effect, intended or not, was elitist. Not in a class sense but in the sense that some had the power to pick and choose who would belong.' But some felt it was not the decision so much as the process that had been faulty. Derya Beyatlı, in the north, said: 'We didn't really explain it to the other group. I guess that was the mistake we made, we should have explained the reason.'

By the time of the London workshop (February 2002) the HAD membership had stabilized around the active nucleus of the inner e-list. The momentous agreement on a constitution, structure and process for Hands Across the Divide would probably not have been so effectively achieved had the group been larger or more politically disparate. But two difficult membership questions remained to be dealt with. One arose in the London workshop itself, the other soon afterwards.

The London workshop was attended by half a dozen women of the London Cypriot diaspora – the ones I had involved soon after my return from the initial seminar. Indeed, it was they who made the practical arrangements for hosting the workshop and had assumed they would be participants. But on the first morning an intensely painful debate occurred in which the members from Cyprus were themselves divided about whether it was appropriate to include the Londoners or not. Some felt the very fact that the latter were keen to be part of the group was valuable and their input as Cypriot women living in less divided circumstances could be helpful. Others felt that diaspora women were unlikely to understand fully the thinking of those who lived under Partition. Besides, the Cyprus-based members by now had a year's experience of each other and many difficult matters still to debate and agree. Incorporating newcomers to the discussion would impede progress. The Londoners for their part were angered by the threatened exclusion. They felt they were being challenged to prove their Cypriot authenticity. They were being constructed as 'not be-longing'.

Eventually a decision was made to include the Londoners, and it proved pivotal. It was a factor in the constitutional decision to designate three membership regions (north of the Line, south of the Line and overseas), that in turn helped us dispense with the standard bi-communal ethnic terminology of 'Turkish Cypriots' and 'Greek Cypriots'. Soon after the return from London, a number of the members resident in Cyprus left for work or study abroad, scattering to Strasbourg, Brussels, New York and elsewhere. The difficult decision that would have been necessary (should they quit the organization?) was averted. They could slip temporarily into the 'overseas region' and continue to play a full part by e-mail. Most members of the group were eventually happy, I think, that HAD was able to reflect in this way the diasporic quality that war and Partition had forced on Cypriots.

The second 'inclusion' question arose soon after HAD's return from London. Those members who disappeared overseas at this juncture were mainly northerners. Replacing them would be hard, for there were far fewer potential women to draw on in the north, for various reasons, including the greater risk involved in political activism. The question of recruiting new members now came on to the agenda with some urgency, first, to bring the northern contingent up to proportional strength and, second, because the constitution is clearly inclusive: 'membership is open to any woman living in Cyprus or elsewhere, who agrees with the aims of the Association'. Already several women had expressed interest in joining.

The appropriate contents of a membership application form had already been widely discussed in the months preceding the London workshop. It had been a useful educational process mulling over the questions it was legitimate to ask a prospective member. Should we ask for passport or ID card numbers? This would be convenient when seeking group permissions to go to Pyla or travel abroad. But why would a women's group want to identify women by the same means as state bureaucracy? Besides, listing their IDs might risk their safety. Again, should we ask women to state their marital status? To some this seemed normal, while others felt it invidious to make distinctions between single, married and divorced women.

With the membership form more or less agreed, however, there remained the equally difficult question of admission procedure. There was anxiety about politically motivated entryism by women opposed to HAD's aims, or about filling up the membership yet again with 'dead wood'. Should it be required for a new member to be personally introduced, proposed and seconded by existing members? How should applications from overseas, from women who might be known to nobody and unable to attend a meeting in person be dealt with? In the end a sensible pragmatic compromise was agreed. As well as getting information *about* the prospective member, emphasis was placed on giving enough information *to* her about the organization and its expectations to enable her to make an informed decision. Neither the dreaded draining away of membership nor the feared influx of unmanageable numbers happened. A few new women, north and south, joined during 2002–03 and began to play a valued part in the organization.

Problem 3. Negotiating a common agenda

There was a huge warmth in the group between women of the north and south, and a lot of pleasure was taken in friendships as they developed. Yet under the surface there stirred memories of the traumas and injustices of the 1960s and 1970s, recounted in Chapters 2 and 3. It is political history after all that produces ethnicity, and ethnic difference did exist in the group however much we might wish to leap over it and leave it behind. We found ourselves thoughtlessly using 'trigger words', terms that raised hackles on one or other 'side'. Someone would incautiously say 'invasion' and someone else would flush with anger. But differences of position, too, were problematic because they gave rise to divergent political trajectories. The women, north and south, came from highly specific and differentiated contemporary situations as we saw in Chapters 4 and 5. They had developed localized political orientations and projects. Mutual knowledge on these was lacking. It took time for each to learn the other's feelings on many issues, and the situations in which they could explore them were too infrequent, too short and too stressed.

There were three factors motivating Hands Across the Divide in the north. One was the *urgency* of their plight relative to Turks and Turkey, the second was the *danger* they felt from the TRNC authorities and the Turkish deep state, and the third was a keen desire to have southern women fully *understand* their situation and help them. Before the mass demonstrations that began in the north in 2002, it came as a surprise to many southerners to find that Turkish Cypriots saw *Turks*, not Greek Cypriots, as 'the enemy'. We saw in Chapter 4 how inward Turkish and outward Turkish Cypriot migration is making some Turkish Cypriots (and this is almost definitive of the left) feel their survival is threatened. To HAD northerners the future seemed reduced to two alternatives, catch the EU train or be absorbed into Turkey. The train looked like pulling out without them. They wanted to act visibly, boldly and fast.

The southerners who had been part of the bi-communalism of the 1900s were not out of tune with this feeling in the north, but for many of the southern women this was their first opportunity to work in partnership with northerners. They did not at first grasp the urgency. They were not ready to leap into action. Derya saw this: 'People are saying, like, we have different agendas, that the Turkish Cypriots are trying to find a solution, let's say, and Greek Cypriots – I'm talking about the views I've heard of – are there because they want to *know us*, they want to meet us, make friends with us. They don't have the urgency.'

The second factor was perceived danger. The media are not censored in north Cyprus, but media freedom is often abused. There is apparent impunity for newspapers who publish libellous comments on bi-communalists and those who speak against the link with Turkey, while the law is readily invoked against opposition newspapers. Two members of HAD were among writers taken to court in December 2002 for merely reporting a dispute over a sacked teacher. People who have links with the south or abroad are watched, and their phones are tapped. People who cross into Pyla see their names being checked against a blacklist. Furthermore, extremist forces with a history of violence are known to be operating in the TRNC, not unconnected to the Turkish military. Certain newspapers, voicing these interests, attack bi-communalists in extraordinarily explicit terms. The following appeared in *Kıbrıslı* on 30 November 2001, eight months after HAD was formed. The author addresses himself to several hundred 'traitors', whose names he claims to have. He likens them to 'a Greek foetus within our very body'. He threatens them with torture: 'Cut out this page and keep it. And if what you so dearly want comes about, and North Cyprus is given to the Greeks, on that day we're going to find you one by one and when we do, please believe me, you will be begging us "let me die". But we won't hear you because our ears will be blocked.'

Pointing a finger at the journalists among the traitors, he warns them:

> We'll use those articles of yours as evidence against you. We'll force you to eat these pages you write in hatred ... Whether you are at home or at work or at the newspaper offices, you should look with suspicion at every passing car. Pick up your phone and you'll hear a threat. You may complain to the world but no one can save you ... On the day they sign a peace agreement, they will be signing your death warrant ... On that day it won't be words that speak but something else ... I give my word that some hundreds among you aren't going to live to see that day.

Three days later *Kıbrıslı* devoted a headline and several pages to an article naming the bi-communalists it was menacing. Several were members of HAD.

It took the women in the south a while to sort out how to evaluate the danger in the TRNC. Northern women themselves were not in total unity on how much or how far they should change their behaviour in response to threats. When they learned about the *Kıbrıslı* article the women in the south quickly proposed to speak out in their own community, condemning media impunity in the north, supporting the bi-communalists. They were shaken to be told, 'Hold back!' by the northerners. And the latter, for their part, were surprised that the southern women did not *see* that their support would make things worse, confirming suspicions that they were in cahoots with Greek Cypriots.

'See' is the key word here. For, as mentioned in Chapter 1, *imagination* is the essence of transversal politics. The making and maintaining of working alliances across differences depend more than anything else on the capacity to step into another person's shoes and see the world from her position. In this respect the northerners felt the southern women were slow to learn. 'How many times do we have to tell them?' Katie recognized this. She said: 'Probably because I don't live in that danger I can't see it, I can't sense it and I can't know what its implications are. Whatever I can know, it's assumptions, it's just *imaginative*.' But Tina felt there was an obligation on both sides to communicate about difference, not just to 'guilt-trip' each other: 'In order for us to be able to understand what living under occupation means, we have to be told. And if we're told a thousand times, that thousand-and-one'th time is still important as well.'

Though they were still not able at this time to visit and see for themselves, gradually, through the words of the northerners, the north came into view in the mind's eye in more detail, with more realism. Rita Pantazi, for instance, said: 'Before I met the women – when people asked me what is happening [in the north] I used to say: "The Turkish Cypriots are suffering." But it was rather like the propaganda explanation that I'd been hearing. Now, I *know what it means*. It has brought it home to me that it is not just propaganda I was saying, you know?'

Empathy came in different ways. Tina was suddenly touched one day by a single phrase she read in a message from Selma Bolayır: 'Our lives lack *dignity*.' Sometimes the seeing came from a shared circumstance. Magda had been impatient when, soon after the attacks in the media, the northern women did not want to risk keeping an appointment with them in Pyla. But she has a young son, Angelo. Sevgül also has a son, Burak. Magda said, 'I don't know if I could have the courage to go to the edge. With my son, I wouldn't.' Sue Lartides drew on her experience as a therapist. She understood the resentment sometimes expressed by the northerners as anger at reliving an old familiar dependency. They were forced to rely on the Republic to carry them along with them into the EU, and, 'It's like, here we go again. Because they've lived that for all of their history. They've always been reliant on someone else, the British or the Greek Cypriots, to give them jobs or whatever it was.'

There had to be reciprocity, however, if the southerners were not to feel, as many of them did at one point or another, that the northerners saw only instrumental value in them. Of course, yes, it was in Greek Cypriot interests too that the Turkish Cypriots should neither become extinct nor get swallowed up by the Turkish state. But, as Magda put it: 'For this to work both our needs have to be met. We need to empower each other. There has got to be a relationship of equality.' What was felt to be lacking was thus partly parity of regard for each other's needs and feelings. Tina said: 'We've tended to be more cautious of what we're saying to the northern group than the northern group are about what they're saying to us.' Nana agreed. She said: 'Actually our needs and our concerns were never discussed.' And Sue said of the relationship: 'I feel it's very one-sided. It feels lopsided.'

The perceived lack of reciprocity was also, however, partly a question of unequal enthusiasm for each other's projects. Some in the south, as we saw above, would have liked to devote more time to exploring differences honestly and to building understanding from the personal level upwards. Some, as we shall see below, would have liked to put energy into building an island-wide women's movement. And some wanted to be more connected to what was going on in the world around them, especially after the events of 11 September 2001. Cyprus, after all, is a crucial Western military base in the Middle East. Iraq is not far to the east. Israel is even less distance away, and the brutal repression of the Palestinian intifada was stirring the women's peace movement all over the world. It is not surprising that some women in HAD, itself a group seeking peace, wanted to join the international protest. Some of the southern women were especially concerned when they heard that Rola, who had spoken at the *Divided Societies* seminar, had been beaten up in the attack on Arabs by Jews in Nazareth. They felt disappointment when some women in the north expressed their *own* disappointment at hearing the southerners were (it seemed to them) willing to act for Palestinians to the neglect of their Turkish Cypriot sisters. Gradually this difference of perspective was ironed out. The vigils organized in the south explicitly linked intolerance in Israel and Palestine with intolerance in Cyprus. And some northerners, too, joined in signing a statement of protest against Israel.

These passionate, exhausting disagreements brought HAD to breaking point more than once over the two years. It is not difficult, sitting at a computer keyboard in London, to survey the scene as I do here, setting out both points of view. But when I was in Cyprus, locked into the separate reality of one or other region, I found myself sharing deeply in local perceptions. It was difficult when on one side of the Line to imagine what was going on in those heads the other side. My sympathies swung to and fro continually. Transversal politics is a very difficult art.

Problem 4. What is a women's politics?

So the Line was impeding women in learning from each other the intricacies of identity – how much and how little each felt herself to be 'Greek Cypriot' and 'Turkish Cypriot' and the variety of things those names can mean when you actually live with them. It was also making it difficult fully to understand the differences of position that living on opposite sites of the Line entails – or indeed the inequalities of position between women *within* either community. It was simultaneously hindering any real exploration of what it meant to be a woman, and what kind of women's politics HAD should practise and promote.

Some members were ambivalent about separating themselves off from men. It seemed to reinforce the very 'gender line' women argue so fiercely against. How can we split the gender ranks when there are so many political problems to solve in Cyprus that concern both women and men? Talking to Gülay, I came to understand this position better. Yes, there are gender-specific 'rights' that we need to be concerned with. For example, women are subject to rape and domestic violence from men and so they need a recognized right as women to bodily security. But Gülay and others who think like her are anxious not to forfeit solidarity between women and men. It is a position supported by left-wing ideology.

Differences over what it meant to be a women's group did not fall on a south/north axis. On both sides of the Line there was talk in HAD of building a women's movement. Myria said: 'There's not been any women's mobilization in the south that I know of. We've tried many times to start something off, which never actually happened. I was hoping this time it would.' In the north, Neriman felt strongly that HAD should be in touch with the average woman. As a former teacher, poet and columnist, she is often invited to talk to groups of women and has a circle of acquaintances that runs to hundreds: 'We are the problem, not them. If we do things right they will start to listen to us, they will come with us … You have to think, these are ordinary housewives. Twenty-four hours a day they are listening to Mr Denktaş, they are listening to their husbands!'

This issue of reaching out to women was, of course, tied up with the question of 'inclusion' that HAD was debating so fiercely in its first year of life. Magda felt: 'We've got to find a way to approach other women, beyond the ten that come to meetings. They're all valuable. We've got to approach maybe the less involved women – what's the expression? – more *everyday* women. Try to bring them in.' But this could be risky if 'security plus political action' were the priorities. And even those whose main concern was not this combination but rather developing bi-communal relationships, could feel that too much stress on feminism might be a diversion. They preferred 'women' to be interpreted as simply '*being* a group of women' and 'doing things women's way'.

At this point in the discussion, two questions arose simultaneously: Are we a feminist project? and, What is feminism? Maria Hadjipavlou teaches and writes on gender issues at the University of Cyprus. As much as anyone in HAD she was pressing for a gender-analytical approach. Her main disappointment in the group was that it continually evaded discussion of gender, and sometimes there seemed to be an anti-feminist ethos. 'When I hear members of the group saying, "I'm not a feminist", that alerts me to see how much we bought into a male understanding of feminism.' Neşe agreed the word feminism was 'connected with a lot of negativity in the society'. She thought instead of talking too much about it we should simply start practising it, and then even women who distanced themselves from feminism would 'come along with it', recognizing it as what they themselves believed in. For her there was logic to a feminist approach to peace, on the grounds that women and men had been differently positioned in relation to armed violence. She saw a danger, of course, in acting politically around the identity 'woman'. Women who are heavily identified with 'motherhood', 'home' and 'homeland' can feed into nationalism, and increase adherence to men in authority, both in the family and in the state. 'Women are considered to be the most reactionary, because they have this role of regenerating the system. But women also can be very revolutionary as well, because they are the victims of the system … It depends on how you mobilize the potential of the woman.'

One reason why we did not easily sit down and work these issues through together was that some women were suspicious of too much talk of 'gender', which seemed to them alienating and 'academic'.

This arose partly from the fact that the women most motivated to get to grips with and clarify the issue of feminism did, in fact, work in university environments. But it is not only academics who need and create political theory. Every movement generates its theory, and its theorists are not necessarily highly educated people. Antonio Gramsci coined a term for grassroots thinkers: 'organic intellectuals' (Gramsci 1971). It helps, if you are active around socialist issues, to have a grasp of concepts such as 'capitalism' and 'profit'. It helps, if you are active around feminist issues, to have a grasp of concepts such as 'gender' and 'patriarchy'. It is no contradiction that those in HAD who were the strongest feminist theorists also wished to see to action. Myria, for instance, wanted HAD to be 'different from the rest, a group that recognizes there's institutional discrimination against women and that they want to do something about it ... If you don't think something needs to be done about it, then I don't think you're a feminist.'

Some, then, saw HAD as a 'women's' group, others wanted it to be a 'feminist' group. That, of course, begs the question as to what feminist action might be said to be. Some assumed it meant action on issues specific to women, such as domestic violence or the education of children. Some would have welcomed such a focus, while others feared it would be a distraction from the historic opportunity to shift the 'Cyprus problem'. Yet others again believed that gender and peace issues were not two political strands but one and the same thing. Georgette said, 'I don't know how to separate them.' Anthoula thought our approach should be 'holistic'; it should deal with the whole spectrum of life, power and politics, not just 'women's issues'. There were several women talking this way: that the apparently political is a women's issue (militarization, for instance, is a gendered culture); and what is apparently a women's issue (single parenting, for instance) is also political. But lurking under the surface were issues on which differences were sensed without being explored. For instance, women might be united in the wish for demilitarization of the island in the long run, but in the short run, depending on their situation, some women would feel unsafe if left unprotected by an army. They would not therefore support, as others might, a demand for their sons to have a right to refuse military service on grounds of conscience.

The key problem was lack of a time and place in which to get together and really work through an agreed group vision. There was always something more urgent demanding our attention, one more lobbying opportunity, one more demonstration called for. When Marie Mulholland came to work with HAD for those two weeks in May 2002 she had tried to kick-start some serious collective thinking about what a specifically women's agenda for peace in Cyprus would be. She predicted that if HAD did not soon discover what beliefs and intentions linked its members, the group would never become a coherent voice for change. Most women agreed with her, though they were at a loss to know how to find the time and focus to address the task. Maria Hadjipavlou, for one, longed to do so. They had always complained, she said, that the Cyprus problem was being allowed to marginalize all other issues in Cyprus, including women's issues. So what was HAD doing, 'recycling the very thing we're critiquing?'

> We're putting on our agenda what the men have already put there. We are following them, we're not saying anything different ... What is the substance, what kind of culture do we want to build? This is not being addressed, and that's what's bothering me. As women, what is our political statement, within a new cultural understanding of ourselves? ... I'm losing hope of generating a feminist intervention which would be *our* voice and *our* culture.

If HAD perpetually failed to produce a detailed platform, however, its members manifested very clearly in their own interactions a proto-feminist belief in the political importance of 'everyday life'. Katie said:

> We're not only political animals, we have lovers, friends, we get hurt every day. We need to make a safe space for each other as women. If it's not that, it's just like any business meeting with its agenda and minutes ... I'm not just a 'bi-communal woman'. I carry lots of different identities. There are lots of other possibilities in me. And if these don't get expression I get frustrated.

The e-mail exchanges were full of attention to each other's personal lives. And a characteristic moment happened in October 2002. Within a span of a few days, Zehra gave birth to a son, Doğa, and Maria's father died. Everyone wanted to be able to cross the Line to celebrate with Zehra, in the north, and to attend Costas Hadjipavlou's funeral in the south. They decided to ask the authorities for permission for these visits. They knew they would be refused, as of course they were. The intention was to make a public exposure of it afterwards. It was Sevgül who wrote the article, an impassioned outcry

against the inhumanity of the political situation. But in addition to the rhetoric, the women also acted directly. Costas had been a refugee from a village in the north he had known by the Greek name Ayios Ambrosios. He had dreamed of being buried there. The women in the north found out the Turkish name of the village. They went there and dug a little earth to scatter on Costas's grave. They handed it to Maria in Pyla, a symbolic act that everyone saw as perfectly in tune with all the other political business habitually transacted between women of south and north in the buffer zone.

8 | Inclusion and diversity

When the Line was opened in April 2003, women, men and children flooded across it, braving long queues to get through the checkpoint. It was like a festival. Everything in the preceding chapters will have made clear why the mood was so celebratory. The separation between the two sides of this small island had been so uncompromising, so inhuman, so long-lasting – this was like rainfall after a drought.

From the experience of those early weeks much was learned. First, it was apparent that many Greek and Turkish Cypriots still held good memories of each other, despite the periods of armed conflict between them. There were few unpleasant incidents and many heart-warming stories of householders, who might well have felt very insecure anticipating a knock on the door by the lawful owner of their home, welcoming the visitors, offering coffee and friendship. In an opinion poll of a random sample of 700 Greek Cypriots and 600 Turkish Cypriots carried out six weeks after the opening, 83 per cent of Greek Cypriots and 60 per cent of Turkish Cypriots who had crossed said they had been treated in a friendly way (*Politis* 2003).

That statistical difference, however, was not without meaning, and there were other significant divergences between Turkish and Greek Cypriots' actions and reactions. The same opinion poll showed that 52 per cent of the population of the north had made a crossing. Since non-naturalized Turks were not allowed to cross, this 52 per cent represented an even higher, though unverifiable, proportion of the Turkish Cypriot population. Two-thirds said they had gone south to see their houses and properties, the remainder had gone for 'tourism', while 3 per cent said they had wanted to apply for Republic passports and identity cards with a view to seeking work in the south and eventually in European Union countries. It cannot be assumed, however, that all Turkish Cypriots, even those who crossed the Line, were happy with the turn of events. Although the report on the poll said nothing about the hesitations of northerners, several told me personally that they felt let down by the politicians who had so arbitrarily and unilaterally changed the rules; left individuals to deal with enmities *they* had created, with the risk of violence involved; and permitted the opening immediately after having rejected a plan for a lasting solution. When the Greek Cypriot authorities responded to the new situation by offering certain supportive measures to Turkish Cypriots, some northerners told me they felt angry and patronized.

The proportion of Greek Cypriots crossing the Line in this first six weeks was smaller – only 39 per cent of Greek Cypriots had taken the opportunity. Seventy per cent of them were refugees from 1974, the poll showed, of whom the 'overwhelming majority' visited the north to see their houses and other properties and to worship in their churches. Only 1 per cent said they had gone for pleasure, and 19 per cent said they would not cross a second time. The majority had boycotted the northern economy: 85 per cent made no purchases and did not eat in a café or restaurant while there. (Even fewer Turkish Cypriots spent money in the south, but it may be assumed this was not because of a principled refusal to contribute to the local economy but because the exchange rate made the south very expensive for them.) The main reason given by Greek Cypriots for not crossing was that they would have to present their passports and thus recognize the 'pseudo-state' (*Politis* 2003).

The opening was welcomed with delight by Hands Across the Divide. Even their suspicions about the political intentions behind the move could not put a damper on the joy. For one thing, the opening greatly eased organizational problems, making it possible to hold meetings in each other's homes instead of having to traipse down to Pyla. Meetings could be frequent, more easily arranged, could involve small groups working on specific projects. They immediately started to look for funding to open a 'women's multicultural internet café' in the centre of Nicosia, as the best means now of fulfilling their constitutional objective of 'the improvement of contact and co-operation between women in the pursuit of peace, equality and human rights in Cyprus'. And they began to push the authorities for further concessions. Why do Greek Cypriots have to present their passports? The north is not a foreign country. Why do we have to be home by midnight? We aren't Cinderellas. They planned to draw other civil society organizations to a demonstration spoofing the Cinderella theme.

At the same time, many Cypriots on both sides of the Line were voicing scepticism and concern about the politicians' motives and apparent irresponsibility. Yiota Afxentiou is a counsellor and psychologist who was displaced from Famagusta when she was fifteen. She described her reactions to me this way:

I am happy but very unhappy at the same time. What will happen now? There's no real basis for a solution yet. The division is still there in our heads – ethnic ideas are deep inside us. Nobody has prepared us for co-existence, or for compromise. The government hasn't been honest with us. Now we're discovering the hard reality that many won't ever be able to 'go back'. Who is acknowledging the pain people are feeling now, seeing their houses again? I think anger will emerge. And nobody is holding those emotions, looking after those feelings.

It was clear that breaching the Line did not mean ending Partition. It guaranteed nothing for the future. Pressure on political leaders for a just and lasting solution to the Cyprus problem had to continue and grow. The aim now must be to use the coming twelve months to snatch an agreement from the fire before the final entry of Cyprus into the EU in May 2004.

When (if) agreement comes, we know more or less what it will involve, because in outline the solution has been on the negotiating table for many years. It will provide for two entities, each with autonomy in internal affairs. There will be an over-arching all-Cyprus authority that gives the state its nominal unity. If the experience of Bosnia is anything to go by, there will be a continuing struggle over the relative authority of the centre and the entities. Some territory will be given up by the north, certainly the ghost town of Varosia, on the east coast, and possibly the citrus-growing region of Morphou in the west, as well. There will thus be a new movement of people, probably involving more turmoil and pain, but neither on the scale nor with the violence of the past.

There will probably be a long period of protection to stop southern wealth buying up the north. Militarism may be trimmed down a little, but it will not go away. There are a lot of Cypriots who long for genuine interrelationship, two evolving cultures closely intermingled, each an agent of change for the other. The reality for a long time to come is more likely to be two zones with two distinct ethnonational identities, though each may acquire a larger minority of the 'other'. Nobody can guess how fast or how completely the physical Green Line will be dismantled. It could be that Line-building is not yet finished, and shiny new fencing will mark out the areas the peace agreement transfers from the north to the jurisdiction of the south. It could be that the existing wire will rust on, with its new official crossing points cut through it. Or it may be that the physical line will be removed so that fields and country roads will flow back into each other, and the beautiful symmetry of Nicosia can be enjoyed again.

A partition may save lives, but it does so at a high cost. 'Partitions do not work as a solution to ethnic conflict. Rather, they restructure the sources of conflict around borders, refugees and diasporas,' wrote Radha Kumar (2000–01: 24). As they are distanced and separated, ethnicities grow more fixed, because there is no longer any necessity for day-to-day, face-to-face, negotiation of each collective identity in relation to the other. All possibility for mutual learning is lost. The world knows less about the effects of undoing partitions, but we can already feel the emotional turmoil being experienced by people of north and south as they venture into each other's space. Identities are being put into question in a way they have not been for twenty-nine years. As people revisit the lost half of their country and reconsider the past, their idea of themselves and the 'other' is being forced to shift. In a post-Partition Cyprus, for sure, new political bids will be made for people's allegiance and identification.

If the theories advanced in Chapter 1 of this book are right, such shifts in ethnic relations can be expected to bring change in gender relations, and may in part be brought about by such change. We get named with an ethnic name that has clear prescriptions for man and woman in it, and we get named as a woman or man of an unmistakably ethnic kind. As patriarchy and ethno-nationalism are partners in theory, sexism and racism are partners in practice. Stasis in one set of relations reinforces stasis in the other; change in one system can unlock change in the other. Women stepping out of line in terms of gender can be specially effective activists for change in the ethnic order. In this final chapter I explore what the experience of members of HAD and other women in Cyprus suggests for a women's movement that might be a collective actor in a future process of peace-making and social reconstruction. As we have seen, HAD did not prove able, in its first two years, to establish a collective vision. This was partly, but not only, due to the difficulties placed in its way by the Line. Other women I interviewed were equally hard-pushed to imagine and describe to me a future with any detail in it, and I think it may be symptomatic of oppression that the oppressor steals away the capability of imagining any other state of affairs. So in this chapter I try, on my own account, to do transversal politics. It is an exercise of situated imagining. I put myself in the shoes of HAD women and try to foresee what Maria had in mind when she spoke of 'a feminist intervention that would be *our* voice and *our* culture', and what Anthoula was thinking when she spoke of 'holism'.

A movement for change

On 31 October 2000, the United Nations Security Council passed a resolution, no. 1325, that was immediately hailed as a landmark by women worldwide. It urged member-states to 'ensure increased representation of women at all decision-making levels in national, regional and international institutions and mechanisms for the prevention, management and resolution of conflict'. It specifically called on 'all actors involved, when negotiating and implementing peace agreements, to adopt a gender perspective, including ... measures that support local women's peace initiatives and indigenous processes for conflict resolution, and that involve women in all of the implementation mechanisms of the peace agreements' (United Nations 2000).

The recent round of peace talks in Cyprus, between January 2002 and March 2003, like the many rounds that preceded them, involved principally two men, the leaders of the Republic and the TRNC, locked in single combat. They were supported by four others on each side, all of them male. The talks were hosted by the United Nations representative Alvaro de Soto and the only women present in the negotiating chamber were two of his staff. The Line is the property of men. One thing, however, was different in this round of talks: there was, especially in north Cyprus, a massive popular movement demonstrating noisily in Nicosia for a solution to the Cyprus problem. Civil society was demanding inclusion in the peace process. Among the organizations and individuals trying to influence the decision-makers from street level were many women, including, as we have seen, women of Hands Across the Divide.

Civil society in Cyprus is unlikely now to fade quietly into the background. More likely, popular demand will continue for a renewal of negotiations and for civil society on both sides of the Line, this time, to be included. The wide consultation process in Northern Ireland is already being cited as a precedent. Perhaps, in this moment of recovery and regrouping, women will begin to lodge demands for the implementation of UNSC Resolution 1325, with two aims. First, they may try to activate the resolution's call for women to be included

Demonstrations, 50,000 strong, organized by the political opposition in north Cyprus in January 2003, called on Rauf Denktaş to sign up to the UN peace proposals and normalize relations with Greek Cypriots. There were many girls and women among the demonstrators (below).

On the morning of 23 April 2003, the northern authorities astonished Cypriots both sides of the Partition Line by lifting the barrier at the checkpoint to allow unimpeded day crossings for the first time for twenty-nine years.

in the processes leading up to a peace agreement. Second, they may start to clarify what their actual input to peace negotiations would be – the substantive content of a post-Partition Cyprus that a women's gendered perspective foresees. For this to happen a coherent women's movement needs to develop. As I finished the fieldwork for this research I reviewed the material I had gathered and on that basis tried to imagine the kind of movement that would logically follow from women's situations. It would be, I guessed, one that actively challenges the male-dominant gender order – that is to say, a feminist movement.

A feminist movement. Here is a difficulty, however. Feminism has been turned into a dirty word by those who do not like to see women stepping out of line, claiming equality, behaving autonomously, creating a new politics. Unsurprisingly, a great many women, and not just in Cyprus, are reluctant to call themselves feminists. There is no consensus on this in HAD. Some women argue, though, that even if we do not take it on as an identity ('I am a feminist'), feminism is indispensable as a programme. However, to invoke 'feminism' is not enough, because there is not just one feminism, there are many, just as there are many versions of socialism or nationalism. And it is open to women, in each new political conjuncture, to distinguish between the different versions and choose the theory and political practice that seem relevant to them. We need concepts, thinking tools, that reflect our reality and serve our purpose. If my understanding of all I have picked up in these many conversations in Cyprus is correct, it will be a movement that is qualified by four terms: it will be holistic, transformative, prefigurative and inclusive.

A holistic movement. When Anthoula said that women's activism needed to be 'holistic', she made it clear she meant it should deal with 'women's issues', but not be limited to them. Our right and proper concern, *as women,* she was saying, is not just body politics, reproductive politics, questions of social welfare and so on, important as those things are; it is the whole spectrum of life, power and politics – including ethno-national strife. Patriarchy is deeply interconnected with other oppressive and exploitative structures. Capitalism, nationalism and patriarchy in particular are mutually supporting, so a critique of gender relations entails a simultaneous critique of the class order and the ethnic order.

A transformative feminism. Women's issues are sometimes addressed by an individualistic kind of feminism that is concerned with a

woman's equal access to the upper echelons of a world defined by
men. A more responsible and collective kind of feminism takes as
its concern the system itself, the systematic marginalization and im-
poverishment of many women, and how it has to change. Similarly,
whereas one kind of feminism sees 'men as the problem', another
sees that many men are themselves damaged by the system, because
it generates particular masculine cultures that, in forming boys into
men, deform them as human beings – in the same way as traditional
dichotomies also produce ridiculously restrictive versions of femininity. Transformative feminism sees patriarchy, not men, as the problem.
Men it sees as potentially part of the solution.

Prefigurative ways of working. Women of Hands Across the Divide,
like many others in women's organizations, say they like being a
women's group because they can 'do things differently' from the way
they are done in a world where men are in control. This means they
want women's issues (such as inequality, marginalization, the demands
of childcare, to name just three) to be tackled here and now in the
functioning of their own organization. What is the point, they ask, of
putting these things in the organization's mission statement if we run
the organization itself in the same old mainstream mode: some members more important than others, some heard while others stay silent,
no care taken to accommodate those with special needs. The ends
we are seeking should be made the means by which we try to reach
them. A prefigurative feminist politics must inevitably place everyday
life, with all its passions and concerns, within, not outside, politics. The
lengthy discussions in HAD about when a meeting may be scheduled
without seriously inconveniencing members' personal lives are not as
trivial as they might seem. Seeing personal life as a legitimate consideration in political life is a necessary part of a prefigurative movement.
Conversely, bringing the personal into politics does not mean abdi-
cating from 'politics with a big P'. What it means is that for women
the Cyprus problem is not 'something else', the thing you campaign
around when you are not 'doing women'. War is a women's issue.
Gender is a peace issue. HAD women engage with the unresolved
ethno-national war through their personal experiences and knowledge, not aside from them.

Inclusive feminism. In Cyprus it is clear that women are looking for
a feminism that can be yoked serviceably to the resolution of ethnic
and national tensions. In Western European feminist movements of the

1970s and 1980s, white women sometimes made the mistake of forgetting their own ethnic specificity, and, with it, forgetting how women of minority ethnic groups experience racism at the hands not only of white men but also of white women. It took many decades for feminists to begin to envision an inclusive theory and practice that could bring together the experiences, aspirations and strengths of women of different ethnic groups, different countries and different regions of the world. Cypriot feminists may be specially alert to ethnic oppression and hatred because they have experienced, from their different standpoints, ethno-national differentiation in such an extreme mode that it led to war and Partition. Yet, as things are, as Myria Vassiliadou points out (writing of the south), through excluding 'other' women, such as lesbians, ethnic minorities, immigrants and domestic workers from Asia and Eastern Europe, women tend to reproduce the values of traditional Cypriot identity to which they themselves have been subjugated as women (Vassiliadou 2003). For this reason a women's movement in Cyprus could scarcely avoid addressing identity, difference and inclusion as central issues for feminism.

Negotiating 'ethnic' identity

Even if the Green Line is dismantled, hugely symbolic as that might be, it will not mean the end of lines. Ethnic lines of some kind – not quite so dichotomous, perhaps, more plural, the hierarchies more complex – will continue to be drawn and redrawn in a future Cyprus. The revised ethnic lines may be less physical, less visible, than today's Partition Line, but they will have far-reaching effects for all that. They will be drawn in identity cards, citizenship and residence regulations, work permits, religious pronouncements, national school curricula and court rulings. The ethnic lines will be cut across, as always, by other lines – in particular the line drawn to differentiate and diminish women, which will continue to be sketched suggestively in every fashion advert, military training manual, vox-pop radio interview and pulp novel.

It could be useful to foresee shifts in this interlocking set of identities. What will matter to women pursuing an inclusive feminist politics is how divisive, inflexible and impermeable the new lines may be compared with the old, what they mean to those who have the power to operationalize them, what they imply for those who are named, shaped, differentiated and excluded by them. Experience in other countries caught up in ethno-national war has taught me that those who want to change 'othering' processes in their world unavoidably start with those in which they live, and on which they therefore have some purchase (Cockburn 1998). They work out carefully who they think they are in relation to each other; as women in relation to men; as bearers of this national name or that. They try to detect how each of us relates to the names we carry, 'Turkish Cypriot', let's say, and 'woman'. Are they something that must be respected as meaningful and enriching to us, part of our sense of self? Or are they something we are merely stuck with, fantasy productions imposed on us by the sales reps of patriarchy and nationalism? How can I find the part of your sense of who you are that is not threatening to my sense of who I am? Can I imagine you might change, I might change? Situated as we are on either side of a conflictual line, can we imagine a common future?

The principal ethnic identities propagated in Cyprus, bidding for people's loyalties, went through periods of flux in the 1960s, and again in 1974. Recently, again, they have been shifting in anticipation of an end to Partition. I heard a lot of women talk aloud about their sense of self in relation to given ethnic identities.

Greek/Greek Cypriot. There are fewer today than in 1974 who still cherish a belonging to Greece as 'motherland'. As you would expect, Efthymia and Andri, of the Independent Student Bastion with its political investment in Hellenism, are among those who do. When I asked them, 'Do you feel more Greek or more Cypriot?', Efthymia answered that Greek 'Cypriot' was a term that was introduced by the British rulers of the island. Before that they had always been unambiguously 'Greeks'. So even now, 'I would give exactly the same answer that you'd get if you asked a Cretan in Crete. Crete and Greece are the same thing. Cyprus and Greece are the same thing too. Every part of Greece has its particularity, and Cyprus is one particular part of Greece.' When I asked, 'Does the word "patriot" have a positive sound for you?', Efthymia answered, 'Of course, yes, but I would hesitate to use it of myself because I am not sure if I am worthy of the people who went before.'

This kind of identity lost its pulling power after 1974 when many Greek-identified people who had supported *enosis*, in addition to being alienated by the *junta*, blamed Greece for its failure to rescue them from the Turkish military. Popular 'Greekness' in Cyprus largely merged into the dual identity, 'Greek Cypriot', for whom the hated 'other' continued to be the Turk. Though modified, the identity remained powerfully nationalist and masculinist. 'The all-male, patriarchal authorities', wrote Myria Vassiliadou, 'have made open efforts to control women's actions in order to achieve their own ends; women's role in the nationalist movement has been significant as they symbolically promoted its interests, mainly ethnic survival' (Vassiliadou 2002: 462).

The experience of loss of home, theft of home, however, has been a point of entry into active nationalist politics for Greek Cypriot women, partly because, as we saw in Chapter 2, history has vested house-ownership in women. The concept of home mobilizes women around an intransigent 'all or nothing' politics of return, the redemption of their property rights in the north. Lia Georgiades told me that return is not a dream, it is *fated*: 'I can't explain it. We can't breathe. We can't breathe because we're living somewhere we feel we don't belong.' This is a painful identity to bear, not just because it sells out the present to the future, but because the future itself is unlikely to bring anything but disappointment. A place is always and only a place in time. Many of those who have taken the chance to cross the Line since the opening have been dismayed to find that time in passing has changed both the place and the returner. 'In this struggle for new ways of living more democratic relationships and new subjectivities,' wrote Jonathan Rutherford, '*there can be* no homecoming. Such a politics must be the discovery and *making* of home' (Rutherford 1990: 25, my italics).

Turk/Turkish Cypriot. As with Greek Cypriots, Turkish Cypriots vary in the stress they put on the two parts of the name. *Turkish* Cypriot is quite a distance from Turkish *Cypriot*. Some sit midway between the two, manifesting a comfortable duality. Latife Birgen, for instance says:

> I consider myself a Turkish Cypriot, because I was born here, brought up here and we have a culture of our own here. But I feel Turkish in the sense that I've been brought up with all the Turkish culture, everything concerning Atatürk, that period. My parents were interested in what was happening in Turkey, and I remember we had pictures of Turkish heroes on our walls during the war of independence ... Turkey is my motherland but Cyprus is my land and I feel Turkish Cypriot.

Some Turkish Cypriots still harbour a deep essentialist animosity for Greek Cypriots. Bahire remembers the horror on the face of a hospital technician when, during a blood shortage, she proposed using a donation of blood from the south for her thalassaemic son Reşat. Greek blood, how could you! The photographs in the official Museum of Barbarism in north Nicosia are spattered with blood, a reminder of what Rebecca Bryant said about the importance in Turkish Cypriot nationalist discourse of Turkish blood, spilled by Greeks on Cypriot soil (Bryant 2002). In the years following the Partition of Cyprus, however, Turkish Cypriots more or less turned their backs on the south, a process sealed by the creation of the TRNC in 1983. They have seen Greek Cypriots on TV, continued to mistrust them, but often enough they have forgotten they were there. Meanwhile, Turkish Cypriots are now divided between those for whom 'Greeks'/ 'Greek Cypriots', still there in the background, have remained the principal 'alien other' in their environment, against whom their group identity is constituted, and those among whom the latter have been replaced by the 'Turk'. Some left-wing women were emphatic in describing Turks to me as intruders, unwelcome instruments of the Denktaş regime.

Or (just) Cypriot? Many left-wing northerners today express their anti-Turkness as 'Cypriotness'. Rauf Denktaş provokes this kind of reaction when he habitually refers to 'his people' as part of the great Turkish nation, and warns them, 'If we are deceived into thinking we are Cypriots we shall boil in the Greek-Cypriot pot' (Dodd 1993b: 149). In the 1960s, Cypriot identity stalled as a project. In 1975 the New Cyprus Association attempted to revive it. Its founding document stated: 'Regardless of their national origins and despite all their real or fictitious differences, Cypriots have common characteristics, interests and aspirations, which determine their identity as Cypriots and which only they themselves can realise and protect' (Stamatakis 1991: 77).

Rita Pantazi remembers how in the late 1970s she and others were active in this nascent Cypriot movement: 'At that time in Cyprus all you would see were Greek flags. So we would go to the big rallies, you know, against the occupation, and we would be this little group of people, the only ones with Cypriot flags. There was nobody else then. They called us traitors.'

Today a Cypriotist movement links *rapprochement*-minded people of north and south. It has the fervour associated with a dissident and denied identity. Those who call themselves Cypriots are longing for reunification, waiting in the wings for history to call them onstage. It is not an ethno-nationalism of the Greek or Turkish kind, stressing purity of blood and descent. It does not dwell on historical roots but on historical change, representing Cyprus as a Mediterranean island whose people are a unique mix resulting from continual waves of invasion. Neriman, for instance, said: 'We are different, we are Cypriots. It's another culture. My story is here. I feel all the other nations who've been here, not only the Turks. Their cultures, the songs they wrote, their history. I feel it all! They're in my fingertips!'

It is an ethnic identity that looks more to the future than the past, imagining into being not a people with an identical origin but one with a common destiny (Yuval-Davis 1997). Being modernist, rather than atavistic, it offers scope for less traditional formulations of gender difference. Certainly, among the crowds demonstrating for a peace agreement in 2002–03 there has been a high proportion of women, many of them young.

Some of the women I spoke with longed for such a Cypriot identity, underpinned by constitutional reality. For some it seemed important to claim a place in a world of nation-states, especially within the European Union. For others, like Tina, brought up in London, it is something 'sacred', an antidote to the experience of racist exclusion in the diaspora:

> When I first came back, I didn't really fit. So I did everything in my power to become accepted here … In England I was a British citizen, I went to school there, you know, everything. But I didn't consider myself British, and a lot of people didn't consider me British. We supposedly came 'home' to Cyprus, which is where our roots are. And yet we're called 'Charlies' here … In England we're foreigners. In Cyprus we're foreigners. What are we – bastards?

Or a plague on all your houses? Some, on the contrary, wanted nothing to do with ethnic or national belonging. Mine Yücel, for instance, would agree with those theorists who see culture not so much as a real differentiator than as a 'dynamic contested resource', used by politicians (Yuval-Davis 1997: 32). She said:

> I'm not really concerned about losing my identity because I don't

really see culture as a binding thing … I feel like I'm a human being and I could live anywhere, provided my needs are met, like, I want to read the books I want to read, I want to say the things I want to say, and do the things I want to do. It's more, like, if it's a place I can't do the things I want to do, I wouldn't like to live there.

Some insisted their sense of self is made up of a myriad little attachments, a complex personhood. Arianna Economou, for instance:

It's all process, it's all being made. So how can I say, 'I'm this?' … There are lots of little 'I am's' … Oh yes, I can put them in order and say, 'I'm a mother, I'm a dancer, I'm a choreographer, I'm a teacher'. But perhaps in the end it's finding the confidence to stand up and say, 'This is me. Little or big, this is me. That's all there is.'

Neşe Yaşın is another who is deeply sceptical of identity politics. Twenty years ago Benedict Anderson gripped our minds with his perception that nation 'is an *imagined* political community' (Anderson 1983: 6, my italics). It depends entirely on enough people believing in it and having the technical and political resources to operationalize that belief. Neşe now uses this same language: 'I have a problem with identities, because they are pre-defined destinies. I believe nation is something imagined, not something real. People suffer a lot because of nation-states. I want the nation-state to disappear.'

Seeing that ethno-national identity threatened to capture her, Neşe tried to evade it by moving to the south, defying the idea that the proper place for a Turkish Cypriot is in north Cyprus. But the identity follows her around. 'Wherever I go, it goes with me.' Aspects of womanhood for her have been almost as constraining. Her biography is the story of ultra-demanding expectations of her as daughter, sister and mother. Finally, she has had to reject, painfully and at a cost, every one of the given, available or compulsory identities. 'I rebelled against the whole lot!'

Who is the new Cypriot?
Is she a woman? The big question facing a group of activist women such as Hands Across the Divide, then, is, What is 'Cypriot' to mean in future? First and foremost, is a Cypriot a *woman*? Is the new identity as much feminine as masculine? Or does it come with the same old gender line built in? When it comes to 'citizenship', women have

often been short-changed. From the eighteenth century onwards, the citizen endowed with 'his' designated rights and responsibilities has been conceived as a man (Lister 1997). It has been a struggle for women everywhere to get the notion of citizen fleshed out as both a woman and a man. Getting the vote for women was only the first step.

I noted above that the Northern Ireland peace agreement is sometimes invoked in considering peace for Cyprus. In the negotiations that led up to it, 'equality' in place of minority status was a principle for Catholics as it is for Turkish Cypriots in Cyprus now. The Irish agreement, and the consultation papers preparing it, had a great deal to say about social inclusion, equality and fairness. The first meaning in the minds of the negotiators was clearly ethnic and religious equality. But women's organizations took up the language, insisting that equality was indivisible. A new Northern Ireland must, they said, guarantee inclusion and fair treatment for all marginalized groups, including those disadvantaged on grounds of gender, marital status, having or not having a dependant, disability, age and sexual orientation (Women Working for Change 1996). It is likely that some women in Cyprus will call for a peace constitution to instal equality with this same encompassing meaning. Netha, when I interviewed her, stressed that equality for women must be part of the peace:

> When I say equality, I envision that everyone whoever they are, living on this island, as a human being has the same rights. A woman, a man, a Maronite, a Turkish Cypriot, whoever. Women are very much a minority here. You don't have a women's voice. Especially in the peace process, and in all of the important institutions of government. We're half the population, but we don't have even a quarter of the voice.

Secondly, in what mode, and in relation to whom, are the new *ethnic* lines likely to be drawn? What is to become of relations between Greek Cypriot and Turkish Cypriot? This will probably be heavily determined by how much life can be breathed into the new unifying constitution. If the two entities keep their backs turned to each other, each hugging its culture as a guarantee of difference and superiority, there will be no reconciliation, merely settlement. 'Cypriot' will remain empty of meaning. But if the all-Cyprus con/federal administration, by popular will as much as by legal arrangements, is invested with real authority, then Cypriot identity might become a strong new reality.

Who else, however, beyond Turkish Cypriot and Greek Cypriot women and men, is 'Cypriot' intended to include? Nobody is in any doubt that the small, ancient Armenian, Maronite and Latin minorities of Cyprus are included in. Roma, here as elsewhere in Europe are not regarded very warmly, but they can hardly after so many centuries be seen as non-belongers. A large question mark, however, hangs over two groups which, although their presence on the island differs in political and economic significance, are growing in number and cannot be quietly ignored. They are Turks in the north, and Asians and other immigrants in the south.

New Cypriot or alien other? The Turks of north Cyprus As we saw in Chapter 4, possibly 50,000 inhabitants of northern Cyprus (the number is disputed) were born of Turkish parents either in Turkey or in Cyprus and now hold TRNC citizenship, which of course includes the right to vote. There are also many more who are temporary residents on the island, including workers and students. As we saw, too, the flow of immigrants has not been politically innocent – it has been to some extent engineered by the authorities, and is certainly welcomed by the right as making north Cyprus more unquestionably Turkish, swelling its population in relation to the south, and enhancing Turkish control. In the circumstances it is not surprising that some Turkish Cypriots feel a profound animosity towards the Turks on the island. They sometimes express it in startlingly racist terms. It is the left of the political spectrum in the north that is predominantly anti-Turk, and indeed people who feel this way often vote for opposition parties precisely because they call for a stop to Turkish immigration and for a policy of 'return'.

When the 41 Organizations, and their supporters in the south, adopted the slogan 'This Country is Ours', they were intending specifically to tell Turkey, 'hands off!' But some women in Hands Across the Divide were already hesitating and asking themselves, 'Who exactly is "us"?' In Chapter 1, I discussed alternative modes of differentiation, choice in the way the other is defined in relation to the self. Not so long ago the leaders of Turkish Cypriots and Greek Cypriots were respectively promoting identities for which the other was an evil alter-ego. Now there are versions of 'Turkish Cypriot' and 'Greek Cypriot' that, espousing Cypriotism, define each other in democratic, complementary mode. Antagonism has become agonism.

It is a huge step forwards. But simultaneously, for both of them, a new antagonistic and hateful other has come to be defined as the not-self.

A Greek Cypriot woman told me 'the settlers moved once to a country that didn't belong to them. If we give them a lot of money, they can move again. They ought to love Turkey, it's their country.' Possibly southerners have been able to sustain such an unambiguous view because, till very recently, they did not meet the Turks in question and could avoid considering the human factor. Turkish Cypriots on the whole feel anxious about the implications. It seems too much like ethnic cleansing to call for the return of tens of thousands of Turks to Anatolia. They look for ways out of a seriously painful dilemma: they do not wish to be unjust, but they do wish to enjoy north Cyprus, their small and hard-won space, as a country for 'ourselves'. Many of those who have moved to Cyprus from Turkey are less urbanized than Turkish Cypriots, and more religious. Some Turkish Cypriots believe them responsible for bringing petty crime to Cyprus. Yet at the same time their natural sense of fair play reminds them that Turks are humans too. Gediz Inan said:

> I have two feelings fighting in me. If I listen to my heart I think
> – some of them have lived here thirty years. Their children have
> grown up here. Some have married Cypriots. It isn't humane to tell
> them to 'go home'. I couldn't do it. But the situation we're in makes
> me feel differently. We're under the political and military control of
> Turkey. The Turkish settlers are used against us. That's why I feel badly
> towards them.

It is a distressingly difficult political and humanitarian problem. Many approach it by deconstructing 'the Turkish settler' into acceptable and unacceptable categories. For example, there are the original wave of migrants, now naturalized, who might stay, while the newcomers should 'go home'. Or the honest and hard-working might stay, but the criminals should go. There is the loyalty test: do they love this country, or not? Alternatively (and here class prejudice slips into the picture), it is Turkish business people, students, those with qualifications and good jobs who are acceptable, while the unskilled who arrive with little money and few prospects have no right to be here. Others remark the irony: these are the very people who are needed to do low-paid labouring jobs, and also the ones compassion would say most deserve any opportunity Cyprus can offer.

The 'settler' phenomenon is deeply gendered. One additional reason some Turkish Cypriot women resent the Turks among them is that many are still tied into religion and the patriarchal family, while they themselves have long been secular and, in terms of family practices, increasingly 'modernized'. Turkish women are, it is said, dominated by their husbands, obliged to cover their heads, not allowed to speak freely. Turkish women spend a lot of time at home, while Turkish men spend a lot of theirs on the street. Especially in the towns one is continually aware of clusters of Turkish men in public spaces. Many look rough, dark and unshaven because they work out of doors in all seasons, while the majority of Turkish Cypriots today are urbanized desk workers. Some Turkish Cypriot women feel them to be a threatening masculine presence because they stare at women in a sexist way that Turkish Cypriot men have learned to avoid.

It is a classic instance of the intersection of identity, position and values. Some Turkish Cypriot and Turkish women might share political values and in other circumstances might look to find what they have in common. In this case, a difference of position in the social and political structure holds them apart. Sevgül is one of few Turkish Cypriot journalists who have been at pains to meet and interview Turkish migrants. She found they do not regard themselves as the unitary group Turkish Cypriots see them as being. Many identify less with Turkey than with the particular region from which they come. They do not all, by any means, agree with the right-wing political parties and the deep state whose agents they are supposed to be. Many feel insecure, lacking the deeds that would give them ownership of homes they have lived in for years. They hear rumours they will be deported. Sevgül concluded that many of them are not so much beneficiaries as victims in the TRNC. Below I represent, from my interviews, three women to whom a non-inclusive feminism would be blind, and to whom a non-inclusive Cypriot identity would deny a belonging they say they need.

Mürüvet Mürüvet, aged twenty, is a Kurd. She lives in a village on the central plain of north Cyprus and is a student at the Eastern Mediterranean University. Her father was an economic migrant who brought his family to Cyprus when Mürüvet was four. They came from the Kurdish area of eastern Turkey, a region seriously deprived of employment, hospitals, schools and other services, because the government

Dress is a differentiating factor among some women in north Cyprus. Münevver, born in Turkey, prefers to wear head cover on working days, though she sometimes removes it for social occasions. Neşe (right) born in Cyprus, is a seamstress and dresses the brides of Famagusta for their 'white weddings'.

discriminates against the Kurdish minority, with whom it is in conflict.

Mürüvet has a good social life in the university, a lot of fun. She contrasts her acceptance there with her rejection by children in the village when she first arrived. She didn't understand why they didn't want to play with her. Now, when her family talk of 'going back one day', Mürüvet resists. She feels she might well be considered a Cypriot after sixteen years living in the village. She and her family can speak just as easily in the Turkish of Anatolia or the dialect of Cyprus, they cook both Kurdish and Turkish Cypriot food. Although her parents are practising Sunni Muslims, she herself is not observant. She says she looks around her at the beautiful world spoiled by war and finds she cannot believe in a god. She is aware, though, that she has the option of wearing jeans and T-shirts only because she is a student. Her friends in the village are all covered.

It is hurtful to Mürüvet that Turkish Cypriots were grateful to Turkey for 'saving them' in 1974, yet now they say 'go home'. She is sad that Cypriot people do not distinguish between Turks and Kurds, and feels Kurdish people are invisible in Cyprus. And she feels politically immobilized, unable to be active either in Kurdish or in Cypriot affairs because of being under surveillance by both governments. But she would like to see the reunification of Cyprus, and to live on the island as a Cypriot among other Cypriots.

Münevver As a child, Münevver lived in a village in Anatolia, where the family kept sheep, while her father worked in a coffee shop in town. He decided to bring his family to Cyprus when Münevver was thirteen. She remembers coming at night in a crowded boat, to a big reception building. They were allocated an empty (Greek Cypriot) flat and her father opened a café. It was a different, urban, more modern life. In the village Münevver had been used to baking the bread and making the cheese. She had pretty much missed out on schooling. Now in Famagusta she was the one to stay in the flat and do the housework, until, at fifteen, she broke with her parents to marry the boy of her choice. She packed oranges for a while. Now she works as a cleaner, and her husband is on social security.

Whereas Münevver was one of seven children and her husband one of ten, they themselves have chosen to have only two, for a better quality of life. Her daughter graduated from university and now teaches in high school. Her son is a soldier, a trumpeter in the military orchestra. She aspires to be a friend to her children, in contrast to her own mother's relationship with her. Turkish families are modernizing, she says. When I met her Münevver, now aged forty, was wearing a neat white embroidered headscarf. But on the sideboard was a recent photograph that showed an alternative and sharply contrasted self: she is at a wedding, wearing a short skirt and bright satin blouse. She has a striking head of hair and is wearing make-up. This duality is part of her sense of who she is. 'That was a wedding,' she said, 'and this is my daily life.' When I asked Münevver if she felt Turkish or Cypriot she said, 'Since I haven't forgotten my past, but I'm living here, it's both.' She and her family think of Turkey as a place to go for a holiday.

Leyla Leyla X, thirty-eight, is a schoolteacher and an active trade unionist. She was born to a prosperous family in Samsun, on the Black Sea coast of Turkey. After studying English linguistics at Ankara University, she married a Turkish Cypriot man, a civil servant, and has a school-age son. She came to Cyprus fourteen years ago. It is perhaps her Marxist Leninist analysis that makes her feel no need of any particular ethnic identity. She sees herself as rather unrooted and foot-loose, and says, 'It doesn't make any difference where you live. It's how you live and with whom, that's what matters.'

Leyla believes the proper thing would have been for Turkey to have helped the TRNC to independence, and then relaxed its hold on the island. She disapproves of Denktaş's policy of favouring inward migration from Turkey, but equally she deplores the racism against Turks in Cyprus. It hurts her to hear Turkish Cypriots make the assumption that any reported crime must have been committed by a *karasakal*, a 'blackbeard'. She sympathizes with the Turkish Cypriot opposition and the movement for reunification of Cyprus. She says, 'I understand that they want to be recognized as Cypriots. But it's going a little bit further than needed, I think. It's becoming a Cypriot nationalism.'

New Cypriot or alien other? Asian immigrants in the south In north Cyprus the jobs that Turkish Cypriots are no longer willing to do are done by Turkish migrants. Many Turkish Cypriot women free themselves from domestic chores by employing Turkish women like Münevver. We saw in Chapter 5 how a shortfall in unskilled manual labour in the south is similarly filled by Sri Lankan, Filipina and Thai immigrants with five-year work permits, and how other economic possibilities are being exploited by impoverished people from Eastern Europe. Women of the Immigrant Support Action group, in interview, told me there are around 25,000 economic migrants with work permits in south Cyprus. 'Informal' migration may bring the total to 40,000. The total population of south Cyprus is around 660,000.

I heard a good deal of resentment and racism against Asians, a rather visible minority, mainly of working age. They include a high proportion of young women, who are to be seen riding their scooters around the streets of Nicosia and walking their employers' dogs. Athena Z said:

> We have the Filipinas and the Sri Lankans and the Russians – we don't like it. If you go back fifteen years, you wouldn't have found anyone that wasn't Cypriot, Turkish Cypriot or British … I mean, I'm not, it's not that I dislike them personally. I have a Filipina girl here, for the house. They are fine, they're OK. But when I go for a walk on a Sunday morning, downtown, by Paphos Gate, you don't see a single Cypriot there; it's like another country. It is when they have their day off, they have a bazaar there [she sighed, and laughed]. We were not used to this kind of thing. I don't like what I see; it's like I'm not in Cyprus. I walk the streets I walked before and it's like somebody has intruded into our space.

Others hesitated to draw such a trenchant line between 'us' and 'them'. Rita, for instance, reminded me that many Cypriots have travelled the world in just this way, searching for a better chance in life, experiencing racism. She pointed out that many Cypriots feel unready for their as yet scarcely-established Cypriot identity to embrace such a huge foreign element. She said:

> I can definitely understand the concerns of people who say, you know: 'How many people are going to be influxing here?' I would like there to be some kind of controlled immigration, so that we would not completely lose the identity of Cypriots, once we gain it. Because at the moment we haven't got it … We have been suffering so long. I want to be Cypriot with Cypriots first.

Entry into the European Union, of course, is going to change the parameters of immigration law. There is scarcely anyone in south Cyprus who has not wanted Cyprus to join, but that is mainly because of its bearing on the Cyprus problem. In terms of European legislation, many have reservations. A particular worry is that, while jobs all over Europe will open up to Cypriots, Cyprus could in turn find itself hosting many foreigners. Since countries on the European mainland are more and more ethnically mixed, many of the new-comers may be expected to be neither white nor Christian. If Turkey is admitted to the EU at some time in the future, Turks too will have a right of residence throughout Cyprus.

Anthoula Papadopoulou, who is active in the Immigrant Support Action Group as well as in HAD, longs to open up Cypriot society to a genuine multiculturalism. More than mere tolerance, what she would like to see is full acceptance of people for who they are, regard-less of the shade of their skin, the colour of their hair or their religion. She supports an open door policy, on the grounds that economic migration is self-regulatory. She helped me meet some of the women whose life choices would be enhanced by an inclusive definition by the Cypriot state of who is a 'Cypriot' and by the European Union of who is a 'European'.

Angela Angela (the name is a pseudonym) is a Filipina. She has already, by changing her name and other means, managed to stay in Cyprus for thirteen years. During those years she has worked unremittingly hard. Out of compassion, she organizes shelter for im-migrant girls and women forced to run away from their employers. Her daughter and son-in-law are now here as immigrant workers and she badly wants them to be able to stay. All three have ongoing strug-gles with the immigration authorities.

Rebecca Rebecca is also a Filipina, a qualified midwife who left her five daughters in the care of her mother while she came to earn money to pay for their upbringing and education. She is the woman (see Chapter 5) who was raped by her employer's friend. She battled to use the law to bring him to justice, refusing to be bought off. She would like to work at the occupation for which she is trained, but there is no possibility under present circumstances of acquiring the additional certification she would need.

Joyce Joyce has worked abroad for many years as a domestic, first in Hong Kong then in Cyprus, while her husband looked after their four children back in the Philippines. Then he started a new family

Thousands of migrants from the Philippines, Thailand and Sri Lanka have come to south Cyprus seeking employment. Many are young women, working as domestics. On Sundays, their one day off, they spread their picnics on the grass of the moat under the Venetian walls of old Nicosia (top left).

with another woman. That he would take a lover, she could accept. But he had promised: no more children. Now her marriage has broken down. She has found a new relationship in Cyprus, with 'a foreigner' like herself. She badly wants to stay and lives in continual fear of deportation.

Mal Mal has achieved what the others long for. Aged thirty-nine, she was a government teacher of English in Sri Lanka. She came to Cyprus where she worked long hours for a seriously unpleasant and disrespectful employer. Eventually she married a Greek Cypriot. Her son, now nineteen, has been able to join her. She at last has a job worthy of her skills, working as a court interpreter, and she feels her future in Cyprus is secure. She will be a Sri Lankan Cypriot.

The Immigrant Support Action Group welcome EU accession because they believe European law may protect Asian immigrants like Angela, Rebecca, Joyce and Mal from some abuses to which they are currently subject. Human rights and democracy, they feel, are more securely embedded in the EU than in Cyprus. It may open up more possibility of eventual citizenship for migrants, and family reunification. Nevertheless, the Schengen agreement that co-ordinates control of immigrants is a tough regime. It is what gives Europe its reputation as a 'fortress' defended against the poorer world (Papadopoulou 2001).

Values versus identity

So, more and less inclusive ways of imagining the identity 'Cypriot' are already evident, even before the peace agreement is signed that could give such an identity a place and time in which to ground itself. 'This Island is Ours' for most Cypriots inevitably and understandably means fulfilment of the destined union of Greek Cypriot and Turkish Cypriot identities. Bi-communalists in Cyprus have sacrificed a great deal for this over the years. Yet some admit there is a danger that the Partition Line of today could be replaced by an equally exclusive fence thrown around the island shore, so that those within are all one of a kind (albeit a duality, bilingual), while others are refused citizenship. If the national identity were to be defined in such a way it is unlikely that there would be any democratizing of relations within, such as those of gender. The result could be one more small sea-bounded, inward-looking, male-dominated community, holding tight to its national identity in a world of nation-states. The geographical fact of being a island, with a 'natural' boundary, fosters this kind of closure.

Some Cypriots would welcome such a future because their greatest worry is lack of an identifiable place to belong to. Their not unreasonable fear is that their Mediterranean island will become a centre of unregulated enterprise, an abstract set of co-ordinates in a global system of military supply lines and economic flows. In such a future, the word 'Cyprus' would not designate a nation, nor even a country, merely a flag of convenience. The knowledge that Cyprus has been traversed by a stream of different peoples for at least 9,000 years fosters this kind of fear.

A key issue Cypriot women such as those of Hands Across the Divide find themselves faced with is whether Cyprus and Cypriotness could mean something different from, and better than, either of these alternatives. Could it be a society that, in being gender-equal and woman-centred, brings other surprises as well?

One thing is now clear about the future: Cyprus (unified or still divided) will become a member of the EU in 2004. That makes it somehow easier to see Cyprus as a microcosm of Europe. The Partition Line that divides a supposedly Christian from a supposedly Muslim region of Cyprus is a shadow of the more ancient and problematic line that passes through the Bosphorus and separates a supposedly Christian Europe from a supposedly Muslim Turkey and Middle East. Those of us, wherever in Europe we live, who want the continent to be more than a closed, white Christian club have almost as much interest in the healing of Cyprus as a Cypriot does. Likewise, those of us who are afraid of exclusive, purity-minded ethnonationalisms and see in the encounter and mixing of different cultures an exciting source of creativity, may learn a lot from Cyprus, as and when its cold war ends. The balancing act of Cypriots trying to enjoy the gains of *rapprochement* or reunification without diving into a new exclusive nationalism will be very much the same balancing act in which a unifying Europe tries to work out its relation to the teeming, diverse, alarming possibilities of the world outside its frontiers.

At the same time, both as women in Cyprus, and as women living elsewhere in Europe, we have a problem of political choice. Those of us who think of ourselves as inclusive feminists are up against both the states we live in and their internal opposition. We have to struggle against the racist immigration and citizenship policies of the nation-states. But we also, more distressingly, find ourselves at odds with the political movements that we might aspire to be part of. The problems encountered with the opposition movements are of three kinds. Some of them fall into the trap of essentialist 'identity politics'. They assume that a 'name' means something real, that those of us who carry it all identify with it, and that it gives us a guaranteed common interest. They appeal to us, 'Workers unite!', 'Muslims unite!', 'Cypriots unite!' Life, on the contrary, teaches us every day that any such name is no more than a label attached to a ragbag of different things, each implying a different politics.

Other movements, including both men and women, are antiracist and oppose nationalist constructions of identity. Yet they are gender-blind, unresponsive to what feminists have been saying: that the way we construct ethno-national identities cannot be changed without changing the way we construct gender identities. Ethnic othering and gender othering occur simultaneously. Dichotomies are catching. Patriarchal gender relations sustain a nationalist ethnic order. Nationalisms tie women into the patriarchal bargain. In this sense an antiracist politics that is not also antisexist, and vice versa, is nonsense. It literally does not make sense.

Thirdly, 'our' movements opposing militarism and war too often ignore the kind of feminist perspective proposed in this book. How can we oppose war without opposing contemporary gender constructions? It is because our societies draw a gender line and place on the outer side (among people we call women) the values of nurture, tenderness and care that they can bring into being on the inner side of the line a category of people (we call them men) who are capable of being schooled into thinking that killing, and being killed, in the name of nation is the ultimate badge of honour and manhood.

So we find ourselves having to be ultra-clear-headed about where we look to find allies. We cannot rely on the identities created by 'lines' to name our allies (and 'enemies') for us. It is not every Turkish Cypriot that a Greek Cypriot can find common cause with, or vice versa – though common cause might be found around a shared economic or social policy. It is not every woman we can find common cause with – womanhood is not a solid basis for a politics of change. But feminism, if carefully defined, can be. It is only by really knowing what our values are, being clear in our own heads and explicit to others, that we can know with whom we can and cannot work. But, and this is the extraordinary gift, such clarity enables us to see partners we might never have thought of – the ones who look different from us, maybe. The ones we thought were too far away to reach. The ones we never noticed because they had been made invisible.

Meantime, as we have seen, there are signs of crisis in the gender order in Cyprus, as elsewhere in Europe. The ideal site for the reproduction of different and unequal genders (proper man, proper woman, proper heterosexual relations) was the traditional patriarchal family. The process was never wholly successful. There was always a credibility gap between what was ideally proposed (a neat dichotomy) and what really exists (deviation and diversity). Now control is slipping rather badly. Capitalist consumerism at times inadvertently undermines it. Daughters glimpsing a new way of living slip the parental leash. When marriage disappoints women, as it often does, they are more likely these days to walk away from it. Yet male dominance, as we have also seen, is adapting to the new times and being massively reproduced. The old masculinist structures are still there – state, military, business. They will persist unless and until men in large numbers default from the current gender order.

Everywhere, though, there are women ready to expose the fraudulence, injustice and violence of the gender order. And in organizing against what Kate Millett long ago called this 'most pernicious of our systems of oppression … and its sick delirium of power and violence', they are taking on those other systems of oppression to which it is indissolubly tied (Millett 1971: 22). Fortunately, there is always a new generation of women willing, even if they sometimes feel themselves a lonely minority, to organize around a feminist programme. Many are sure that the best source of strength for the future is on the one hand the inclusion of women of different cultures living in the same national space, and, on the other, alliances between women living in different regions of the world. HAD's meeting with WINPEACE showed that in Greece and Turkey there are women's movements that, were they more in touch with the changing aspirations of Cypriot women, could be helpful allies. In Cyprus besides, Cypriot women could draw strength from partnership with Filipina women who, after all, come from a country with one of the oldest, biggest and boldest women's movements in the world. They could find something in common with Sri Lankan women, because they too have experienced ethnicized civil war, displacement and attempted partition, and women's organizations in Sri Lanka actively worked for a peace agreement.

Conversely, those of us in other European countries working out tactics for opposing militarism and war have a lot to learn from the experience of women making a bid for peace in Cyprus. Imperialism, nationalism, patriarchy – these are not things of the past. Their weaponry grows more devastating year by year. As I drafted this chapter in the spring of 2003, the USA and Britain were preparing to fly their war planes to Baghdad. Some of us were acutely aware at that moment of the urgent need for effective working alliances between women of Western Europe and that not-so-other, not-so-distant Middle East. Cypriot women could not be better placed to make such links.

References

Anderson, B. (1983) *Imagined Communities*. London and New York: Verso.

Anthias, F. (1989) 'Women and Nationalism in Cyprus', in N. Yuval-Davis and F. Anthias (eds), *Woman–Nation–State*. London: Macmillan.

——(1992) *Ethnicity, Class, Gender and Migration*. Aldershot: Avebury.

Anthias, F. and N. Yuval-Davis (1989) 'Introduction', in N. Yuval-Davis and F. Anthias (eds), *Woman–Nation–State*. London: Macmillan.

——(1992) *Racialized Boundaries*. London and New York: Routledge.

Bacchi, C. L. (1990) *Same Difference: Feminism and Sexual Difference*. Sydney and London: Allen and Unwin.

Bahcheli, S. (2003) 'Study "Sees Truth of the Maligned Turk"', *Cyprus Today*, 24–30 May.

Balibar, E. (1991) 'Is There a Neoracism?', in E. Balibar and I. Wallerstein (eds), *Race, Nation and Class*. London: Verso.

Berdahl, D. (1999) *Where the World Ended: Re-Unification and Identity in the German Borderland*. Berkeley: University of California Press.

Berger, J. (1972) *Ways of Seeing*. London: BBC and Penguin Books.

Bolger, D. (2002) 'Gender and Mortuary Ritual in Chalcolithic Cyprus', in D. Bolger and N. Serwint (eds), *Engendering Aphrodite: Women and Society in Ancient Cyprus*, CAARI Monographs Vol. 3. Boston, MA: American Schools of Oriental Research.

Brah, A. (1996) *Cartographies of Diaspora: Contesting Identities*. London: Routledge.

Brah, A., M. J. Hickman and M. Mac an Ghaill (1999) 'Thinking Identities: Ethnicity, Racism and Culture', in A. Brah, M. J. Hickman and M. Mac an Ghaill (1999) *Thinking Identities: Ethnicity, Racism and Culture*. Basingstoke: Macmillan.

Brannon, L. (1999) *Gender: Psychological Perspectives*. London: Allyn and Bacon.

Brewin, C. (2000), *The European Union and Cyprus*. Huntingdon, Cambridge: Eothen Press.

Broome, B. J. (1997) 'Designing a Collective Approach to Peace: Interactive Design and Problem-Solving Workshops with Greek-Cypriot and Turkish-Cypriot Communities in Cyprus', *International Negotiation*, 2: 381–407.

Bryant, R. (2002) 'The Purity of Spirit and the Power of Blood: A Comparative Perspective on Nation, Gender and Kinship in Cyprus', *Journal of the Royal Anthropological Institute* (N.S.), 8: 509–30.

Bunimovitz, S. and A. Yasur-Landau (2002) 'Women and Aegean Immigration to Cyprus in the 12th Century BCE', in D. Bolger and N. Serwint (eds), *Engendering Aphrodite: Women and Society in Ancient Cyprus*. CAARI Monographs Vol. 3. Boston, MA: American Schools of Oriental Research.

Butalia, U. (2000) *The Other Side of Silence: Voices from the Partition of India*. London: Hurst and Co.

Butler, J. (1990) *Gender Trouble: Feminism and the Subversion of Identity*. New York: Routledge.

Byman, D. L. (1997) 'Divided They Stand: Lessons about Partition from Iraq and Lebanon', *Security Studies*, 7, Part 1: 1–29.

Catselli, R. (1975) *Refugee in my Homeland*. Nicosia: Chrysopolitissa Editions.

Close, D. H. (2002) *Greece since 1945: Politics, Economy, Society*. London: Pearson Education.

Cockburn, C. (1991) *In the Way of Women:*

Men's Resistance to Sex Equality in Organizations. London: Macmillan.

—(1998) *The Space Between Us: Negotiating Gender and National Identities in Conflict*. London and New York: Zed Books.

Cockburn, C. and L. Hunter (1999) 'Transversal Politics and Translating Practices', *Soundings: A Journal of Politics and Culture*, 12: 88–93.

Connell, R. W. (1987) *Gender and Power*. Cambridge: Polity Press.

—(2002) *Gender*. Cambridge: Polity Press.

Connolly, W. E. (1991) *Identity/Difference: Democratic Negotiations of Political Paradox*. Ithaca, NY, and London: Cornell University Press.

Constantinou, C. M. and Y. Papadakis (2001) 'The Cypriot State(s) *in situ*: Cross-ethnic Contact and the Discourse of Recognition', *Global Society*, 15(2): 125–48.

Cyprus Social Research Centre (1975) *Cypriot Woman, Rise and Downfall*. Nicosia.

Cyprus Weekly (2003a) Menelaos Hadjicostas, 'Turks Expel Prelate from Morphou Church', 16–22 May.

—(2003b) Demetra Molyva, 'Business Doubles for Cabarets and Hotels in the North', 2–8 May.

de Beauvoir, S. (1972) *The Second Sex* [1949]. Harmondsworth: Penguin Books.

Diamond, L. and R. J. Fisher (1995) 'Integrating Conflict Resolution Training and Consultation: A Cyprus Example', *Negotiation Journal*, 11: 287–301.

Dodd, C. H. (1993a) 'Historical Introduction', in C. H. Dodd (ed.), *The Political, Social and Economic Development of Northern Cyprus*. Huntingdon: Eothen Press.

— (1993b) 'The Ascendancy of the Right, 1985–1993', in C. H. Dodd (ed.), *The Political, Social and Economic Development of Northern Cyprus*. Huntingdon: Eothen Press.

—(1998) *The Cyprus Imbroglio*. Huntingdon: Eothen Press.

Donald, J. and A. Rattansi (1992) 'Introduction', in J. Donald and A. Rattansi (eds) *'Race', Culture and Difference*. London: Sage Publications.

Dudink, S. (2002) 'The Unheroic Men of a Moral Nation: Masculinity and Nation in Modern Dutch History', in C. Cockburn and D. Zarkov (eds), *The Postwar Moment: Militaries, Masculinities and International Peacekeeping*. London: Lawrence and Wishart.

Durrell, L. (1957) *Bitter Lemons*. London: Faber and Faber.

Ehrlich, T. (1974) *Cyprus 1958–1967*. Oxford: Oxford University Press.

Eisler, R. (1987) *The Chalice and the Blade: Our History, Our Future*. London: Unwin Hyman.

Enloe, C. (1993) *The Morning After: Sexual Politics at the End of the Cold War*. Berkeley: University of California Press.

— (2000) *Maneuvers: The International Politics of Militarizing Women's Lives*. Berkeley: University of California Press.

Ertekün, N. M. (1981) *The Cyprus Dispute and the Birth of the Turkish Republic of Northern Cyprus*. Nicosia: K. Rüstem and Brothers.

Fausto-Sterling, A. (2000) *Sexing the Body: Gender Politics and the Construction of Sexuality*. New York: Basic Books.

Fine, R. and S. Rai (eds) (1997) *Civil Society: Democratic Perspectives*. London and Portland, OR: Frank Cass.

Firestone, S. (1979) *The Dialectic of Sex: The Case for Feminist Revolution* [1971]. London: Women's Press.

Goodwin, J. (1999) *Lords of the Horizons: A History of the Ottoman Empire*. London: Vintage.

Gramsci, A. (1971) *Selections from the Prison Notebooks*. London: Lawrence and Wishart.

Groom, A. J. R. (1993) 'The Process of Negotiation 1974–1993', in C. H. Dodd (ed.), *The Political, Social and Economic Development of Northern Cyprus*. Huntingdon: Eothen Press.

Gülçür, L. and P. Ilkkaracan (2002) 'The

"Natasha" Experience: Migrant Sex Workers from the Former Soviet Union and Eastern Europe in Turkey', *Women's Studies International Forum*, 25(4): 411–22.

Güven-Lisaniler, F. (forthcoming 2003) *Assessing the Status of Women, a Step towards Equality: Gender Profile in Employment and Education, North Cyprus*. Nicosia: Turkish Cypriot University Women's Association.

Güven-Lisaniler, F. and L. Rodriguez (2002) 'The Social and Economic Impact on North Cyprus of Accession to the European Union', in Thomas Diez (ed.), *The European Union and Cyprus: Modern Conflict, Postmodern Union*. Manchester: Manchester University Press.

Güven-Lisaniler, F. and S. Uğural (2002) 'Occupational Segregation: The Position of Women in the North Cyprus Labor Market', *Kadın / Woman*, II(1). Eastern Mediterranean University, Famagusta, Cyprus.

Hadjipavlou-Trigeorgis, M. (2001a) 'Cypriot Women's Contribution to Conflict Resolution: Successes and Limitations', paper presented to the conference on 'Women, Conflict Resolution and Democratization', Council of Europe, Commission of Equality between Men and Women, Strasbourg, 19–21 September.

— (2001c) 'The Contribution of Bi-communal Contacts in Building a Civil Society in Cyprus', in A. Eagly, R. Baron and V. L. Hamilton (eds), *The Social Psychology of Group Identity and Social Conflict: Theory, Application and Practice*. Report of a conference in honour of Professor Herbert Kelman, November, Manhattan Beach, CA: APA Publishers.

— (2002) 'Cyprus: A Partnership between Peace Education and Conflict Resolution', in G. Salomon and N. Baruch (eds), *Peace Education: The Concept, Principles and Practices around the World*. Mahwah, NJ: Lawrence Erlbaum.

— (forthcoming) 'Cypriot Citizens' Reconciliation Efforts: A Critical Appraisal', in A. Ackerman (ed.), *Reconciliation in Global Perspective: Theory and Practice*. Baltimore: Johns Hopkins University Press.

Hall, S. (1996) 'Introduction: Who Needs Identity?', in S. Hall and P. du Gay (eds), *Questions of Cultural Identity*. London, Thousand Oaks and New Delhi: Sage Publications.

Haraway, D. (1991) *Simians, Cyborgs and Women: The Reinvention of Nature*. London: Free Association Books.

Hart, E. and M. Bond (1995) *Action Research for Health and Social Care: A Guide to Practice*. Buckingham and Philadelphia: Open University Press.

Hawkes, J. (1968) *Dawn of the Gods: Minoan and Mycenaean Origins of Greece*. New York: Random House.

Hitchens, C. (1997) *Hostage to History: Cyprus from the Ottomans to Kissinger*. London and New York: Verso.

Jayawardena, K. (1986) *Feminism and Nationalism in the Third World*. London and New Jersey: Zed Books.

Jorgensen, D. L. (1989) *Participant Observation: A Methodology for Human Studies*. Newbury Park, London and New Delhi: Sage Publications.

Joseph, J. S. (1997) *Cyprus: Ethnic Conflict and International Politics: From Independence to the Threshold of the European Union* [1985]. Basingstoke: Macmillan.

Jung, D. with W. Piccoli (2001) *Turkey at the Crossroads: Ottoman Legacies and a Greater Middle East*. London and New York: Zed Books.

Kandiyoti, D. (1988) 'Bargaining with Patriarchy', *Gender and Society*, 2(3): 274–90.

Kaufmann, C. D. (1996) 'Possible and Impossible Solutions to Ethnic Civil Wars', *International Security*, 20(4): 136–75.

— 'When All Else Fails: Evaluating Population Transfers and Partition as a Solution to Ethnic Conflict', in B. F. Walter and J. Snyder (eds), *Civil Wars, Insecurity and Intervention*. New York and Chichester: Columbia University Press.

Keane, J. (1998) *Civil Society: Old Images, New Visions*. Cambridge: Polity Press.

Killoran, M. (1998) 'Good Muslims and "Bad Muslims", "Good" Women and Feminists: Negotiating Identities in Northern Cyprus (or, the Condom Story)', *Ethos: Journal of the Society for Psychological Anthropology*, 26(2): 183–203.

Kumar, R. (1997a) 'The Troubled History of Partition', *Foreign Affairs*, 76(1): 22–34.

—(1997b) *Divide and Fall? Bosnia in the Annals of Partition*. London and New York: Verso.

—(2000–01) 'Settling Partition Hostilities: Lessons Learnt, the Options Ahead', in *Divided Countries, Separated Cities*, special edition of *Transeuropéennes: Revue Culturelle Internationale*, 19/20: 9–28.

Lewis, F. (1995) 'Reassembling Yugoslavia', *Foreign Policy*, 98: 132–44.

Lister, R. (1997) *Citizenship: Feminist Perspectives*. London: Macmillan.

Loizos, P. (1981) *The Heart Grown Bitter: A Chronicle of Cypriot War Refugees*. Cambridge and London: Cambridge University Press.

Lutz, H. (2002) 'At Your Service Madam! The Globalization of Domestic Service', *Feminist Review*, 70: 89–104.

Matthews, J. (1984) *Good and Mad Women: The Historical Construction of Femininity in 20th Century Australia*. Sydney, London and Boston: Allen and Unwin.

Mellaart, J. (1975) *The Neolithic of the Near East*. New York: Scribner.

Mertan, B. (2000) 'The Position of Women in the Eastern Mediterranean University: A Case Study', *Kadın/Woman*, 1(1): 1–9. Famagusta: Eastern Mediterranean University.

Millett, K. (1971) *Sexual Politics*. London: Sphere Books.

Morvaridi, B. (1993) 'Demographic Change, Resettlement and Resource Use' in C. H. Dodd (ed.), *The Political, Social and Economic Development of Northern Cyprus*. Huntingdon: Eothen Press.

Nearchou-Ellinas, L. (2001) 'Cyprus National Report on the Role of Women in Economic Development: Dimension of Equal Opportunities between Men and Women within the Euromediterranean Partnership'. Nicosia, Cyprus.

Oberling, P. (1982) *The Road to Bellapais: The Turkish Cypriot Exodus to Northern Cyprus*, Social Science Monographs. Boulder, CO (distributed by Columbia University Press, New York).

O'Malley, B. and I. Craig (1999) *The Cyprus Conspiracy: America, Espionage and the Turkish Invasion*. London and New York: I.B. Tauris.

Onofriou, A. (2002) 'In Search of Voices: Policing the Borders of Legitimate Sexuality and Gendered Subjectivities among Cypriot Students'. PhD Thesis, Institute of Education, London.

Papadopoulou, A. (2001) 'The Effects of EU Accession on Migration'. Paper presented to the conference 'After EU Accession: the Changing Face of Civil Society in Cyprus', Intercollege, Nicosia, 10–11 May.

Pateman, C. (1988) *The Sexual Contract*. Cambridge: Polity Press.

Patrick, R. A. (1976) *Political Geography and the Cyprus Conflict: 1963–1971*. Ontario: University of Waterloo, Department of Geography.

Pieterse, J. Nederveen (1997) 'Deconstructing/reconstructing Ethnicity', *Nations and Nationalism*, 3, Part 3: 365–96.

Platon, N. (1966) *Crete*. Geneva: Nagel Publishers.

Politis (2003) Acnielsen-Amer and Kadem opinion poll on behalf of *Politis*. 'Who Goes, Who Doesn't and Why?' 9 June *Politis On-Line*, <www.politis-news.com>

Pollis, A. (1979) 'Colonialism and Neocolonialism: Determinants of Ethnic Conflict in Cyprus', in P. Worsley and P. Kitromilides (eds), *Small States in the Modern World: The Conditions of Survival*. rev. edn. Nicosia: New Cyprus Association.

Polyviou, P. G. (1980) *Cyprus: Conflict and Negotiation 1960–1980*. London: Duckworth.

Pyrgos, M. A. (1993) *The Cypriot Woman at a Glance*. Nicosia: Pyrgos Public Relations.

Rattansi, A. (1994) '"Western" Racisms, Ethnicities and Identities in a "Postmodern" Frame', in A. Rattansi and S. Westwood (eds), *Racism, Modernity and Identity on the Western Front*. Cambridge: Polity Press.

Reason, P. (1998) 'Three Approaches to Participative Inquiry', in N. K. Denzin and Y. S. Lincoln (eds), *Strategies of Qualitative Inquiry*. London, Thousand Oaks and New Delhi: Sage Publications.

Republic of Cyprus (2000) *Cyprus National Report on the Implementation of the Beijing Platform for Action*. Nicosia, Cyprus.

—(2001) 'Cyprus: Plan of Action on Gender Equality', unpublished paper. Ministry of Justice and Public Order 3.5.08 (12). 21 June. Nicosia, Cyprus.

Rich, A. (1980) 'Compulsory Heterosexuality and Lesbian Existence', *Signs* 5(4): 631–60.

Rodriguez, L., F. Güven-Lisaniler and S. Uğural (2003) 'Migrant Sex Workers and State Regulation in North Cyprus', Eastern Mediterranean University, paper presented to the conference 'The Languages of Gender', University of Cyprus, 16–17 May, Nicosia.

Rutherford, J. (1990) 'A Place Called Home: Identity and the Cultural Politics of Difference', in J. Rutherford (ed.), *Identity: Community, Culture, Difference*. London: Lawrence and Wishart.

Sainsbury, S. (2003) 'Do You Know They Call Us "Mavroulla"?: Asian Women Experiencing Domestic Work in Cyprus', paper presented to the conference 'The Languages of Gender', University of Cyprus, 16–17 May, Nicosia.

Sant Cassia, P. (2001) '"Waiting for Ulysses": The Committee for Missing Persons', in O. P. Richmond and J. Ker-Lindsay (eds), *The Work of the United Nations in Cyprus: Promoting Peace and Development*. Basingstoke and New York: Palgrave.

Sirmen, A. (1979) 'The Notion of the Small State: Cyprus, Its Security and Survival', in P. Worsley and P. Kitromilides (eds), *Small States in the Modern World: The Conditions of Survival*, rev. edn. Nicosia: New Cyprus Association.

Solomos, J. (1989) *Race and Racism in Contemporary Britain*. London: Macmillan.

Stamatakis, N. A. (1991) 'History and Nationalism: The Cultural Reconstruction of Modern Greek Cypriot identity', *Cyprus Review*, 3(1): 59–86.

Stavrinides, Z. (1976) *The Cyprus Conflict: National Identity and Statehood*. Nicosia: Loris Stavrinides Press (reissued 1999 by Nicosia: Cyprus Research and Publishing Centre).

Stavrou, S. (1997) 'Cypriot Women at Work', *Cyprus Review*, 9(2): 57–81. Nicosia: Intercollege.

Stoetzler, M. and N. Yuval-Davis (2002) 'Standpoint Theory, Situated Knowledge and the Situated Imagination', *Feminist Theory*, 3(3): 315–33.

Turkish Republic of Northern Cyprus (1999) *Census of Population. Social and Economic Characteristics of Population, December 15, 1996*. Nicosia: TRNC Prime Ministry, State Planning Organization, Statistics and Research Department.

United Nations (2000) Security Council Resolution 1325, 31 October. New York: United Nations.

Vassiliadou, M. (1997) 'Herstory: The Missing Woman of Cyprus', *The Cyprus Review*, 9(1): 95–120.

—(2001) 'Narratives of Gender Consciousness: A Qualitative Approach to Feminist and Other Identities', paper presented at the 24th Annual Scientific Meeting of the International Association of Political Psychology, 'Cultures of Violence, Cultures of Peace', Cuernavaca, Mexico, 15–18 July.

—(2002) 'Questioning Nationalism: The

Patriarchal and National Struggles of Cypriot Women Within a European Union Context', *European Journal of Women's Studies*, 9 (4): 459–82.

—(2003) 'Cypriot Women and Other "Others": Through the Front Door', in S. M. Michalis and T. Tasos (eds), *Cyprus in the Modern World*. Melbourne: National Centre for Hellenic Studies and Research, La Trobe University.

—(forthcoming) 'Inside the Cypriot Family Fortress: A Fine Line between "Old" and "Restored" Designs for Women'. Department of Sociology and Gender Studies, Intercollege, Nicosia.

Volkan, V. D. (1979) *Cyprus – War and Adaptation: A Psychoanalytic History of Two Ethnic Groups in Conflict*. Charlottesville: University Press of Virginia.

Welz, G. (2001) '"One Leg in the Past, and One Leg in the Future": A Society in Transition', *Cyprus Review*, 13(1): 11–30.

Wolleh, O. (2001) *Local Peace Constitu-encies in Cyprus: Rapprochement by the Bi-communal Conflict Resolution Trainer Group*, Report No. 8. Germany: Berghof Forschnungszentrum für Konstruktive Konfliktbearbeitung.

Women Working for Change (1996) 'Proposals for Equality Proofing the Peace Package', unpublished paper. Belfast.

Women's Research Centre (1995) 'Turkish Cypriot Women: Obstacles, Needs and Hopes', Report to International Women's Rights Action Watch for CEDAW review, prepared by Sevgül Uludağ. Nicosia, Cyprus.

Woodward, S. L. (1999) 'Bosnia and Herzegovina: How Not to End Civil War', in B. F. Walter and J. Snyder (eds) *Civil Wars, Insecurity and Intervention*. New York and Chichester: Columbia University Press.

Yuval-Davis, N. (1997) *Gender and Nation*. Cambridge: Polity Press.

—(1999) 'What is "Transversal Politics"?', *Soundings: A Journal of Politics and Culture*, 12: 94–98.

List of abbreviations

AFE	Anexartiti Foititiki Epalxi | Independent Student Bastion
AKEL	Anorthotikon Komma Ergazomenou Laou | Progressive Party of the Working People
BKP	Birleşik Kıbrıs Partisi | United Cyprus Party
ÇAĞ-SEN	Kıbrıs Türk Devlet Çalışanları Sendikası | Turkish Cypriot State Employees' Union
CEDAW	Convention on the Elimination of All Forms of Discrimination Against Women (UN)
CTCW	Council of Turkish Cypriot Women | Kıbrıs Türk Kadınlar Konseyi
CTP	Cumhuriyetçi Türk Partisi | Republican Turkish Party
DIKO	Dimokratiko Komma | Democratic Party
DISY	Dimokratikos Synagermos | Democratic Rally
DP	Demokrat Parti | Democrat Party
EDEK	Eniaia Dimokratike Enosis Kentrou | United Democratic Centre Union
EDI	Kinima Enomenon Dimokraton | Movement of United Democrats
EMU	Eastern Mediterranean University | Doğu Akdeniz Üniversitesi
EOKA	Ethnike Organosis Kyprion Agoniston | National Organization of Cypriot Fighters
GODIK	Gynekia Organosi Dimokratikou Kommatos | Women's Organization of the Democratic Party
GODISY	Gynekia Organosi Dimokratikou Synagermou | Women's Organization of Democratic Rally
GOED	Gynekia Organosi Enomenon Demokraton | Women's Organization of the United Democrats
HAD	Hands Across the Divide
IMTD	Institute for Multi-Track Diplomacy
ISAG	Immigrant Support Action Group
MAP	Milliyetçi Adalet Partisi | National Justice Party
NGO	Non-governmental organization
NMWR	National Machinery for Women's Rights
POGO	Pangipria Omospondia Gynekeion Organoseon | Pancyprian Federation of Women's Organizations
POP	Pangipria Organosi Prosfigou | Pancyprian Association of Refugees
Protoporia	Protoporia Women's Association (associated with DISY)

PWU	Patriotic Women's Union | Yurtsever Kadınlar Birliği
RoC	Republic of Cyprus
TCAUW	Turkish Cypriot Association of University Women | Kıbrıs Türk Üniversiteli Kadınlar Derneği
TCWA	Turkish Cypriot Women's Association | Kıbrıs Türk Kadınlar Birliği
TCWWA	Turkish Cypriot Working Women's Association | Kıbrıs Türk Çalışan Kadınlar Birliği
TKP	Toplumcu Kurtuluş Partisi | Communal Liberation Party
TMT	Türk Mukavemet Teşkilatı | Turkish Resistance Organization
TRNC	Turkish Republic of Northern Cyprus | Kuzey Kıbrıs Türk Cumhuriyeti
UBP	Ulusal Birlik Partisi | National Unity Movement
UHH	Ulusal Halk Hareketi | National People's Movement
Ülkü Ocakları	Grey Wolves
UNFICYP	United Nations Peacekeeping Forces in Cyprus
UNSC	United Nations Security Council
WCIP	Women's Civil Initiative for Peace | Kadınların Barış İçin Sivil Girişimi
WINPEACE	Women's Initiative for Peace
WMPFS	Women's Movement for Peace and a Federal Solution | Barış Ve Federal Çözum İçin Kadın Girişimi
WRC	Women's Research Centre | Kadın Araştırmaları Merkezi
YBH	Yurtsever Birlik Hareketi | Patriotic Unity Movement
YDP	Yeni Doğuş Partisi | New Revival Party

Index

Zed Books titles on gender, conflict and peace studies

Butalia, U. (ed.), *Women Seeking Peace: Voices from Kashmir*

Cockburn, C., *The Space Between Us: Negotiating Gender and National Identities in Conflict*

Jacobs, S., R. Jacobson and J. Marchbank (eds), *States of Conflict: Gender, Violence and Resistance*

Joseph, A., K. Sharma, (eds), *Terror, Counter-Terror: Women Speak Out*

Meintjes, S., A. Pillay and M. Turshen (eds), *The Aftermath: Women in Post-conflict Transformation*

Moser, C. and F. Clark (eds), *Victims, Perpetrators or Actors? Gender, Armed Conflict and Political Violence*

Turshen, M. and C. Twagiramariya (eds), *What Women Do in Wartime: Gender and Conflict in Africa*